The Many Lives
of Scary Clowns

The Many Lives of Scary Clowns

Essays on Pennywise, Twisty, the Joker, Krusty and More

Edited by Ron Riekki

McFarland & Company, Inc., Publishers
Jefferson, North Carolina

LIBRARY OF CONGRESS CATALOGUING-IN-PUBLICATION DATA

Names: Riekki, R. A., editor.
Title: The many lives of scary clowns : essays on Pennywise, Twisty, the Joker, Krusty and more / edited by Ron Riekki.
Description: Jefferson, North Carolina : McFarland & Company, Inc., Publishers, 2022 | Includes bibliographical references and index.
Identifiers: LCCN 2022000762 | ISBN 9781476680910 (paperback : acid free paper) ∞
ISBN 9781476644523 (ebook)
Subjects: LCSH: Horror films—History and criticism. | Clowns in motion pictures. | Clowns on television. | BISAC: PERFORMING ARTS / Television / Genres / Science Fiction, Fantasy & Horror | PERFORMING ARTS / Film / Genres / Horror
Classification: LCC PN1995.9.H6 M3156 2022 | DDC 791.43/6164—dc23/eng/20220204
LC record available at https://lccn.loc.gov/2022000762

BRITISH LIBRARY CATALOGUING DATA ARE AVAILABLE

**ISBN (print) 978-1-4766-8091-0
ISBN (ebook) 978-1-4766-4452-3**

© 2022 Ron Riekki. All rights reserved

No part of this book may be reproduced or transmitted in any form or by any means, electronic or mechanical, including photocopying or recording, or by any information storage and retrieval system, without permission in writing from the publisher.

Front cover image © 2022 Shutterstock

Printed in the United States of America

*McFarland & Company, Inc., Publishers
Box 611, Jefferson, North Carolina 28640
www.mcfarlandpub.com*

This book is dedicated to my
favorite clown of all, Bill Irwin

Table of Contents

Acknowledgments ... ix

Introduction
    Ron Riekki ... 1

Part One: Television and Film Clown Horror

A Clown in the Living Room: The Sinister Clown on Television
    Kevin J. Wetmore, Jr. ... 15

Killer Klowns vs. the Blob: Klowning Around in the Generation Gap
    Dale Bailey ... 35

Corpses, Rejects, Afterlives: Welcome to Zombieland
    Jason V. Brock ... 49

"Art for Art's Sake": Art the Clown, Visuality, and the Cruelty of Allegoresis
    Mattius Rischard ... 56

Clowns, Bogeymen, and the Anxiety of Strangers: Analyzing the Cautionary Elements of Jon Watts' *Clown* (2014)
    Debaditya Mukhopadhyay ... 74

Out of the White (Terror) and into the Black (Presence): Difference as Monstrous in Stephen King's *It: Chapter Two*
    Kim Hester Williams ... 82

Part Two: Real-Life Clown Horror

The Return of the Killer Clowns: A Field Guide to Surviving the Zombie Clown Apocalypse
    Jennifer K. Cox ... 99

The Transcendental Anonymity and Moral Ambiguity
   of Phantom Clowns
   JOANNA PARYPINSKI   119

From Scream to Screen: "Killer Clown" John Wayne Gacy
   on Film
   BENJAMIN RADFORD   132

Part Three: Interviews and Accounts

Interview with Kevin Kangas (*Fear of Clowns*, 2004)
   RON RIEKKI   145

Stitches (2012)
   EOGHAN MCQUINN   152

Interview with Jaysen Buterin (*Kill Giggles*, 2020)
   RON RIEKKI   154

About the Contributors   159
Index   161

Acknowledgments

I see this book as the finale to a two-part series, the first being *The Many Lives of* It: *Essays on the Stephen King Horror Franchise*. I'd like to give a huge thanks to everyone at McFarland, especially Charlie Perdue, Kristal Hamby, and Beth Cox. Thank you for allowing me to commit four hundred pages in these two books to the study of clown horror. I know there are some big fans of this specific genre. I'd like to thank the contributors to that first volume that focused solely on Stephen King's *It*, including Ralph Beliveau, Laura Bolf-Beliveau, Jason V. Brock, Rebecca Frost, Cory R. Goehring, Michelle Leigh Gompf, Dominick Grace, Hayley Mitchell Haugen, Rebecca Janicker, Eric Junnola, Conny Lippert, André Loiselle, June Pulliam, Brian W. Smith, Gregory Stevenson, Katherine A. Troyer, Kevin J. Wetmore, Jr., and, of course, horror icon Joe Mynhardt. (Congrats, by the way, to Kevin for his essay from that collection being listed on the HWA Bram Stoker Award member recommendations list.)

In the carnival/clown horror genre, there are, of course, many people I don't know but who I find to be just as inspiring to me as the people listed above, including the likes of Tod Browning, Tim Burton, Dan "The Cabinet of Dan Caligari-neta" Castellaneta, Danny Elfman, Matt "Bat" Groening, Al Jean (of Farmington Hills), John Carroll Lynch, Andy Muschietti, Clarence Aaron "Tod" Robbins, Henry Selick, Bill Skarsgård, Deane Taylor, Benjamin Wallfisch, and many more. I just had to be sure to tip my clown hat to them.

Lastly, thank you to my parents, who have consistently encouraged my doing these crazy books that I put together.

I also have to give a huge thank you to my boss at NBC/the Golf Channel who, during down time during prep for the filming of the 2020 PNC Father Son Challenge, allowed me to work on this book. I missed Tiger Woods doing his practice round with his son, but I got a ton of copyediting done. (And I got to see Tiger later during the actual tournament. Another tip of the hat to him. He's amazing.)

Lastly, to all of the horror fans out there. Definitely out of all the genres, horror fans are, by far, the coolest.

How many clowns does it take to change a light bulb?
Two. One to change the bulb. The other to hide the body.

Introduction

Ron Riekki

In Chicago, I spent two years completely dedicating my life to comedy. For me, no film has captured the experience of trying to become a professional comedian better than Todd Phillips' *Joker*. Comedians so often get brutal with their comedy perhaps because trying to be a comedian *is* brutal.

I went to an open mic night at a bar in Schaumburg, Illinois, and the bartender informed me that the host hadn't arrived yet. I waited and the host never arrived. Another comedian did though: Kyle Kinane. This was over a decade ago. Kyle looks basically the same then as he does now, a mix of Willem Dafoe's Thomas Wake in *The Lighthouse* and one-man band Seasick Steve—three old souls who all had beards even when they were neonates. Kyle was completely unshaken at the emptiest open mic in history. (By the way, if you don't know the name Kyle Kinane, then you don't know comedy, but at that time, he was completely unknown. As unknown as I still am.) The bartender told me and Kyle that the open mic was in a back room of the bar. We went to it. No one was there either. And no host. Just me and Kyle and a room packed full of ghosts. The conversation went something like this.

"Wanna still do it?"

"There's a mic."

"It'll be good practice."

"Yeah, if we can do our standup to an empty room, it'll show we can do it to any audience."

"We can't get less than zero people to attend a show."

"You do your set, then I'll do mine. And when I do my set, you leave the room. And when you do your set, I'll leave the room."

We agreed that's what we'd do. We both wanted the experience of having done the shittiest open mic of all-time. Or one of the shittiest. I'm sure there's been worse. But this was close.

I went outside and could hear Kyle inside the empty room running through his jokes. What impressed me was that he did his full five minutes. Then I went in and did my five minutes, speaking to the chairs. After, stubbing out his cigarette, Kyle said he was leaving, and he did.

I went for another year of comedy after that. I didn't quit right away, but I did quit. Kyle didn't though. He kept plugging away. Ten years later, he's done *Comedy Central Presents Kyle Kinane* and *Workaholics* (as Sewer Dwayne) and *Comedy Bang! Bang!* (as Lenny Spruce) and *Aqua Teen Hunger Force* (as Dr. Balthazar) and a hell of a lot more. I remember watching a YouTube video online, right around the time when I was thinking of quitting, and Kyle was on it, saying how much doing comedy sucks, how bad you're treated, how awful the money is. I quit right after I saw that video. I thought I'd put in enough time with so little to show for that commitment. I'd done hundreds of open mics, had actually done a tour of northeast US colleges with two other comics through Kramer Entertainment where I learned I did love comedy, but I didn't love the road—and that's so much of what being a comedian is. I'd also gotten to do some paid showcases thanks to a Chicago booker named Dave Odd, an ex-insult comic who also didn't have much triumph in comedy and now forages for mushrooms for his produce company.

While I was in Chicago, I routinely did open mics with Kinane, as well as Pete Holmes, T.J. Miller, Kumail Nanjiani, John Roy, Prescott Tolk, Nick Vatterott, and so many more who have now stamped their names all over comedy. What I noticed when I was at rooms like the Lyon's Den was just how violent the comedy could be, with comics breaking VHS tapes and bottles over their heads, punching themselves, going into the crowd and lying down on the greasy floor, and attacking the crowd with f-words, c-words, x-words, every letter in the alphabet. It was *bodily* comedy—fueled by nicotine and alcohol and drugs and the tension that comes with new sobriety and a total embracing of their neuroses. The Lyon's Den served as home for many punk gigs, and that punk aesthetic bled into the comedy. The topics often got into murder and chaos and misanthropy and you got the feeling that a multitude of the comedians needed rehab and counseling and to simply go on a date, something normative, like a yoga membership. Instead their days were minimum wage or unemployment, and their nights were begging for laughs, basking in it when it did happen, enjoying seeing comics you had the suspicion would become at least quasi-famous in the future, the thrill of seeing them testing out new material, the train wrecks of it, the most beautiful train wrecks you can imagine. I remember comedian Mike Wiley doing death metal comedy, yes, smashing bottles over his head, bottles I thought were real, but then, later, after much coaxing for him to tell me, him admitting that they were fake, telling me to be careful with one I was handling, saying they were expensive. He had a gas station job and yet he was buying expensive fake bottles just for a laugh at an open mic. I love comedians. I also remember how the majority of those comics are completely forgotten by the comedy world, have faded away and back into "normal" lives; they did four-minute sets straight out of the Jim Rose Circus sideshow and those days were gone, are gone.

I loved every night I got to spend at the Lyon's Den.

What's been intriguing is seeing how many of those comics who did make names for themselves have stepped so easily into sci-fi and horror. With T.J., there's *Underwater*, *Ready Player One*, *The Gorburger Show*, *Hell and Back*, *Transformers: Age of Extinction*, and *Cloverfield*. With Kumail, I think of *Men in Black: International*, *The Twilight Zone*, *Middle-Earth: Shadow of War*, *Mass Effect: Andromeda*, *The X-Files*, *The Walking Dead* video game, and *Hell Baby*. There's something about comedians where they can so smoothly operate in the horror genre. (I'm tempted to do a long list here of examples, but I'll hold off just giving three that immediately come to mind: Bill Hader, *It: Chapter Two*; John Landis, *An American Werewolf in London*; John Krasinski, *A Quiet Place*.) In some ways, it's the same genre; horror, comedy, and punk/metal are all from the same family. It's about shock a lot of the time, eliciting a reaction through any means necessary, often through the opening of a vein, be it metaphorical or, if needed, literal. At horror movies, I routinely hear laughter, often in unexpected places. And horror soundtracks are full of punk and metal bands. And, yes, comedy shows can easily delve into horror. Andrew Dice Clay, David Cross, Daniel Tosh, Sarah Silverman, Bill Hicks, Doug Stanhope, Dave Chappelle—these are comedians who can get savage. Imagine Jason Voorhees in a comedy club. As the prime example, consider how easily Jordan Peele moved from Comedy Central's *Key and Peele* to the center of horror that *Get Out* became upon its release. Hollywood should be begging the best comedy writers to write horror scripts, because comedy and horror are twins, standing there, shoulder-to-shoulder, in a hallway of the Overlook hotel, waiting for their younger brother, punk, to arrive on his tricycle so that all mayhem can truly break loose.

Actually, that pairing of Jason Voorhees and a comedy club came true for me. One night in L.A., I dropped in on an improv show to find Derek Mears, the actor who played Jason in the 2009 film version, as one of the improv performers onstage. Luckily—thank you to whoever that nameless, shadowed person who did it—someone in the audience yelled out "horror" as the suggestion for the night's show and they took that suggestion (with a sly, approving, evil grin from Derek) and I got to see one of the coolest things I've ever seen in theater: an improv show that wasn't so much funny as it was authentically and unexpectedly frightening. The actors used shadows and atmosphere and the clichés of horror to transcend those clichés. The murders, even though comic overall, had intense moments of the ghastly, with Derek largely contributing, his continued devilish grin as he seized each moment by coming up with what would make us uncomfortable: slow approaches and masterful use of darkness and his body and face that are perfectly made for both comedy and horror—his 6'5" body, his shirt demonstrating freakish muscles, his Michael Berryman-ish face that's also childlike. I remember a Second City Mainstage actress telling me after class at Improv Olympic that the best improv performers have baby faces, something lighthearted just looking at them. Derek has that quality, a mix of theatre and threat, an intriguing face made for both comedy and horror films. I studied him and this slow build to the murders onstage that was all so, honestly, deeply tense and intense. It was unlike any improv show I'd ever seen. And I found myself hoping for less comedy, more horror, because improv horror is something I'd never even fathomed before. And it worked. Brilliantly.

When I think of the best moments I've ever experienced in the world of theater—and that includes such highlights as an American Repertory Theatre version of *The Merchant of Venice* starring Will LeBow (whom I love) and an Edison Community College production of *Dark of the Moon* that gave me honest-to-God chills—the absolute pinnacle is strangely enough in the clown horror genre.

In Chicago, a friend of mine recommended I go to see Soiree DADA. I came late to the performance in a tiny theatre, walking in from the brightness outside to the darkness inside, discombobulating me. What discombobulated me even more was that the actors were mid-scene and they all stopped performing and stared at me. The show completely stopped. I'd walked in late and they acknowledged this. A bizarre book called *The Clown Egg Register* describes the four main types of clown makeup—Tramp, Character, Auguste, and Whiteface. Personally, Whiteface gives me the creeps. I think of historical Whiteface Clowns like Francesco Caroli, Tommy Keele, Paul Jung, Harty, Clown Foottit, Billie Merchant "Little Billy," Lulu Adams, Percy Huxter, Grimaldi, Rainbow, Sven Bronett, and Jean Barrel; I know they're supposed to be comical, and I'm sure they were, but images of those sorts of clowns are equally creepy. Not horrific, but, for sure, creepy. Maybe it's the corpse-like appearance of the skin, how it looks like the person is in shock, medical shock, on the way to death, if not already dead. And everyone on that stage in Chicago was in various forms of extreme whiteface. And they were all looking at me. I ran out of the theater, into the brightness and traffic noise of the street outside. I paced. I thought about leaving, but I'd already paid for my ticket. This time, I decided, I'd go back inside, but much more meekly, silently, so that hopefully they wouldn't even notice. I waited, then reentered the theater and, just like the last time, the actors all stopped mid-scene and stared at me. And they stayed immobile, just their eyes following me like portraits you'd find in a haunted mansion. Until, slowly, whispering apologies, I sat down next to my friend who was sitting near the center of the audience, right in the middle, forcing me to brush my legs against the knees of those nearby, to bother everybody so that I felt ashamed of arriving late. Then the worst thing possible happened. The actors onstage all began walking towards me, from all different directions, like a trained Vietnam War unit, coming from different angles so that I couldn't escape. One of the clowns walked straight at me, climbing over chairs, stepping over people, until all of them came around me, every one of them, sliding down my row, and they circled me, and just stared, their faces inches from mine, all around me, the audience roaring with laughter, and me, horrified. The cast paused, letting this moment sink in. Then they turned, walked back to the stage, and picked up the performance where they left off, as if nothing at all had happened.

That's theater.

That was the most I've ever felt in a theater in my life, this shot of dopamine and epinephrine that ran through my body. It was exhilarating and uncomfortable.

And it was clown horror.

There's an inherent theatricality to clowns. The costume differentiates them so much from humans with the multi-colors and just pure strangeness. They're impossible not to look at if they're in a room. And it's not hard to hope they don't look at you.

When I took a Witchcraft, Magic, and the Occult course at Central Michigan University when I was earning my Bachelor's in religion, my professor, Dr. Robin Hough, talked to us about "liminality," how during Halloween our costuming puts us in a state that's between normal everyday life and the supernatural. This costuming was critical for shamans, for putting a foot into the netherworld. Clowns do this, border halfway between human and monster. Whether or not it's intended. And when clowns perform, it tends to be for liminal moments, such as birthday parties, where a person is transforming to a new age. Or in massive church-like carnivals, with their revival-tent feel.

There's also an element of poverty to clowns, such as the Hobo/Tramp theme previously mentioned or Homey D. Clown or all of the Walter White–face clown horror films where a down-on-his-luck nobody—always a "he"—gets transformed into an "I am the danger" serial killer. In real life, clowning tends not to be a job where the person makes much money, so you have this individual struggling to survive in society, portraying a poverty-stricken character, while being lowly paid to perform. The class issues of clowning rarely get explored in commentary, but they're at the heart of the clown narrative. Clowns are Others.

There's also the tendency for clowns to have facial features or bodies that are non-normative. One of the reasons I think I went into comedy was because of my body. I'm tall. Freakishly tall. I get asked daily—not exaggerating, *daily*—what my height is. I've learned multiple different replies, depending on my mood. Sometimes I just say, "I'm 6'6'" and other times I say, "6'7"," not wanting to explain how I'm somewhere in between the two. Other times, if I'm in a different mood, I say: "I'm 6-6-6," pausing before I deliver that third six.

I moved to the Hollywood area one year with the same delusions of most who make that move, unsure how I'd survive, and a friend of mine had recently been an extra in one of *The Pirates of the Caribbean* films, telling me how it was good money and showing me photos of herself in elaborate pirate wench dresses that made her look like she was a cross between being ready for the runway and being a runaway. She looked so intensely different in those photos—transformed, otherworldly. She glowed showing me each photo, recounting what it was like to have professional costume designers and makeup artists spending so much time on her. She said I should put in my photos for Central Casting, so I did. Quickly, I received a call. ABC was interested in me for the TV show *Pushing Daisies*. I'd be a background actor. They thought I had the perfect body for the circus. I took it as a compliment, sort of. During the shoot, I got to meet other jugglers and bearded ladies and a "little person" stripper, and everyone had such memorable faces, unforgettable bodies. It was a "freak show," except we all felt normalized being around one another. It felt like home. Quickly came other calls, where *Criminal Minds* said I looked like I was someone who would be in a cult. *Terminator: The Sarah Connor Chronicles* felt like I was someone who you'd find at a funeral. *The Middleman* felt like I was someone who might survive the apocalypse. Each call had a hint of insult that I just got used to, appreciating that they were interested in me. I met director Steve Balderson at the Crimson Screen Horror Film Festival. He cast me as a killer in his film *Short Straw*. Then I met director John Johnson at the same horror film festival a couple years later and he cast me as a serial killer in his film *Flesher*. They just looked at me and thought, "Killer." With Octobers approaching, I've walked down the street and gotten asked if I wanted to be a "scare-actor" in haunted houses. When I turn around corners, even during the day, I will legitimately scare people. And I'm not even that tall. I'm not Wilt Chamberlain or Kareem Abdul-Jabbar, but I guess it's just a thing where you gravitate to where you're supposed to be, like a magnet. And I've continued to stumble my way further into horror. After I gave a guest lecture at the University of Houston at Victoria—a very non-horror lecture on the importance of regional literature—I was in Jeff Sartain's office and saw his poster of *The Evil Dead*. I casually mentioned that a collection of academic writing on that franchise would make a good book. Jeff nodded, and then the nod turned more definitive, and he said, "Yeah, it would." I said we should do it then and he said sure. *The Many Lives of* The Evil Dead: *Essays on the Cult Film Franchise* was born. That casually. This is the fourth book in that *The Many Lives of* series, having gone on to explore *It* and *The Twilight Zone* as well. And it's allowed me to delve into films and TV that I love. *Evil Dead 2* (1987), *It* (2009), and *The Twilight Zone* (1959–1964) were all mind-blowing for me, and in ways where I felt they were due respect in academia, that they were films and TV that could be analyzed and re-analyzed, revealing even deeper meanings that perhaps wouldn't be there on the first viewing.

I should say this. I'm not afraid of clowns. Not at all. The most horrific ones, to me, are just a bit creepy, at best, but not scary. When I've "performed" in haunted houses—and, yes, I've been in several, "acting" in them in Michigan, Illinois, and California—they've had the obligatory clown horror scenes and, although they were always the number one favorite among the attendees, they never actually scared me. Even when the clown-actors would try to. What would happen, instead, is I'd just be highly intrigued. I didn't want to run away from their faces; instead, I wanted to lean forward, study their masks or makeup. Horror, when it's done very well, to be honest with you, is quite beautiful. In the film *Flesher*, I remember a scene where I was doing a surgical removal of actress Erica Mary Gillheeney's face and the precision of special effects artist Sean Krumbholz's work was awe-inspiring to me. I'm the same way at haunted houses when I go through them and I'm not an actor. I want to stop and admire a well-made set, which I did once at one of the Busch Gardens Howl-O-Scream haunted houses and found that a security guard quickly appeared and followed obnoxiously close behind me for the rest of the walk-through. I wasn't trying to cause mischief; I just admire a high-quality mask, an impressive costume, an intriguing prop. The best of clown horror offers all of that. I could imagine a set designer, costume designer, or makeup artist drooling even more heavily than Bill Skarsgård as Pennywise with the opportunity to work on the sets of *Killer Klowns from Outer Space* or *It* or *Clown* or *American Horror Story*. Clowns and carnivals—as I got to witness on the set of *Pushing Daises* for their "Circus, Circus" episode—explode with color, which is something that horror so often doesn't do, being much more interested in darkness and night. The combination of "clown" and "horror," though, allows for an intriguing combination, like chocolate and peanut butter, red beans and rice, spaghetti and meatballs, monsters and mash. And clowns imply comedy so that Pennywise, for me, is at his best when there's a sense of dark humor to what he's doing, like waving with a severed hand or dancing the creepiest (yet strangely funny) jig you can imagine. The best clown horror films and TV don't forget about the clown elements and just go strictly for horror. They do a tightrope balancing act between the two. On the other hand, the worst clown horror is just horror: no clown, no fun, no color, just drab serial killer redundancy with, usually, no story. But when it's instead done well, it's amazing. Thank goodness (and badness) for Pennywise, the Joker, Krusty, Beetlejuice, *Fool's Fire*, and that brief moment of the Clown with the Tearaway Face in *The Nightmare Before Christmas*. Those clowns are part of some of my favorite films and TV of all-time. And it makes me want to delve further into the genre to find out what else out there is scaring me and making me laugh simultaneously, which is such a wonderful combination.

Because I couldn't find any sort of extensive list online, I put together a collection of films and television in the clown horror genre. To qualify, films had to be at least sixty minutes in length, with the notable exception of bracketed very early short films. For television, I don't list single short episodes of shows in the clown horror genre except for the inclusion of some episodic TV with multiple episodes in the genre. (These films and shows reflect what I could hunt down as of December 21, 2020. Of course, there was much debate on my part on what should or should not be included as part of "clown horror," but these are what I decided to include.)

Timeline of Clown Horror in Film and Television

1910—[Note: 1910's *Hop-Frog*, directed by Henri Desfontaines, may just be the beginning of clown horror cinema]
1917—*Klovnen*
1920—[Note: "The Ouija Board," 5-minute short with a clown in a haunted house]
1921—[Note: only 7 minutes in length, the mischievous clown in 1921's "Invisible Ink" is worth mentioning as one of the early horror-ish clowns, also note *The Exorcist*-ish head-spinning scene]
1924—*He Who Gets Slapped*
1928—*Laugh, Clown, Laugh*; *The Man Who Laughs* [note: the apocalypse-inducing clown in the 6-minute "Koko's Earth Control"]
1932—*Freaks*
1933—[Note: although only seven minutes in length, "Koko the Clown" is one of the earliest filmic horror clowns as seen in Betty Boop in "Snow-White"]
1942—[Note: Gacy born]
1949—*Edgar Allan Poe Centenary*
1954—*The Phantom of the Big Tent*
1960—*Circus of Horrors, Masterworks of Terror*
1965—*Master of Horror*

1966—*Psycho-Circus*
1968—*Yellow Submarine*
1976—*The Clown Murders*
1978—*Halloween, KISS Meets the Phantom of the Park*
1979—*Macbeth* (many versions of Macbeth have the Porter as not clown-ish enough such as the 1971 version or with considerable lines cut such as the 1948 version, but this Royal Shakespeare Company version blends hell and clown)
1980—*Terror on Tour* [note: Gacy sentenced to death]
1981—*The Funhouse, The Killing of America*
1982—*Pagliacci, Poltergeist*
1983—*The House on Sorority Row*
1986—*Slaughter High* [note: *It* novel published]
1987—*Blood Harvest, Funland, Tales from the Quadead Zone*
1988—*Beetlejuice, Ghosthouse, Killer Klowns from Outer Space, Out of the Dark*
1989—*Beetlejuice* (TV version), *Clownhouse, Santa Sangre* [note: Insane Clown Posse is formed in Detroit]
1990—*It* [note: the first "Treehouse of Horror" on *The Simpsons*]
1991—*Shakes the Clown* [note: Krusty's first appearance in a "Treehouse of Horror" episode]
1992—*Demonic Toys, Evil Night, Fool's Fire, To Catch a Killer*
1993—*Dark Carnival, The Nightmare Before Christmas*
1994—*Funny Man, Serial Killers, The Crow* [note: Gacy dies]
1995—*Dead Presidents, Edgar Allan Poe: Terror of the Soul*
1996—*Mr. Ice Cream Man*
1997—*The Game, Insane Clown Posse: Shockumentary, Spawn*
1998—*Carnival of Souls, Night of the Clown*
1999—Biography—*John Wayne Gacy: A Monster in Disguise, Blood Dolls, The Clown at Midnight, Serial Killers: Profiling the Criminal Mind, Super Badass*
2000—*Camp Blood, Camp Blood 2, Killjoy, Sideshow, Vulgar*
2001—*Scary Movie 2, Slashers*
2002—*Killjoy 2, Urban Massacre*
2003—*Gacy, House of 1000 Corpses, Killer Klowns from Kansas on Krack, Maniacal, SICK: Serial Insane Clown Killer, Sssshhh...*
2004—*Dead Clowns, Fear of Clowns, Feast of Fools, Hellbreeder, Puppet Master vs. Demonic Toys*
2005—*DeadHouse, The Devil's Rejects, Supernatural, Within the Woods: Camp Blood Trilogy*
2006—*Axegrinder, M.O.N., Mr. Jingles, When Evil Calls*
2007—*100 Tears, Clown, Dead Silence, Devil Girl, Drive Thru, Fear of*

Clowns 2, Final Draft, Fraternity Massacre at Hell Island, Frayed, Freakshow, The Fun Park, Hack!, Hellscape, House of Fears, Masters of Horror: We All Scream for Ice Cream, Methodic, Mr. Halloween, Secrets of the Clown

2008—*Amusement, The Dark Knight, Torment, Twilight Syndrome*

2009—*Clownstrophobia, The Hole, Jingles the Clown, Killer Clown, Zombieland*

2010—*8213: Gacy House, Closed for the Season, Cut, Dahmer vs. Gacy, Dead American Woman, Dear Mr. Gacy, Doll Boy, Hellweek, Killjoy 3, Klown Kamp Massacre, The Last Circus*

2011—*The Cabin in the Woods, Jack the Ripper, Born to Kill?—John Wayne Gacy: The Killer Clown, The Task*

2012—*All Dark Places, Grimas, Into the Zone: The Story of the Cacophony Society, Killjoy Goes to Hell, Laughter, Scary or Die, Serious Serial Killers, Silent Hill: Revelation, Slasher House, Sloppy the Psychotic, Splash Area, Stitches*

2013—*All Hallows' Eve, Blood Slaughter Massacre, Down with Clowns, Gingerclown, Killer Holiday, Prank*

2014—*American Horror Story: Freak Show, Among the Living, Bongo Killer Clown, Camp Blood: First Slaughter, Circus of the Dead, Clown, Clown Kill, The Damned Thing, The Documentary of OzBo, The Houses October Built, Judy, Killer Legends, Killer Party, Mockingbird, Theatre of Fear*

2015—*Badoet, Cannibal Clown Killer, Cleaver: Rise of the Killer Clown, The Funhouse Massacre, Fun Time, Kruel, Krampus, The Legend of Wasco, Loon, Lucifer's Angels, The Piper, Scooby-Doo! and Kiss: Rock and Roll Mystery*

2016—*31, Batman: The Killing Joke, Camp Blood 4, Camp Blood 5, Camp Blood 666, Clowntown, House of Whores 2: The Second Cumming, Insane, Joker's Poltergeist: The Aurora Massacre, Poltergeist, Sorority Slaughterhouse, Space Clown, Suicide Squad, Terrifier, Toxic Apocalypse, Yamishibai: Japanese Ghost Stories' "Merry-Go-Round"*

2017—*American Horror Story: Cult, Behind the Sightings, Circus Kane, Clowntergeist, It, The Joker, It Kills: Camp Blood 7, Land of Smiles, The Night Watchmen*

2018—*8 Ball Clown, Clown Footage, Crepitus, The Bad Man, Gags, World's Most Evil Killers: John Wayne Gacy*

2019—*Cleavers: Killer Clowns, Clown, Clownado, Clown Doll, Clownface, Clown Motel, Clown Nightmare, Haunt, It: Chapter Two, Joker, Wrinkles the Clown*

2020—*Camp Blood 8, Clownery, Clown Fear, Clown Motel Vacancies,*

Introduction (Riekki)   11

The Clown Movie, Drown the Clown, Homecoming Massacre, Killer Clowns, Kill Giggles, Night of the Wicked Clown, On Halloween, The Tales of Strango the Clown, Terrifier 2

Commonly, I've heard that it's King's *It* miniseries in 1990 that started the clown horror genre. Others give that beginning of the genre to King's 1986 novel. And then others with the infamous clown of *Poltergeist*. But the real beginning of the clown horror genre in film is 1917's *Klovnen*, a Danish film directed by A.W. Sandberg. Although much forgotten, the murderous clown of the film precedes Pennywise's filmic debut by more than seventy years.

But the real root of clown horror I would argue, at least in terms of American cinematic clown horror, stems from Gacy, especially the over-mythologizing of his clown persona, Pogo. The mix of zeitgeist and poltergeist that has been patched together to become Gacy's Pogo has allowed the image to stick, an image that gets toyed with, reinvented, moved from screen to screen, from script to script. My own distaste and discomfort with clown horror that lacks any sense of humor is that it feels like it moves closer and closer to a sort of Gacy documentary, fictionalized; whereas, clown horror that moves further to the side of comedy is so much more appealing. Putting together this collection, I would get emails and comments on how deeply the fan base and love of Krusty is—because Krusty is the anti–Gacy. Drab serial killer clown horror without story, just random acts of violence, parallels Gacy's drab, colorless life where there is no heroic storyline there, just, again, random acts of senseless violence. Krusty inhabits an intensely colorful world, a cartoon world, in fact, where jokes aren't delivered every minute, like in slower-paced sitcoms, but, rather, seemingly every few seconds with a combination of both spoken and visual humor—the opposite of the long, slow feel of humorless serial killer clown horror. My favorite episodes of *The Simpsons* are always from "Treehouse of Horror." The "bizarre dream-like quality" (Sims) of "Treehouse of Horror" is so distant from the empty nightmare of Gacy. For me, balancing the "clown" and the "horror" of "clown horror" is the secret recipe to success in the genre.

In this collection, a diverse group of academics give their own take on their favorites and least favorites in the genre. Kevin J. Wetmore, Jr., introduces the scary clown on television. Mattius Rischard makes a strong argument for Art the Clown in *Terrifier,* how a colorless no-story serial-killer clown horror film is, in fact, actually art. Dale Bailey pays homage to the nostalgia of *Killer Klowns from Outer Space*. Kim Hester Williams rips the mask off of Pennywise and the Joker and reveals the importance of understanding how race is at the center of those narratives. And Benjamin

Radford, Debaditya Mukhopadhyay, Jason V. Brock, Jennifer K. Cox, and Joanna Parypinski give their own unique takes on the films of Rob Zombie, Jon Watts' *Clown*, and how real-life scary clowns have morphed from Gacy into the "phantom clowns" and "zombie clown apocalypse" of recent horror clown sightings, that same real-life scary clown subject matter tackled from two different perspectives by Cox and Parypinski. Along with interviews with icons of the genre Kevin Kangas and Jaysen Buterin and a short nonfiction recounting of the making of *Stitches* by Eoghan McQuinn, the book hopes to creep up on the subject matter from multiple angles. I hope fans of the clown horror genre enjoy these pages.

Work Cited

Sims, David. "*Treehouse of Horror*: An Appreciation." *The Atlantic*. October 28, 2015. theatlantic.com. Accessed December 20, 2020.

PART ONE

Television and Film Clown Horror

A Clown in the Living Room
The Sinister Clown on Television
Kevin J. Wetmore, Jr.

"I think of him all the time as a smile gone bad."
—Tim Curry, on Pennywise the Dancing Clown

The television clown runs the gamut, from children's show clowns like Bozo to Pennywise, Twisty and Pretzel Jack, who are as likely to turn your intestines to balloon animals. Who would invite such insane creatures into the living room, into the heart of the home? Clowns have been a part of television since its inception, mostly as part of children's programming, although the figure of the clown as sad or sinister has also been present in adult programming from the beginning as well. This inherent televisuability of clowns is odd, considering their origin. The clown, after all, is a theatrical creature, one developed on stages and in circuses. As Jon Davidson notes:

> At first sight the clown whose aesthetic had been built in the medium- or large-scale spaces of circuses would not sit comfortably on the small screen. The strong visual elements—necessitated by distance—circular spaces, and the acoustics of the circus were alien to the tiny flat space of the television screen with its volume control in your own living room [Davidson 111].

While clowns appeared as characters in films, the television clown evolved from the big top to the small screen, bringing his (the pronoun use is intentional, most early television clowns were male, even if the character was coded as female) antics into a more confined medium.

Television takes outside entertainment (film, narrative, news, etc.) and brings it into the home in a much smaller, controlled format; consequently, in a sense, the television clown is an embodiment of television. Television in one sense restricts the clown who is, in person, much more anarchic and makes the clown safe for the children at home. Television provides distance that makes the clown less threatening. Yet, as the clown evolved, it also found ways to be no less dangerous, and perhaps even a bit more sinister, not least of which because we have now invited that clown into our living room.

The sinister clown on television functions differently than the monster clown of film, primarily due to the medium. Television, historically, is much more highly regulated than film, with the Federal Communications Council and individual network standards and practices limiting for much of television history what clowns (or any monsters, in fact) could do. Television clowns tend to threaten violence much more than perpetrate it. The clown on television is sinister; whereas, the cinematic clown tends to be much more monstrous (see Ron Riekki's essay in this volume). Sinister and monstrous clowns both invert everything the historic theatrical clown was supposed to be: harmless, amusing, fun aimed primarily at children, with the purpose of making people laugh. The sinister clown is not silly, he is disturbing.

The clown has been a television presence since the inception of the medium, with Bozo first broadcasting in 1949. While clowns might be sad, infantilized, or anarchic, their potential for evil became manifest in the late seventies and forward. The emergence of the horror of John Wayne Gacy/Pogo the clown and the 1978 trial of Paul Kelly, son of Emmett Kelly, Jr., beloved hobo clown "Weary Willie," of two of his partners, in which Paul Kelly was diagnosed with what was then called "Multiple Personality Disorder," cast into the public mind the idea of the evil clown. Although the trope of the monster clown had been presented on film and television before the late seventies, most notably the child Michael Myers, dressed as a clown, killing his sister in *Halloween* (1978), the reality of evil clowns seemed to confirm the trope. These factors, combined with the appearance of Stephen King's *It* in 1986, followed by the television miniseries adaptation in 1990, opened the floodgates to evil clowns.

This essay takes two theses as a given: first, all clowns are sinister, regardless of intent. Even clowns on children's programming contain a sinister element. *Ralph Breaks the Internet* distinguishes between "scary clowns" and "happy clowns," but both look alike. We don't know if clowns are "happy" or "scary" until they do something, in fact, until we engage with them for a while. Pennywise, for example, always seems happy and nice when he first encounters a victim. Clowns contain an element of uncertainty. We do not know if they are "happy" or "scary," and even the happy ones are potentially scary. This incongruity makes all clowns suspect. Second, television clowns, like virtually all clowns are grotesque and carnivalesque/Bakhtinian creatures designed to frighten in a fun way to distract us from the truly terrifying—our own demise. We shall take their sinister-ness as a given, and in this survey we shall consider Bakhtinian approaches to television clowns to understand what makes them sinister.

Clowns on television are underrepresented in scholarship. Indeed, even children's television clowns have remarkably little written about them. In his wonderful volume *Bad Clowns*, Benjamin Radford only gives ten pages out of the entire volume to television "bad clowns," which include, apparently, Pennywise, Krusty, Homey, Yucko, and Bozo, all but the first are less "bad" than poorly behaving, and the last one really isn't a bad clown, some rumors just allege he is; only Pennywise is a truly "bad" clown (Radford 66–75). This essay, while making no claims to be comprehensive, hopes to offer a somewhat larger study of sinister clowns on television.

Mikhail Bakhtin, in considering carnival clowns, offers a useful way to think about sinister clowns on television. According to Bakhtin, clowns are "folk carnival humor" that include ritual and spectacle (*Rabelais*, 5). Clowns are neither normal nor natural; they employ ritualistic elements and visual and aural elements to entertain, delight, and provoke laughter (and terror). The clown is a low figure, a form of folk culture, not high culture, and the clown's presence is a kind of lowness. Bakhtin reminds us that laughter towards clown is debasing, mocking; we laugh at, not with, clowns (*Problems* 127). The clown is the victim, but if horror has taught us anything, it is that victims often then become perpetrators themselves.

Central to carnival are the themes of death and renewal, and the clown is linked to both (Bakhtin, *Problems*, 124). He will often undergo symbolic death, only to emerge to laughter. Yet in horror culture, this symbolic death of the clown transforms into the clown as manifestation of its victim's death and becomes much more sinister and, further, much more real. Evil versions take this carnival aspect and transform it into death without rebirth. Death by clown taken comedically results in rebirth, death by clown taken realistically and in a sinister sense results in no rebirth, only death.

Lastly, Bakhtin notes there is no distinction in carnival between performer and spectator (*Problems*, 122). Clowns make us part of the performance whether we want to or not. When we add all of these elements up: the clown is a grotesque figure who is low, worthy of our laughter and mockery, who breaks down barriers between performer and audience, but who also embodies death and rebirth. When these qualities are exploited in a negative, evil way, the clown turns sinister and monstrous. The television clown in particular is Bakhtinian—low, worthy of our laughter, and yet sinister and possibly fatal without the chance for rebirth. In manifesting these qualities, these clowns represent a variation of terror management theatre. In laughing at the clown, we laugh at our own death, even as we fear it. The clowns we will consider in this essay are virtually all Bakhtinian clowns.

As for the first thesis, that all clowns are inherently sinister, in his analysis of the genre through the lens of evolutionary psychology, *Why Horror Seduces*, Mathias Clasen sees not just evil clowns as scary but all clowns, primarily because of our evolutionary psychology:

> Nonetheless, the evil clown is an effective horror monster, and we can make sense of its effectiveness by considering the figure in light of evolved defensive dispositions. The evil clown is a supercharged version of the conspecific predator, a homicidal human exhibiting unpredictable, psychotic behavior. The clown masks its inner life, its intentions and motives, by obscuring its face with paint, thus making it unreadable and unpredictable. Humans decipher other humans' inner states from reading their faces. [...] When we are blocked from reading a face, the result is unease or even dread [42–3].

Clowns in general are disturbing because their makeup masks them, making them unreadable and, therefore, unreliable. Even child-friendly clowns such as Bozo or Clarabell are suspect, as they, too, mask their intentions and motives through makeup, rely upon child-like anarchic behavior, and we do not know the person behind the mask. For adults, clowns have the potential to be very scary as they wear masks and have access to children and in no other profession is that behavior acceptable (Durwin). We fear clowns for what they can do to us or what they can do to the vulnerable ones we love.

Joseph Campbell reminds us that clowns and devils are often interchangeable. Both are tricksters and both are funny and scary: "Universal too is the casting of the antagonist, the representative of evil, in the role of clown. Devils—both the lusty thickheads and the sharp, clever deceivers—are always clowns" (251). This means there are two sides of the same coin: if clowns are evil, then evil is clownish. The clown is often portrayed on television in an antagonist role, from Pennywise terrifying adults who first encountered him as a child to Bozo tricking children, to Clarabell communicating through shooting seltzer water into people's faces; the clown is adversarial. Humor and horror are part of the same categories.

Like Campbell, Noël Carroll sees the clown and the monster as beings on the same spectrum: "If, typically, clowns function in incongruity comedy in a manner analogous to the way in which monsters function in horror fictions—i.e., as the objects of the relevant mental states—then our question can be focused concretely by asking: what does it take to turn a clown into a monster or to turn a monster into a clown?" (Carroll 156). Carroll's argument is that clowns "are already categorically incongruous beings. They can be turned into horrific creatures by compounding their conceptually anomalous state with fearsomeness" (156). The example, par excellence, is Pennywise from Stephen King's *It*, a clown with sharp teeth who can also transform into other things. The only thing it takes to make a clown sinister is for it to become even just slightly fearsome, which would seem to indicate an inherent horrific potential in every clown; all clowns are capable of being monsters. Lastly, Carroll makes an important point for television clowns: clowns have horrific potential for children because children "have not yet mastered the conventions of so-called comic distance" (156). The first television clowns (Bozo, Clarabell) were aimed at children. The very things that make clowns appeal to children—their anarchic, madcap, and, dare I say, childlike behavior behind a mask of makeup—are also the very things that render the clown terrifying. Children do not know how to laugh at the low, as they themselves are low status within society. The clown is both like and not like them. It is like them in that it is low status, not taken seriously, and behaves in a manner often inappropriate. It is not like them in that it is monstrous and terrifying for doing the same exact behavior. Even the friendly clowns may take on a sinister aspect when lacking comic distance.

For the purposes of this study, let us break the trope of the television clown down into three types: the series clown, the episodic clown, and the anthology clown. The series clown is a recurring character on a regular television program, often, but not always aimed at children. Such clowns include Bozo, Clarabell (from *Howdy Doody*); Homey D. Clown (*In Living Color*); Krusty the Clown (*The Simpsons*); Der Clown (*Der Clown*); Brozo, el payaso tenebroso ("Brozo, The Shady Clown"); and Twisty (*American Horror Story*). This category might also include such clown-esque characters such as the Joker (Cesar Romero) on *Batman*. The episodic clown is a non-recurring character on a regular series show, including clowns on such programs as *Supernatural, Millennium, Scooby Doo, Buffy the Vampire Slayer, Seinfeld,* and *Animaniacs*. Lastly, the anthology clown is a character on an anthology show—one that does not feature a recurring cast or setting and tells a different narrative each week. Horror anthology shows have proven particularly popular, as the genre lends itself to the "television short story format," since effect is the purpose of horror. As such, sinister clowns show up on *The Twilight Zone, One Step Beyond, Tales from the Darkside, Tales from the Crypt,* and *Are You Afraid of the Dark?* A fourth category is needed for one clown who is in a category by himself: Pennywise.

Pennywise the Dancing Clown, before two feature films in 2017 and 2019, was first seen in 1990 in a made-for-television miniseries based on Stephen King's *It*. Delivered in two parts over concurrent evenings on ABC, eighteen million households saw Pennywise the Dancing Clown, which could transform into anything that frightened you and had a ravenous maw filled with sharp teeth, threaten the seven members of the Losers' Club as both tweens and adults. Boasting several significant and well-known television actors of the time (Richard Thomas, Harry Anderson, John Ritter, Seth Green, Tim Reid, and Jonathan Brandis, among others), the adaptation of Stephen King's 1986 novel was sanitized for television, yet still terrified.

In an article for *Vanity Fair* in anticipation of the new adaptation of *It*, entitled "How the Original *It* Miniseries Traumatized a Generation of Kids," Laura Bradley argues that the miniseries cemented the sinister clown on television and the miniseries terrified viewers not through gore (although there was more of that than in the average made-for-television film) but rather through creating empathetic characters and then terrifying them psychologically while never losing the physical threat of the clown (Bradley). The reviews at the time were glowing, and the nostalgia for the miniseries continues to be strong. Especially effective in making Pennywise terrifying was the performance of Tim Curry, whose previous best-known roles, Dr. Frank-N-Furter in *The Rocky Horror Picture Show* (1975) and Darkness, the devil creature from *Legend* (1985) inform Pennywise. He is seductive and playful, yet evil incarnate. He became the model for all television clowns (see also Riekki, *The Many Lives of* It: *Essays on the Stephen King Horror Franchise*).

The Series Television Clown

Although created in 1946 for a series of books and albums, Bozo the Clown is far better known for his advent on television in 1949, running in various incarnations over the world until 2001. The character is arguably different than other clowns (and characters, for that matter), as it was franchised by its creators and, thus, there were multiple simultaneous "Bozo the Clowns," rather than a single entity called Bozo. By 1956, dozens of local stations had local Bozo the Clown shows. In 1965, Larry Harmon developed and syndicated *Bozo's Big Top*, the first national show for markets without a local Bozo. This means that, at heart, Bozo is an unstable character. His appearance and voice varied from city to city. Bozo was also a national presence with a local identity. This also means there is no history of Bozo, only a handful of autobiographies by local Bozos.

Benjamin Radford reports on an urban legend about a moment on the Bozo show during a live broadcast in Boston, in which a child loses a game on the show and is offered a consolation prize, to which the young boy responds, "Cram it, clown," and Bozo allegedly called the kid an "unprintable name" (73). Most likely this event never happened, but the fact that it is a rumor that has spread about multiple Bozos in various forms shows our own willingness to believe that beneath the playful exterior, clowns are vulgar, grotesque, sinister, and child-hating.

From the same period as Bozo, Clarabell Hornblower served as a sidekick of Howdy Doody on his show (1947–1960). Howdy Doody was a marionette who hosted a television program that pioneered the interaction between humans and puppets in children's television. Clarabell was a clown who was a sidekick to a puppet (raising the anxiety factor for those disturbed by clowns and puppets, since both are liminal, categorically incongruous figures). Clarabell was further incongruous by having a girl's name, but clearly played by male performers [Bob Keeshan (1948–1952), who later achieved fame as Captain Kangaroo], Robert "Nick" Nicholson (1952–1954), and Lew Anderson (1954–1960), the last of whom returned to the role in the brief revival series *The New Howdy Doody Show* (1976–77). Clarabell was mute—the clown that communicated through a horn and gestures, although during the final episode he revealed that he knew how to talk and spoke his only words in the series: "Goodbye, kids." Clarabell was unruly and liked to squirt authority figures with a seltzer bottle, often showing an anarchic side.

What both Bozo and Clarabell did was normalize clowns in the living room for the first generation of children to grow up with television. They were friendly and entertaining. In an interview with Frank Avruch, who played Bozo in Boston, Jay Blocher informed Avruch that Blocher's uncle claimed to have tried to pull off Bozo's wig on air and Avruch scolded him. Avruch responded, "More than likely, I didn't scold him but I'm sure the Ringmaster did. 'Cause if I scolded him in front of the other kids, Bozo would be a meanie. So we couldn't do that. Bozo had to be just wonderful, kind and good and America" (Blocher). But he is also "bold and loud" (Blocher). The show wanted Bozo to be "wonderful, kind, good and America," which is an interesting combination. Partly the concern over keeping Bozo kind and good is the idea that the clown's appearance can be scary—large, flaming red hair, a giant red mouth and emphasized eyes make him both comic and eerie. Avruch also acknowledges the anarchic, unsettled nature of the role, confessing, "I can almost liken it to Hallowe'en, when you wear a costume. You sort of lose all your inhibitions" (Blocher). Bozo and Clarabell both model the children's television clown for the shows that followed, but they also embodied the child-friendly clown with an edge. What happens when a clown loses his inhibitions?

What followed in the wake was a variety of local clown shows, eventually leading to parodies of these shows in popular culture in the eighties and nineties, when those who watched *Howdy Doody* and *Bozo the Clown* as children in the fifties and sixties began to have children of their own. One of the most obvious parodies of the local television clown is the misanthrope Krusty the Clown from *The Simpsons*. He hosts his own television show for children with a live audience, but things often go horribly wrong. One of his sidekicks, Sideshow Bob tries to frame him for robbery and since has tried to kill both him and Bart Simpson, whenever possible. Krusty has been involved in money laundering, prostitution, child exploitation, extortion, robbing, plagiarism, gambling, and many, many other crimes. His personal life is a disaster with many former wives and a heart attack. Even when attempting to exploit his past as a television clown, Krusty always manages to transform it into something salacious or horrible sounding: "Hi kids, welcome to 'Krusty's Komedy Klassics' KKK? That can't be good" ["Simpsoncalifragilisticexpiala(Annoyed Grunt)cious"]. Krusty is a bad clown par excellence.

It is in the third annual Halloween show, "Treehouse of Horror III," that the evil clown motif shows its most obvious form on *The Simpsons*. In a sequence entitled "Clown without Pity," a parody of the "Talky Tina" *The Twilight Zone* episode, although the title is a reference to *Town without Pity* (1962), a film about four soldiers on trial for rape in occupied, postwar Germany and not relevant to *The Simpsons* episode at all, Bart is given a talking Krusty doll that is possessed and evil. It repeatedly attempts to kill Homer, or at least place him in embarrassing situations, like running out of the bathroom naked in an attempt to escape the doll. Disturbed by the doll's behavior, they call the hotline. Gary Lewis and the Playboys' "Everybody Loves a Clown" is the hold music, positing the title sentiments and then asking, "why don't you?" Finally, a repair man shows up, and tells them, "Here's the problem, pally; you got this doll set to evil," and pulls up the clown's shirt. On his back is a switch between "Good" and "Evil" and the repairmen switches it back to "Good." After that, the doll is well-behaved, if put upon ("Treehouse of Horror III"). The entire sequence is a parody both of killer-doll movies and killer-clown stories, but only works as a parody if one knows the original.

Terrifying clowns have shown up in other places in *The Simpsons*, most notably in the fourth season episode "Lisa's First Words," in which Homer, meaning well, builds Bart a horrific clown bed, its mouth open on the headboard, as if to devour anyone who sleeps on it. Bart imagines the clown on the headboard coming to life and saying, "If you should die before you wake," followed by a maniacal laugh. The scene then cuts to Bart sitting on the floor, his arms pulling his knees close to his chest, rocking in terror, repeating "Can't sleep, clown will eat me," which has now become a series of memes ("Lisa's First Word"). In short, Krusty, the evil Krusty doll, the clown bed, and other evil clowns have continually been exhibited on *The Simpsons*, and every last one is a parody of the sinister and grotesque. In the most Bakhtinian sense, that means that Krusty, the clown bed, and evil Krusty doll are sinister and Bakhtinian, since a parody of things sinister becomes sinister and grotesque in and of itself, resulting in the "Can't sleep, clowns will eat me meme"; as with clowns themselves, we laugh, but look over our shoulder and try to keep our distance without looking like we're keeping our distance. You don't want to attract the clown's attention, after all.

Also, from the nineties is Homey D. Clown, played by Damon Wayans on *In Living Color*. His real name is Herman Simpson, and he first appeared in a sketch entitled "Birthday Party" on the ninth episode of the first season, entitled "Introducing…. Homey D. Clown." Homey would mock, denigrate, and even hit kids, often with an air-filled bladder or a sock full of coins. A standard trope consists of Homey asking if the kids wanted to see him perform a standard clown activity, often one which would demean the clown. The kids would cheer and say they wanted to see it, and Homey would invoke the catchphrase for which he would become known: "Homey don't play that." Homey would then assert as a Black man he might be a clown, but he would never play the fool and demean himself for the entertainment of others.

The character was a clever satire on white expectations of Black performers, particularly comedians. Yet the character was more than that. When a little girl asks why he is a clown, he responds, "I guess it's because I got so much love to give. And it's part of my prison work release program." Until recently he had been in prison. Homey is bitter, disrespectful, and untrusting of institutions, authority, and white people. He is very much a clown in the Clarabell tradition, but one infused with racial consciousness and well aware of how his audience perceives him. Homey is a Bakhtinian clown who rejects the role of Bakhtinian clown. He is grotesque and ritualistic; he knows socially he is "low," but refuses to be the object of laughter, derision, or mockery. Instead, the audience laughs at Homey mocking those who would laugh at him. In an odd inversion, by refusing to be a Bakhtinian clown, Homey might be the most Bakhtinian.

In subsequent episodes, Homey is shown being disrespectful to his parole officer, with whom he is also having an affair, running a questionable carnival that allows him to abuse children (and adults), filling in for Santa at the mall (completely disrupting the tropes of sitting on Santa's lap and telling him what you want for Christmas), and getting scouts to rebel against their scoutmaster—all of which is anarchic, popular, and rebellious. Audiences laugh at Homey D. Clown, but we do not want to be on the receiving end of his attention. He is aggressive, belligerent, violent (especially towards children), and has a criminal past, all of which makes him suspect, dangerous and, dare I say, somewhat sinister, again, if one is on the receiving end of his anger.

A German television series, *Der Clown*, ran from 1998 to 2001 featured the exploits of an international police agent who disguises himself using a plastic clown mask to strike fear in the hearts of the criminals he fights. Agent Max Zander was the target of a car bomb attack, which killed his friend instead. Since his enemies believed him dead, Max decides to go underground and fight crime as "Der Clown." The poster for the series featured a man in a sinister grinning clown mask, aiming a rocket launcher. Der Clown is a rather brutal, ex-special forces soldier, so the series often featured scenes of Der Clown shooting, stabbing, and blowing up people. While the audience was clearly intended to be on the side of Zander, his appearance as Der Clown functioned in the same manner as Batman: designed to create fear in his opponents by not knowing whom they were fighting and by taking a form that at least some would find terrifying. It is a show whose gimmick was that the main character exploited the trope of the monster clown to fight crime.

The final clown we will consider in this section is something of an anomaly, in that he has his own television series and is also a serious journalist. On Mexican television since 2000 is the program *El Mañanero*, hosted by Brozo, al payaso tenebroso (Brozo, the Shady Clown), played by journalist Victor Trujillo. He is "a misogynistic, alcoholic, course and malignant character," transgressive and aggressive (Alonso 16, 76). Brozo is a corruption of "broza," slang for "vulgar people," that also evokes "Bozo," but is intended as "the antithesis of the stereotypical and fondly-remembered Bozo, the friendly clown" (Alonso, 79–80).

Trujillo developed Brozo within the Mexican tradition of clowns as satire, and purposefully made him sinister and threatening. He has long green hair, but bald on top (in the manner of Bozo's red hair), a red nose, and a round red mouth. Brozo was allegedly born in Santa Martha Acatitla prison in Mexico City, where his mother, Brozamama was serving time for attempted murder (Alonso 80). (Even his backstory is social satire, designed to call attention to the problem of women giving birth to and raising children in prison, see Garsd). Trujillo/Brozo confronts politicians, businesspeople, and the leaders of any institution to call attention to corruption. He refers to himself as "the Shady Clown," and behaves boorishly, politically incorrectly, and vulgarly, but does so in the name of being "the influential buffoon who confronts the powerful" (Alonso 85). Brozo is a truly Bakhtinian clown in every sense; he is grotesque, he inverts social order, he is the lowest of the low mocking the highest of the high for the purpose of social change, and the audience watches, enjoying the clown debasing himself in order to debase the political and social elite even more. The irony being, by being so grotesque and foul, he is actually not sinister, unless, of course, one is being interviewed by him.

The Episodic Clown

The episodic clown is a non-recurring character on a regular series show, manifesting in two forms, which can sometimes overlap. In episodic shows that feature supernatural or unexplained adversaries (i.e. "monster-of-the-week" shows), the evil clown gets a turn as the monster of the week (see: *Supernatural* and *Scooby-Doo, Where Are You?*). In other shows, often comedies, the presence of a clown demonstrates that a series regular is terrified of clowns (see: *Seinfeld* and *Animaniacs*). Or, in the case of *Buffy the Vampire Slayer*, there is a new monster each week, and Xander is scared of clowns. Episodic clowns can be live action or animated.

The model for episodic clowns might be found in the various incarnations of Scooby-Doo. In the original series, *Scooby-Doo, Where Are You?*, a ghost clown appears in the episode "Bedlam in the Big Top." As with all *Scooby-Doo* narratives, the revelation at the end of the episode is that the villain is neither ghost nor clown—after being invited to investigate Mr. Blackstone's Circus, which has proven accident-prone as of late, and audiences scared off by a ghost clown, which hypnotizes people with a gold coin. After the various members of Mystery, Inc. have been hypnotized into thinking they are circus performers, they set a trap and capture the ghost, who is revealed to be Harry the Hypnotist, who had been fired from the circus for theft. While the story is formulaic and silly, the clown is presented as menacing. Not only is it a ghost and creepy in appearance, it has the ability to hypnotize and make its victims do things they would not ordinarily. In the subsequent show, *The New Scooby and Scrappy-Doo Show*, Scooby is joined by his nephew Scrappy in investigating and solving mysteries. In "Crazy Carnival Caper," a man named Jerry disguises himself as a clown to steal a ruby from a science experiment. As with "Bedlam in the Big Top," the evil clown is merely a disguise for a common criminal, but the construction of clowns remains the same: they are criminal, scary, and not to be trusted.

In the *Animaniacs* episode "Clown and Out," it is revealed that Wakko Warner is terrified of clowns, which, of course, given cartoon logic, means he must be exposed to them frequently until he no longer is, or it is no longer funny that he is. In episodic television such as this, the revelation that a regular character is scared of clowns is often used as a source of humor in the horror. *Seinfeld* (1989–1998), for example, the most popular and celebrated sitcom when it was on, had two episodes that featured clowns: "The Opera" and "The Gymnast." In the former, Kramer encounters "Crazy" Joe Davola, dressed as a clown who, while perhaps not fully sinister, is certainly antagonistic and creepy. Elaine is dating him, not knowing he is the man also threatening Jerry and Kramer. Crazy Joe appears dressed in the manner of an Italian opera clown, specifically Pagliacci, and threatens Kramer, who reveals he is terrified of clowns, making Crazy Joe's conversation with him all the more sinister. In the latter, backstage at the circus, as Jerry and Katya have a discussion in the foreground, in the background Kramer steals a clown's hat and then returns it as he reiterates his fear of clowns. The clown in "The Gymnast" is not sinister or Bakhtinian, except to Kramer himself, who finds them scary no matter what.

Similarly, Xander Harris from *Buffy the Vampire Slayer* (1997–2004) suffers from coulrophobia. In the first season episode entitled "Nightmares," a boy in a coma begins manifesting the nightmares of the characters on the show. Whereas many of the characters' nightmares are played for horrific effect, Xander's are meant to serve as comic relief. Among the bad dreams Xander must face is a nightmarish clown, which is eventually defeated, leading Xander to sneer, "You were a lousy clown. Your balloon animals were pathetic. Everyone can make a giraffe." The clown is threatening, nightmarish, and indeed sinister. In both the case of *Seinfeld* and *Buffy*, one gets the sense that the revelation that a primary character suffers from coulrophobia predominantly for the comic effect. While Crazy Joe and the nightmare clown are threatening, the audience is clearly meant to find Kramer and Xander's fears funny, not empathetic. We laugh at, not scream with, which is still in keeping with Bakhtinian clown theory.

A clown makes a brief appearance in the episode "Dead Letters," the third episode of the first season of *Millennium*, a spin-off of *The X-Files* that ran on Fox for three seasons (1996–1999). In the opening sequence, protagonist Frank Black's daughter Jordan is terrified by a sinister clown crawling across the ceiling, which allegedly gave nightmares to the young actress who played the character. While crawling across the ceiling makes the clown uncanny, the makeup makes the clown sinister and grotesque.

The long-running series *Supernatural* (2005–2020) has thus far featured sinister clowns in two episodes. In season two's "Everybody Loves a Clown," at Cooper's Circus, a small-town carnival, a demonic clown seduces children into opening the door to their home so it can enter and kill their parents. As the brothers Winchester investigate, they discover that a rakshasa, a shapeshifting entity from Hindu mythology, has taken the form of a clown to eat people. As in previous series, we learn that younger brother Sam suffers from coulrophobia, Dean teasing him, "I know what you're thinking, Sam. Why did it have to be clowns? You didn't think I remember, do you? Come on, you still bust out crying when you see Ronald McDonald on the television" ("Everybody Loves a Clown"). Sam reminds Dean that he is afraid of flying, to which Dean responds that his fear is based in reality: planes can crash. Sam rejoins, "And apparently clowns kill!" asserting that his fear is also based in reality. As with all other episodes of *Supernatural*, once the brothers discover the true nature of the monster, they are able to defeat and kill it. The point of the episode is that a dangerous supernatural being takes the form of a clown (echoing *It*), that clowns are dangerous and must be carefully monitored. The monster was merely disguised as a clown to gain access to people's homes or to the children, which one can read as both a metaphor for child predators and as a confirmation that the clown is always more than what they appear to be and are truly categorically incongruous: they seem to be something they are not, but share enough qualities with the thing they seem to be that they violate our categories.

In season seven's "Plucky Pennywhistle's Magical Menagerie," the brothers Winchester investigate deaths in a small Kansas town that lead them to the eponymous family pizza place. "Pennywhistle" already contains the echo of "Pennywise," and the targeting of children and adults is also suggestive of *It*. Through investigation, the brothers learn that children draw their fears on a mural at Plucky Pennywhistle's Magical Menagerie, and that fear then comes to life and kills a hated parent. Given Sam's fear of clowns, it is not unexpected that he is attacked by a group of evil clowns. Adding to the terror that simple coulrophobia creates in Sam, there are multiple clowns dressed similarly like hobos, grinning malevolently (and let us remember the thin line between a smile and baring one's teeth as a threat display), bleeding glitter and attacking with seltzer bottles. As noted above from Carroll, all it takes to make clowns monstrous is to transform the elements they already have by making them fearsome. The clowns in this episode are fearsome horror clowns. As with the earlier episode, however, and linking Sam Winchester with Kramer and Xander Harris, Dean's constant teasing and mocking of his brother's fear of clowns, reminding him that "99.99% of clowns *don't* attack you," and that the clowns are actually fairly easily defeated by hunters, we are meant to find his fear a form of comic relief. Again, we laugh at, not with, and while the clowns may be sinister and meant to provoke some level of fear, in the end, the fear of clowns is ironically meant to be funny, except to Sam.

American Horror Story introduced Twisty the Clown (John Carroll Lynch) in season four, *American Horror Story: Freak Show*, although the character was not named aloud until season seven, *American Horror Story: Cult*. Twisty is a serial-killing clown who also holds children prisoner in an abandoned school bus. Twisty's real name is not known. What is known is that he was dropped on his head as a child. Running away from home as a teen, he became a clown with Rusty Westchester's Traveling Carnival. Audiences, especially children, loved Twisty. Jealous, some of the other freaks started a rumor he was a child molester (see above—the fear of adults that clowns have access to children). He lost his job and returned home to find his family dead. With no way of supporting himself, he tried to commit suicide by putting a shotgun in his mouth, but only succeeded in blowing his lower jaw away. Horribly disfigured, Twisty wears a mask that covers his lower face with a painting of a mouth filled with sharp teeth on it. He continually wears a filthy clown suit, clown makeup, and the horrid smile mask, while dragging a sack filled with weapons and clown toys.

In *Freak Show*, we first see Twisty find a young couple, kill the boy, and kidnap the girl. It is later revealed he wanted her for a babysitter for the other children he has kidnapped. In his mind, Twisty saves children from bad parents, and they should love him in exchange for their rescue. Twisty attempts to entertain his captives, but when they respond with terror, he rages. In the kind of logic only *American Horror Story* seems to have, Twisty is then hired by Gloria Mott to entertain her son, Dandy, despite the fact that Twisty is clearly a demented monster. Hitting Dandy with a juggling pin, Twisty returns to the bus in the woods, stalking children on Halloween and threatening the town. Finally, Edward Mordrake, who has a hidden, secret demon head attached to his body, arrives, using his magic to help Twisty tell his story to the children. Mordrake, learning from his demon head that Twisty is the one he needs to get revenge, kills the clown. His ghost is then invited to join the haunted freak show.

Twisty is one of several "ghost clowns," who began as a real monster clown. In the follow-up series *American Horror Story: Cult*, Twisty has become a figure of pop culture with his own line of toys and a graphic novel series. His ghost returns to threaten the child Oz, who is obsessed with Twisty, despite one of his mothers suffering from coulrophobia. We might also note that in *American Horror Story: Hotel*, John Wayne Gacy is a character who arrives to spend a night in the eponymous inn. Gacy is played by John Carroll Lynch, the same actor who plays Twisty, linking the two serial killing clowns.

American Horror Story takes the evil clown motif and expands it by making Twisty deformed by his suicide attempt. He is grotesque; he brings death and his own form of rebirth. The show repeatedly shows him as sinister, stalking children and adults, often only seen in the shadows and in the dark. So disturbing is Twisty that Clowns of America, International, the nation's largest clown organization, made a formal complaint to FX, the network that produces *American Horror Story* (Abramovitch). CAI president Glenn Kohlberger claims the series exploits coulrophobia, sensationalizing it, and perpetuating the "killer clown" trope (Abramovich). In fairness, Twisty is arguably the most violent, disturbing, dangerous television clown in history, certainly rising to the level of Pennywise, if not as widely viewed as *It*. Nevertheless, Twisty is a truly Bakhtinian, sinister presence on television, the embodiment of the sinister clown.

The Anthology Clown

Our third category is the anthology clown, a clown episode on an anthology program. The clown may not always be sinister in intention, but clowns, as this essay has argued, are inherently sinister by nature, rendering intention secondary. Possibly the first sinister clown on television that was intentionally sinister appeared in the anthology program *One Step Beyond*, which ran on ABC from 1959 to 1961. In the second season, on March 22, 1960, the episode "The Clown" aired, depicting a jealous older husband, Tom Regan, being abusive towards his young new bride Nonnie in a bar, and acting aggressively towards any other male who talked to her. Pippo the Clown, a mute who mimes, enters the bar and hands out balloons advertising the arrival of a travelling circus. Although Pippo's makeup is somewhat disturbing, with a large oversized mouth and buck teeth painted on his lips, emphasizing him as a devourer of sorts, Nonnie takes a shine to him when he gives her a balloon. Tom grabs scissors and cuts off a lock of the hair for the clown. Terrified at her husband's violence, Nonnie flees and comes across the circus. She takes shelter in Pippo's trailer, but Tom finds them and murders her with the scissors, fleeing the trailer as Pippo holds her body. As Tom runs from the scene of the crime and returns to the bar, he keeps seeing Pippo reflected in mirrors, trying to strangle him. No reason is given why this is happening, or if the visions of Pippo are real or merely manifestations of Tom's guilt over having murdered his wife. Eventually, Tom stops by a river and sees Pippo once again reflected behind him in the water, who strangles him and holds his head under the water. Pippo has never left his trailer, yet is soaking wet. Pippo is arrested for Tom's murder, Tom is arrested for Nonnie's, and show host John Newland reminds the viewers, "Look, a clown. Yes, usually his only function is to make us laugh. It is certainly not to disturb the secure curtain of reality." He points out that the clown was in his trailer, yet the clown was wet, and Tom will spend a long time in a jail cell, and somehow this is all "reality."

The episode is a wonderfully effective portrayal of the clown turned sinister. Though Pippo is childlike and seemingly playful and harmless, his makeup shows he is a giant maw, a mouth ready to devour and consume. He is, in fact, grotesque. Nonnie's delight in his antics rapidly transforms to Tom's terror at his presence in mirrors and in places he should not be. As Newland's closing host monologue reminds us, clowns tamper with "the secure curtain of reality," and are untrustworthy. Pippo is quite sinister and disturbing in appearance and action. While he himself does not murder, it appears as if he could strangle Tom for the murder of Nonnie, if not for the police finally arriving to arrest Tom.

The only *The Twilight Zone* episode to deal with a clown featured a clown that was incidentally sinister and served as an antagonist figure but was not meant to be seen as malevolent or evil. Nevertheless, he is creepy. The 1961 episode "Five Characters in Search of an Exit" (tangentially named after two absurdist plays: Luigi Pirandello's *Six Characters in Search of an Author* and Jean Paul Sartre's *No Exit*) featured five archetypal people trapped in a cylindrical room, open at the top: a soldier (specifically a major), a ballerina, a hobo, a bagpiper, and a clown. The five are trapped in the room. The major is the protagonist. He does not know why he is in the room. The others do not either, but it is the major who insists that something insidious must be happening and attempts to organize the others into an escape. The clown serves as an antagonist of sorts. Wearing a potted plant for a hat, featuring Italian-style clown makeup and carrying a small umbrella, he ridicules the seriousness of the major with mock seriousness himself: "I'm a clown. Which is neither here, there, nor anyplace. I could be a certified public accountant, a financier, a left-handed pitcher who throws only curves. What difference does it make? We're here, because we're here, because we're here. Because-we're-here" ("Five Characters in Search of an Exit.") The clown is not sinister, but he is antagonistic, confrontational without being direct, and argumentative. Where the other characters seem resigned to their fate and the major seeks to lead a breakout, the clown is actually in a positive state because he is with others. He can entertain, challenge, breed laughter, or mock. Whether in a cylindrical room, a big-top circus or a sidewalk, so long as there are others around, the clown is all right.

The major believes they are in hell. The hobo believes they are in purgatory. The great twist, of course, is revealed when they do escape (with the clown helping). The major is able to climb out of the open top of the room. He drops over the wall, and the show reveals that he is a doll who has fallen to the sidewalk. A girl picks him up and returns him to the charity toy barrel in which the other four dolls are. In keeping with the dramas that inspired the title, the episode appears to ask existential questions leading to the discovery that we are, metaphorically speaking, just dolls in a barrel that think we are bigger and more alive than we are. Only the clown, bemused by the situation instead of horrified by it, is not horrified. This clown is not sinister, but he is Bakhtinian, as is the situation, discovering a death (the characters go from being live actors to inanimate dolls at the end), and then rebirth, as it is clear they repeat this cycle over and over, completing the existential horror of the episode. There is no escape, there is no exit.

Tales from the Darkside, George Romero's syndicated short horror anthology, featured a clown story in its first season, although the clown was not sinister, but pathetic. In "If the Shoe Fits" (Season 1, Episode 18), politician Bo Gumbs believes people will only vote for someone who is entertaining, so he performs his "aw shucks" southern politician persona to the hilt. Before a big campaign rally, a hotel bellboy presses his suit, which comes back as a clown suit, complete with oversized bow tie, large lapels and buttons, a paper dickey instead of a shirt, rainbow suspenders, and giant clown shoes. Only he can see the suit as a clown suit, to all other characters it appears normal. As he attempts to remove the suit he begins "clowning around," taking pratfalls and being ridiculous. Eventually, the car comes to take him to the rally and it is a small clown car. The metaphor is a subtle as a sledgehammer—politicians are clowns who employ superficial charm and performance techniques to win elections when their own agenda is much more selfish and insidious. While Bo Gumbs is not a sinister clown in the sense of the other clowns discussed here, he certainly is a Bakhtinian one, grotesque and debased. We laugh at, not with Bo Gumbs, but the underlying horror is the implication that the episode reflects the American political system. We indeed vote for grotesque clowns.

Not to be outdone, *Tales from the Crypt*, HBO's horror anthology series offers a clown puppet, combining two Bakhtinian horror tropes (puppet and clown) into one; in 1992's "Strung Along," a fourth season episode in which aging, retired puppeteer Joseph Renfield is afraid his younger wife Ellen is having an affair with his young assistant, David, Joseph spends much of his time taking to his most famous creation, Coco the Clown, a classic clown-type puppet with a sense of revenge. While the episode employs many of the standard puppet/doll/ventriloquist dummy elements (changes of expression on the puppet's face even though it is painted on, doll changing position when people are not looking, doll appears to be staring, finally inanimate object begins to speak and move on its own), the episode is able to effectively convey the horror of this little clown figure encouraging violence from the puppeteer. As with narratives of this sort, the question remains if Coco was, in fact, alive, or if all of Coco's words and actions were in Joseph's head. While Dave and Ellen trick Joseph into having a heart attack by making him think Coco stabbed Ellen to death, the two of them are subsequently killed and strung up like puppets themselves. Without being grotesque or evil-looking, Coco, a sweet, traditional-looking clown, comes across as sinister, not just because of what happens in the episode, but in the relationship between Joseph and Coco (or is it Joseph and his own subconscious)?

Lastly, the Nickelodeon series *Are You Afraid of the Dark?*—about a small group of friends ("The Midnight Society") telling each other horrific tales around a campfire—features a few sinister clowns, beginning with its own credit sequence. The theme song and opening credits have a shot of a scary clown puppet that flashes across the screen as part of a series of scary images: a swing in an empty playground slowly swaying, shutters beating against the wall in a rainstorm, children's laughter over the image of an abandoned skateboard in an attic, and the camera then moves to pan down a hobo clown puppet with a sinister grin The flash of a clown hints at the grotesque and carnivalesque nature of the tales to follow.

In "The Tale of Laughing in the Dark" (the second episode of the series), the clown Zeebo is introduced, who will be referenced in several other subsequent series. In the tale told in this episode, Josh, his friend Weegee and his sister Kathy visit Playland Amusement Park. The ghost train ride in the park is called "Laughing in the Dark," and Kathy refuses to ride as she has heard it is haunted by the ghost of a clown named Zeebo. Josh mocks her and in turn is dared to go into the haunt by himself by a carny who runs the ride. The group leaves, but they research the carnival the next day and learn there actually was a clown named Zeebo who, after stealing the circus payroll was chased by police into Laughing in the Dark. Dropping his cigar, he burnt the ride down with himself in it. His spirit allegedly remains in the haunted house, which has been rebuilt with a mannequin that looks like Zeebo at the exit. Josh accepts Weegee's challenge to go through alone, as the carny had dared him to and promises to bring the replica Zeebo's nose out with him. Josh goes through and takes the nose, but in doing so has angered the spirit of Zeebo, who haunts him. After several days of smelling cigars, hearing maniacal laughter and strange voices, including one that repeatedly says, "Put it back," Josh replaces the nose and leaves a box of cigars as a peace offering. The ending hints that Zeebo may be a real ghost or the carny who challenged Josh might be behind it all.

Regardless, the episode does a few things not seen before and many that have been. Zeebo is a ghost, as well as a doll, as well as a real clown (back in the twenties); thus, there are multiple Zeebos in the story. The idea that the clown is a ghost, however, is new. Zeebo is a sinister clown, not merely because he is undead, but also because he was a criminal, and because his life was somewhat salacious (as represented by the smoking of cigars, always a marker of decadence, corruption and depravity in narratives aimed at young viewers). Zeebo is sinister and Bakhtinian, threatening and grotesque.

Zeebo is referenced in a videogame called "Zeebo's Big House" in the subsequent season three episode, "The Tale of the Crimson Clown." Brothers Sam and Mike are terrorized by the eponymous clown. To buy a videogame, Sam steals the money Mike was going to use to buy his mother a present. In the antique store window, next to the toy store, Mike points out a clown figure and tells Sam it is the "Crimson Clown" and it will come scare Sam until he is good. When they return home, the clown doll is in Sam's room. The Crimson Clown proceeds to terrify Sam throughout the night until he apologizes and begs for another chance, waking again to find that time has reversed and he never stole the money. The story is a cautionary one, a typical fairytale about doing the right thing; always being honest, otherwise the monsters will get you. Nevertheless, the doll itself is a creepy clown that becomes far creepier at six feet tall. The clown is sinister, grotesque, but also serves to threaten Sam with death, until his "rebirth," in which he discovers he has been given a second chance. That would have not happened without a Bakhtinian clown terrifying him.

Conclusion

As Bakhtin reminds us, carnivalesque death is a way to combat fear of actual death (Rabelais 91). A grotesque and buffoonish death as seen when one is killed by a clown is both "droll and monstrous," and a means to laugh at our own death (Rabelais 91). When we view sinister clowns on television or through other media, we may be scared, and we may laugh, but we do both as they are preferable to thinking about the seriousness of our own demise. Sinister clowns on television, like much of everything else on television, are a distraction, one designed to keep us from thinking too much about things that are genuinely terrifying and threatening. Regardless, the very nature of the clown keeps him sinister, even when he is not intended to be. We invite the clown into our living room, but we are equally glad the television also turns off.

Works Cited

Abramovitch, Seth. "Professional Clown Club Attacks 'American Horror Story' Over Murderous Character." *The Hollywood Reporter*, October 15, 2014. Web. Accessed November 12, 2019.
Alonso, Paul. *Satiric TV in the Americas: Critical Metatainment as Negotiated Dissent*. Oxford: Oxford University Press, 2016. Print.
American Horror Story: Cult. Twentieth Century Fox. 2018. DVD.
American Horror Story: Freak Show. Twentieth Century Fox. 2015. DVD.
Bakhtin, Mikhail M. *Problems of Dostoevski's Poetics*. Trans. Caryl Emerson. Minneapolis: University of Minnesota Press, 1984. Print.
_____. *Rabelais and His World*. Trans. Hélène Iswolsky. Bloomington University Press, 1984. Print.
"Bedlam in the Big Top." *Scooby Doo, Where Are You?* Writ. Ken Spears, Joe Ruby, and Bill Lutz. Dir. Joseph Barbera and William Hanna. CBS. November 15, 1969. Television.
Blocher, Jay. "Hey Kids, It's Bozo: Interview with Frank Avruch." *TV Party* (August 2010): http://www.tvparty.com/. Web. Accessed November 13, 2019.
Bradley, Laura. "How the Original *It* Miniseries Traumatized a Generation of Kids." *Vanity Fair*, August 31, 2017. Web. Accessed November 12, 2019.
Campbell, Joseph. *The Hero with a Thousand Faces*. 1949. Novato, CA: New World Library, 2008. Print.
Carroll, Noël. "Horror and Humor," *The Journal of Aesthetics and Art Criticism* 57:2 (Spring 1999): 145 160. Print.
Clasen, Mathias. *Why Horror Seduces*. Oxford: Oxford University Press, 2017. Print.
"The Clown." *One Step Beyond*. Writ. Gabrielle Upton. Dir. John Newland. ABC. March 22, 1960. Youtube.
Der Clown—Die Serie. Universum Film GmbH, 2006. DVD.
"Clown and Out." *Animaniacs*. Writ. Nicholas Hollander and Paul Rugg. Dir. Alfred Gimeno. Fox Television. November 4, 1993. Television.

"Crazy Carnival Caper." *The New Scooby and Scrappy-Doo Show*. Writ. Gene Ayers. Dir. Oscar Dufau, George Gordon, Carl Urbano, John Walker, and Rudy Zamora. ABC. October 15, 1983. Television.

Davidson, Jon. *Clown: Readings in Theatre Practice*. New York: Palgrave Macmillan, 2013. Print.

"Dead Letters." *Millennium: The Complete First Season*. Writ. James Hong and Glenn Morgan. Dir. Thomas J. Wright. Twentieth Century Fox Home Video, 1996. DVD.

Durwin, Joseph. "Coulrophobia and the Trickster," *Trickster's Way* 3:1 (2004). Web. Accessed October 24, 2019.

"Everybody Loves a Clown." *Supernatural: The Complete Second Season*. Writ. John Shiban. Dir. Phil Sgriccia. Warner Home Video, 2006. DVD.

"Five Characters in Search of an Exit." *The Twilight Zone: The Complete Third Season*. Writ. Rod Serling. Dir. Lamont Johnson. Image Entertainment, 1961. DVD.

Garsd, Jasmine. "As more women are incarcerated in Mexico, so are their babies." *PRI.com*. April 5, 2018. Web. Accessed November 23, 2019.

"The Gymnast." *Seinfeld: The Complete Sixth Season*. Writ. Alec Berg and Jeff Schaffer. Dir. Andy Ackerman. Sony Pictures Home Entertainment, 1994. DVD.

"If the Shoe Fits." *Tales from the Darkside: The Complete Series*. Writ. N. Ward and Armand Mastroianni. Dir. Armand Mastroianni. Paramount Home Entertainment, 1985. DVD.

"Introducing… Homey D. Clown" *In Living Color*. Writ. Keenan Ivory Wayans et. al. Dir. Paul Miller. Fox Television, June 17, 1990. Television.

It. Writ. Tommy Lee Wallace and Lawrence D. Cohen. Dir. Tommy Lee Wallace. Warner Home Video, 1990. DVD.

"Lisa's First Word." *The Simpsons: The Complete Fourth Season*. Writ. Jeff Martin. Dir. Mark Kirkland. Twentieth Century Fox Home Video, 1992. DVD.

"Nightmares." *Buffy the Vampire Slayer: The Complete Series*. Writ. David Greenwalt. Dr. Bruce Seth Green. Twentieth Century Fox Home Video, 1997. DVD.

"The Opera." *Seinfeld: The Complete Fourth Season*. Writ. Larry Charles. Dir. Tom Cherones. Sony Pictures Home Entertainment, 1992. DVD.

"Plucky Pennywhistle's Magical Menagerie." *Supernatural: The Complete Seventh Season*. Writ. Andrew Dabb and Daniel Loflin. Dir. Mike Rohl. Warner Home Video, 2012. DVD.

Radford, Benjamin. *Bad Clowns*. Albuquerque: University of New Mexico Press, 2016. Print.

Riekki, Ron, ed. *The Many Lives of* It: *Essays on the Stephen King Horror Franchise*. Jefferson, NC: McFarland, 2020. Print.

"Simpsoncalifragilisticexpiala(Annoyed Grunt)cious." *The Simpsons: The Complete Eighth Season*. Writ. Al Jean and Mike Reiss. Dir. Chuck Sheetz. Twentieth Century Fox Home Video, 1997. DVD.

"Strung Along." *Tales from the Crypt: The Complete Series*. Writ. Yale Udolff and Kevin Yaeger. Dir. Kevin Yaeger. Home Box Office Home Video, 1992. DVD.

"The Tale of Laughing in the Dark." *Are You Afraid of the Dark? The Complete First Season*. Writ. Chloe Brown. Dir. Ron Oliver. Cookie Jar Entertainment, 1992. DVD.

"The Tale of the Crimson Clown." *Are You Afraid of the Dark?: The Complete Third Season*. Writ. Darren Kotania. Dir. Ron Oliver. Cookie Jar Entertainment, 1994. DVD.

"Treehouse of Horror III." *The Simpsons: The Complete Fourth Season*. Writ. Al Jean, Mike Reiss, Jay Kogan, Wallace Wolodarski, Sam Simon, and Jon Vitti. Dir. Carlos Baeza. Twentieth Century Fox Home Video, 1992. DVD.

Killer Klowns vs. the Blob
Klowning Around in the Generation Gap
Dale Bailey

The 1988 film *Killer Klowns from Outer Space*—the only commercially released movie by the trio of writers, directors, and producers known as the Chiodo brothers—is easy to dismiss as an affectionate send-up of cult films that has become a cult film itself. Given the gleefully absurd title, which echoes the titles of half a dozen '50s-era sci-fi/horror films—*It Came from Outer Space* (1953), *It! The Terror from Beyond Space* (1958), and *I Married a Monster from Outer Space* (1958), among them—it's easy to see why critic Bill Osgerby lumps the movie in with "ironic pastiches" such as 1991's *Chopper Chicks in Zombietown* (139). But *Killer Klowns* is more than an exercise in irony, and it's not entirely a pastiche. It's also a critical revision of the 1958 teen classic *The Blob*, as director Stephen Chiodo points out in "The Making of Killer Klowns," a feature included in the film's 2018 *Special Edition* Blu-ray release. Chiodo notes that the movie reworks "essentially *The Blob*, [producer] Jack Harris's *The Blob*." In both films, he adds, "kids try to communicate to the authorities that there [are] monsters." The key word, of course, is "try."

Despite this fundamental similarity, the pictures diverge in tone. *The Blob* is clearly a product of Eisenhower-era conservatism. It plays its far-fetched story straight. *Killer Klowns*, though it too is the product of a conservative decade in American history, embraces its ridiculous premise: the monsters really *are* Killer Klowns from outer space. Their spaceship looks like a circus tent, their weapons include balloon animals and popcorn guns, and they cocoon their victims in pink cotton candy for later consumption.

This absurdist twist on the earlier film is crucial. For while it's true that the plot of the Chiodo brothers' would-be masterpiece maps broadly onto that of *The Blob*, key changes reflect troubling transformations in the

American teenage experience. In this context, two facets of the movies provide especially fruitful lines of inquiry. One is the role adults play in each film. The other is the nature of the monsters the teenage protagonists must repel.

These Kids Today

As Thomas Patrick Doherty points out in *Teenagers and Teenpics: The Juvenilization of American Movies in the 1950s*, adolescents in the late 1950s were an increasingly important demographic for Hollywood producers. Films such as *Invaders from Mars* (1953), *Invasion of the Saucer Men* (1957), and *The Giant Gila Monster* (1959) pitted youth against age, forcing them to reconcile in the face of an invasive threat. *The Blob*, in its depiction of teens in conflict with skeptical adults, is a clear iteration (and almost certainly the best one) of this basic plot. Other films, such as *I Was a Teenage Werewolf* (1957), *Teenage Zombies* (1959), and *Teenagers from Outer Space* (1959), frame friction between teens and adults in slightly different, but fundamentally similar ways. Clearly tension between the Greatest Generation and their youthful progeny was in the air.

The concept of the teenager was a relatively new paradigm for understanding the transitional years between childhood and adulthood. The *OED* informs us that the word "teenager" itself was first used early in the twentieth century, but the *Dictionary of American Slang* points out that it didn't enter everyday American vernacular until after World War II, when our understanding of American young adulthood underwent a radical shift (Wentworth and Flexner 538–539). Jonathan Green reiterates this argument, noting that "the modern concept of the teenager as representing a segregated social group is a creation of the 1940s, if not the decade that followed; [...] it required rock 'n' roll for the teenager proper" (352). Prior to the 1950s, young people were usually seen as either children or young adults. But in the '50s, adolescence began to be seen as a liminal space between those two cultural categories: adolescents were no longer children, but they had yet to be granted full adult autonomy. The roots of this transformation are far more complex than the advent of rock and roll, of course, though the influence of the developing musical genre should not be underestimated. But two other key changes in American culture seem even more crucial. Access to cars dramatically changed adolescent courtship rituals and the post-war economic boom created a generation of youthful consumers prosperous enough to invest their money—and their sense of identity—in a nascent adolescent consumer culture that has, in the decades since, come to be a defining force in music, television, and film.

The angst adults experienced because of this incipient transformation in their children is evident in the genesis of another new concept, the juvenile delinquent, apparent in noted psychiatrist Fredric Wertham's lamentably successful attack on the "nefarious" influence of horror comics (believed to be a contributing cause of juvenile delinquency), in the Broadway musical *West Side Story* (1957), and in films such as *Rebel Without a Cause* (1957) and *The Wild One* (1953), in which Marlon Brando, asked what he is rebelling against, snarls, "Whaddya got?"

Both sorts of movies were *about* teenagers. But films such as *The Blob* were *for* teenagers. And despite their dubious merits as cinematic art, they voiced anxieties shared by many teens: adults didn't understand them; worse yet, adults often distrusted them; and, worst of all, adults sometimes actively exploited them in deeply destructive ways. Many of these threads are woven together in *The Blob* and reflected in its reinvention as *Killer Klowns*.

The first acts of the two films track almost scene by scene. But *Killer Klowns* alters its source material to set up important thematic contrasts. For example, *The Blob*'s opening credits play over a tame quasi-rock song called "Beware of the Blob," written for the film (by Burt Bacharach and Mack David) and performed by studio musicians who've been dubbed "The Five Blobs." Though the opening credits of *Killer Klowns* also feature a song tailored for the film, the Chiodo brothers replace the "tasteful" restraint of "Beware of the Blob" with a blast of irreverent punk from The Dickies, an established band that had already recorded such flippant songs as "If Stuart Could Talk" (1983), about a loquacious penis. As its title suggests, their debut album, *The Incredible Shrinking Dickies* (1979) mined the same vein of sophomoric humor. "Beware the Blob," designed by adults to appeal to teenage listeners, is an artifact of the established order. The eponymous theme song of *Killer Klowns* thumbs its nose at that order. It's a punk rock song by a youthful band that specialized in mocking adult sensibilities. Though both films are set in quintessential American small towns—*The Blob* in "Downington" and *Killer Klowns* in "Crescent Cove"—teen culture in those towns has changed dramatically over the course of three decades.

This transformation is also evident in the films' parallel Lover's Lane sequences. *Killer Klowns* presents far more suggestive material than the modest necking depicted in the earlier film. *The Blob*'s protagonists, Steve and Jane, exchange only a single kiss before Jane turns away, spooked by her date's ardor. The entire scene is played with utter sobriety, in every sense of the word. Modesty and sobriety play no part in *Killer Klowns*. A local DJ, audible over a car radio, refers to the kids on Lover's Lane (here called the Top of the World) as "make-out artists." The *mise-en-scène* bears out his description. Hatchbacks hang open, with legs dangling out suggestively, and kids help themselves to cans of beer. Mike and Debbie, our stand-ins for Steve and Jane, haven't quite gotten to the "making-out" stage of the evening, but they're clearly moving in that direction. They're lying in the back of Mike's SUV, sharing a bottle of wine and canoodling atop an inflatable raft that looks comfortably soft, if somewhat less than seaworthy.

The arrival of Mike's friends the Terenzi brothers makes the risqué elements here explicit. The Terenzi brothers are driving a rented ice-cream truck surmounted by a giant clown statue named Jojo. Brandishing popsicles, the brothers use the truck's PA system to pitch their wares to the lovers who've sought solitude at the Top of the World:

> I'm Jojo the ice cream clown,
> With the bestest ice cream in town.
> We'll give you the stick,
> You give it a lick,
> And it'll tickle you all the way down!
> Ice cream, ice cream!
> We brought our goodies here to you
> A tasty treat for while you screw!

The last line is delivered with a pelvic thrust. As with the title of The Dickies' album, this bit of doggerel, not to mention the gesture, isn't subtle. Nor is the Terenzi brothers' departure, under a fusillade of empty beer cans, a detail suggestive of adolescent rejection of childhood pleasures in favor of adult ones, such as sex and alcohol, that are not yet fully available outside the remote teenage haven at the Top of the World.

We've come a long way from the sharply delineated (and deeply conservative) social mores depicted in *The Blob*. Unlike Steve and Jane, Mike and Debbie inhabit a complex and ill-defined interstitial space that partakes of childhood (the ice-cream truck) and adulthood (sex and alcohol) alike, a reading reinforced by Catherine Driscoll's observation that "the transitions of adolescence leave adolescents stranded between categories, functions, and meanings" (112). This interstitial gap between childhood and adulthood is the social and psychological equivalent of no man's land, a liminal field of fire between the entrenched safety of the clearly defined social roles on either side. An invasion of Killer Klowns only complicates matters.

Kids, Cops, and Parents

Both *The Blob* and *Killer Klowns* employ a standard horror formula, focusing on the eruption of a disruptive force, a monster, into an established order that must gather its strength to repel or destroy the threat, restoring the world to its original, uncorrupted state. But who is going to mount such a response if the only witnesses to the attack are mere ... teenagers?

This is the principal issue in both movies.

Yet the parameters of the problem—and its solution—differ dramatically. Marlon Brando might have been spitting rebellion in *The Wild One* as early as 1953, but five years later word is only beginning to trickle down to the kids in *The Blob*. In Downington, the generation gap is more like a sidewalk crack. This accounts for the contrasting function of parents in the two films. In *Killer Klowns*, parents are nearly absent, reflecting core anxieties of the late '80s; in *The Blob*, parents are still very much on the scene. Jane's father may be fuming when he arrives at the police station to collect her, but in an era when any hint of sexual impropriety could derail a young woman's life, his ill-temper makes sense. It springs from concern for his daughter's welfare. As a young man, Steve doesn't face the same exacting standard of sexual purity. This may account for the more affable relationship he enjoys with his folks, who arrive at the police station puzzled rather than angry. "Steve is not in the habit of telling lies," his father—Pop, Steve calls him—tells the police.

It's hard to imagine the characters in *Killer Klowns* calling their fathers "Pop." It's hard to imagine them even having fathers. By the 1980s, "latchkey kids"—children left unsupervised while both parents worked—were a matter of increasing cultural anxiety, as a 1985 *The New York Times* editorial called "Help for the Latchkey Kids" suggests. As early as 1976, the United States Department of Commerce estimated that thirteen percent of American children between ages seven and thirteen came home from school to empty houses—a number that "alerted educators, politicians, and people from all walks of life concerned with the welfare of youth," as a 1986 article for *Family Relations* informs us (Robinson et al. 473). By the time *Killer Klowns* came out in 1988, the *Chicago Tribune* was reporting that "[m]ore than 60 percent of America's households have no parent at home during the day," adding that "[f]or parents, educators and policymakers, the rising number of children in 'self care' is a troubling phenomenon" ("Latchkey Kid Is King").

Killer Klowns reflects the pervasive unease occasioned by this trend. It depicts a universe essentially void of parents, in which teenagers are exposed to adult temptations—and their associated risks—without adult guidance. Even amidst the Klown crisis, no one thinks to consult a parent. No one worries that a parent will wonder where they are. And when Mike drops Debbie off at home in a misguided attempt to protect her, no parents are present to advise her that it's never a good idea to take a shower in a horror movie. The only parent we see in the film is having dinner with friends at Big Top Burger, a local fast-food restaurant, and she's so tied up in conversation with another adult that she almost doesn't notice when a Klown tries to lure her little girl outside into the playground.

The authorities in *Killer Klowns* are little more reliable, another significant shift between the two films, each of which presents viewers with a contrasting pair of police officers. In *The Blob*, Lieutenant Dave, Downington's commanding officer, has no intrinsic distrust of teenagers; he just can't bring himself to countenance a farfetched tale of predatory goo. His junior officer, Sergeant Bert, is the only adult in the movie who doubts the kids simply be*cause* they're kids. But when he insists that Steve and Jane's story is part of an elaborate adolescent prank, Lt. Dave pushes back, pointing out that it's not "a crime to be seventeen years old."

Thirty years later, *Killer Klowns* flips this dynamic, highlighting the chasm that has opened between teenagers and adult authorities. Now men like Sgt. Bert are in charge. Deputy Mooney, the presiding officer in Crescent Cove, categorically equates adolescence and delinquency. His disdain for teenagers is evident from his first scene, when he dismisses a young man crossing the street as a "little son of a bitch." A more telling sequence directly parallels an episode in *The Blob*. In the earlier film, Lt. Dave gently reprimands Steve for an ill-advised car-racing stunt. "What am I going to do with you kids? You know I don't wanna haul you in," he says ruefully, before sending Steve on his way with a fatherly injunction: "No more horseplay. Now get outta here." Mooney, on the other hand, can't—or won't—distinguish youthful hijinks from malicious criminality. At the station with two young college students he's collared for drinking in the park, Mooney is egregiously hostile, though the young men are presented as sober and polite, if mildly annoyed. "It's scum like you that are killing this town," Mooney snaps, before physically assaulting the teenagers. After Mooney's youthful fellow deputy, Dave Hansen, intervenes, one of the students risks a mild protest. "What's the problem?" he asks, eliciting this charming riposte: "You're the problem, you little shit!"

Both Sgt. Bert and Mooney are driven by paranoia and insecurity, a correspondence reinforced by *Killer Klowns*' callbacks to the earlier film's dialogue. Like Sgt. Bert, Mooney dismisses Mike and Debbie's story as a prank, fearing, in an almost direct quote from *The Blob*, that they're trying to "make fools of the police department," and adding, in a line that will pay off later in the film, "you're not going to make a dummy out of me." He worries, like Sgt. Bert, that the teenagers "have the whole town in on this." He later accuses Hansen and his "college flunkies" of trying to "break [him] down," repeating verbatim a phrase Sgt. Bert employs in much the same context. These explicit parallels highlight the degree to which the Chiodo brothers relied on the earlier movie in scripting their own. They also amplify its critique of *The Blob*'s conviction that any conflict between teenagers and adults can be resolved, and work to establish the grave consequences of such a failed reconciliation.

Those consequences become clear when emergency calls begin to pour in. Mooney, unlike Sgt. Bert, has no higher-ranking officer at hand to rein him in. Sgt. Bert ultimately comes around. Mooney does not. He responds to reports of the Klown invasion with smirking disbelief, finally lighting a cigar (a symbol of smug patriarchal authority), picking up a gun magazine (likewise), and letting the phone ring unanswered. When a Klown shows up at the station, Mooney reacts with fury, still convinced that he's the victim of an elaborate practical joke. The Klown douses Mooney's cigar, exposing the deputy's impotence with a classic clown gag: a plastic flower that sprays a jet of water into the observer's face. Soon afterward, the paranoid deputy finds himself gorily repurposed as a Klown's ventriloquist's dummy, reprising in the most literal way the anxiety he revealed earlier in the film. "Don't worry, Dave," the Mooney-dummy tells his fellow officer, "all we want to do is kill you." The "we," of course, can be read two ways: Mooney is obviously being forced to voice the murderous hostility of the invading Klowns, but the pretext of compulsion allows him to express openly the repressed animosity he feels toward Deputy Hansen.

That fact that his malice is directed specifically at his junior officer is also important, for Dave Hansen's claim to adult status is not entirely settled. Despite his official post, he has a lingering affinity with the teenagers of Crescent Cove. In *The Blob*, Dave's moral analog, the sympathetic Lt. Dave—the name repetition can hardly be coincidental—is in charge. Deputy Dave, however, shares neither Lt. Dave's commission nor his age. He and Mooney may be appointed at the same rank, but Mooney's threat to report his fellow deputy to the unseen "Chief" suggests that Mooney still carries more weight. Mooney's contemptuous epithet for him—"Mr. Police Academy"—underscores his rookie status on the force. Perhaps most important, Dave is young enough to have dated Debbie. When he throws in his lot with Mike and Debbie and takes up the battle against the Killer Klowns, he symbolically surrenders the power inherent in adult authority, making explicit the film's argument with *The Blob*'s faith that teenagers and adults can come together to defeat the incursion of a monstrous threat.

The symbolic qualities of those monsters reinforce the two films' conflicting visions of the potential for reconciliation between adolescents and adults. In *Killer Klowns*, they also highlight the costs and consequences incurred when such a reconciliation proves impossible.

Monsters and Metaphors

According to Judith Hess, "Genre films [...] serve the interests of the ruling class by assisting in the maintenance of the status quo," a point

Stephen King echoes in *Danse Macabre*, writing that "when we discuss monstrosity we are expressing our faith and belief in the norm[....] The writer of horror fiction is neither more nor less than an agent of the status quo" (41). Critic Andrew Scahill also contends that "horror can easily be the mouthpiece of the status quo." It's not insignificant that the phrase "status quo" turns up in all three comments. Even Jon Towlson, who identifies a subversive strain of horror movies in a recent study, concedes that the "majority of horror films […] can and should be considered reactionary" (5). King sums matters up with his usual mordant directness: "[m]onstrosity," he argues, "fascinates us because it appeals to the conservative Republican banker in a three-piece suit who resides within all of us" (41).

At first glance, *The Blob* and *Killer Klowns* confirm this understanding of the genre: the monster embodies a disruptive threat; the heroes work to preserve the existing order. Closer scrutiny reveals that *Killer Klowns* presents a thematic challenge to its predecessor. *The Blob* is a deeply conservative film. *Killer Klowns* is a profoundly subversive one. Nowhere is this more evident than in the monsters their teenage protagonists square off against.

Those monsters couldn't be more different. In a brief overview of *The Blob* in the *Historical Dictionary of Science Fiction Cinema*, M. Keith Booker observes that the eponymous creature "bears certain metaphorical resemblances to Cold War visions of an all-devouring communism" (77). This is an understatement. The Cold War subtext is virtually transparent. Like the specter of nuclear war, the Blob, as safely ensconced in its meteor as an atomic warhead atop an ICBM, brings death from the sky. Like the threat of a fifth column of deadly communist sympathizers, the Blob oozes unseen among us, hidden in the grocery stores, diners, and cinemas Americans frequent daily. Like Senator Joseph McCarthy on the prowl for communists, Steve and Jane spend most of the movie *looking* for the Blob; only in the last twenty minutes do they actually confront and combat the enemy. And, of course, the Blob itself, a bloated, shapeless, crimson monstrosity, is literally a Red Scare that at the film's close is not killed—"I don't think it can be killed," Lt. Dave says—but merely frozen (like the Cold War itself) and expelled from the country to the icy Arctic.

It's hard to read *The Blob* in more complex terms. Divorced of its immediate Cold War context, it partakes of no larger tradition of cultural significance. Before 1958, we had no Blobs, and apart from an inferior sequel, *Beware! The Blob* (1972), and a 1988 remake (in which the Blob is the product of Cold War science gone awry), we have had no Blobs since (though rumors of a reboot persist). When the movie's first teenage viewers walked into the darkened theaters of Eisenhower's America, they could hardly have known what a Blob was, much less what it signified. Unlike many other monsters, it had no preexisting cultural associations, cinematic or otherwise. As a consequence, it seems uniquely a product of its era.

Precisely the opposite is true of clowns—including those of the Killer variety. Clowns draw upon a long and rich transcultural history. Michael Bala notes that "[c]lowns have been traced back as far as Egypt's Old Kingdom Fifth Dynasty, some 4,500 years ago" (50), and Louise Peacock states that "clown roles have demonstrably existed in scripted dramas since the plays of Aristophanes" (13). Janet Davis locates the circus clown's "historical roots in traveling medieval troupes and the European tradition of the court jester" (170). Andrew Stott traces our modern conception of the clown to Joseph Grimaldi, an early nineteenth-century actor who slathered himself in white greasepaint, took to a Covent Garden stage, and capered his way into wealth and celebrity (7–8). But whatever his innovations, Grimaldi was clearly working in a well-established tradition. He may have modified the idea of the clown. He did not cut it from whole cloth.

Stott attributes Grimaldi's popularity in part to his dual reputation as a jester by night and a depressive by day (9). But such contradictions were central to the clown's identity well before Grimaldi gamboled onto the scene. Bakhtin argues that clowns stand "on the borderline between life and art, in a peculiar midzone [...] neither eccentrics nor dolts" (8). Anthropologist Don Handelman writes that the clown's ritual progenitor is "an ambivalent figure of danger and enticement, gravity and hilarity, solemnity and fun" (323). Theologian Wolfgang Zucker confirms this perspective: "Self-contradiction [...] is the clown's most significant feature." They are "clumsy and inept, but, simultaneously, incredibly agile and endowed with astonishing skills; ugly and repulsive, yet not without elegance and attractive charm" (307–308). Further, they express "contempt for, and a principal opposition to all order[.... The clown's] lord is the 'Lord of Disorder,' as the devil was called in medieval literature" (313).

Monsters harbor similar contradictions, and a parallel abhorrence of order. Noël Carroll, author of *The Philosophy of Horror*, asserts that lethality is a necessary—but insufficient—characteristic of monstrosity; true monsters, he contends, must also be "impure," a state arising from the embodied "conflict between two or more standing cultural categories" (43). Zombies are both alive and dead; werewolves, animals and men. And both violate the moral order by transgressing primal taboos against the consumption of human flesh. As critic Jeffrey Jerome Cohen puts it, such creatures are "disturbing hybrids whose externally incoherent bodies resist attempts to include them in any systematic structure[....] The monster is dangerous, a form suspended between forms that threatens to smash distinctions" (6).

Carroll identifies clowns as such hybrids, arguing that they are the icon of humor most suited for transformation into a monster ("Horror and

Humor" 155). The Killer Klowns bear him out. Fundamentally interstitial beings, Killer Klowns are also, unequivocally, *clown* clowns. Like their circus analogs, they drive clown cars, put on puppet shows, and caper about on big, floppy clown feet. One of them rides a pint-size bike, complete with training wheels and a horn. Yet they are also, undeniably, monstrous Killer Klowns. They inspire the eerie disquietude that we often feel in the presence of "beings" that inhabit what Japanese robotics professor Masahiro Mori has described as the Uncanny Valley, a space occupied by simulacrum that simultaneously adhere to and violate human form and features, such as mannequins, dolls, ventriloquists' dummies, and marionettes (98–100). In their madcap destruction of Crescent Cove, the Klowns express their opposition to any system of human order by turning harmless clownish behavior to destructive ends, as when they demolish a pharmacy with an inspired bit of slapstick that The Three Stooges would have applauded. And they transgress near-universal norms, values, and fears almost every time they're on screen—and not merely prohibitions against violence, murder, and cannibalism. They violate primal anxieties associated with bodily integrity (a biker's decapitation), blood (they drink it), and sexuality (the scene at Big Top Burgers is laden with undertones of child abduction and sexual abuse, while rape is a clear subtext of Debbie's shower scene). They even kill a dog (yet another reversal of *The Blob*, in which the "little dog," as Jane calls it, survives), violating perhaps the most sacred taboo of American cinema, as evidenced by the online movie database called "Does the Dog Die?" (doesthedogdie.com).

As clowns and not-clowns, the Killer Klowns are not unlike their teenage adversaries, who are neither children nor adults. Both Klowns and kids simultaneously embody multiple contradictory states. This parallel plays out in complex ways that sharply contrast with *The Blob*'s moral simplicity. Doherty argues that the adolescent audience for '50s-era horror movies felt a kinship with the genre's monsters based on their own experience of a "biological state [that] must have seemed equivalently capricious and uncontrollable. The sudden swellings and shrinkings of adolescence, the inhabitation of a body with a mind of its own, beset all sorts of screen creatures" (119). In this light, it's hard not to see the Klowns as a manifestation of the hormonal turmoil churning inside the film's teenage viewers. The Klowns' heads are misshapen lumps, often sitting on their shoulders minus the convenience of a neck. Their facial features are bulbous and distorted; their skin is an oily, impure white; their shark-like teeth are jagged and yellow. Every teen who ever stood before a mirror staring down a fresh efflorescence of acne and a date with the orthodontist has seen something like a Killer Klown staring back from the other side of the glass.

But the metaphorical density of the Klowns transcends simple physical correspondence. Jojo, the clown mounted atop the Terenzi brothers' ice-cream truck, suggests a more ominous symbolic function. The truck is doubly the vehicle of the Terenzi brothers' teenage liminality. While it clearly embodies the temptations of childhood, it also represents the pull of the adult world. The Terenzi brothers have rented the ice-cream truck not to sell ice cream, but, as they put it, to "get girls." This puerile seduction strategy indicates their naiveté about adult sexual desire; the phrase "get girls" reinforces this conclusion by yoking that desire to the infantilizing word "girls." The "girls" they have managed to pick up further bolster such a reading. Their babyish plumpness emphasizes their sexual innocence. They may be eating popsicles (childhood) in a way suggestive of fellatio (adulthood), but their explicit rejection of any sexual advance—"what kind of girls do you think we are?" they ask—renders them entirely innocuous, a safe bet for a couple of adolescent boys more comfortable with the idea of sex than with its reality. Though the Terenzi brothers long for sexual consummation, they also fear it.

This attraction-repulsion dynamic is consonant with the structure of monster narratives generally. Cohen asserts that "[w]e distrust and loathe the monster at the same time we envy its freedom" to transgress cultural taboos (17). In this understanding of the genre, the monster is an outward reflection of inward division; it enables us both to express and repress our forbidden desires. Both the ice-cream truck and the sequences set at the Top of the World sanction such a reading. The truck's comforting associations with childhood make it an unthreatening space in which to rehearse adult pleasures. Jojo, the massive clown on the roof has an altogether different function; it establishes an affinity between the film's adolescent protagonists and the invading Klowns. The truck safely contains the carnal energies of its teenage drivers; the clown (the Klown) looming over it personifies the danger those energies pose to the existing order should they escape—a danger expressed outwardly in the mayhem the Klowns visit upon Crescent Cove.

Given the amorous heat the teens are generating at the Top of the World, one could argue that the existing order has already disintegrated before the film begins. The adults in *The Blob* would see it that way; the Klowns' extermination of the young lovers seems to confirm it. As Wes Craven's *Scream* (1996) points out, if you wish to survive a horror movie "you can never have sex," a lesson the kids who've gone up to the Top of the World learn too late. Such are the consequences when parents don't close ranks with their kids to repel the monstrous invasive threat. But, unlike the Blob, the Killer Klowns are invaders only in the most literal sense. A more careful reading of the film shows that the real threat is to be found inside Crescent Cove itself, in a culture riven by panic about absent parents and unsupervised children. Two years after *Killer Klowns from Outer Space* debuted, director Chris Columbus parleyed that panic into a Christmas blockbuster. *Home Alone* (1990) wrung laughs out of its cartoonish depiction of an abandoned eight year old defending his house from a pair of inept burglars. It's not insignificant that the film's young hero bests his feckless housebreakers with the sadistic glee and Rube Goldberg ingenuity characteristic of Crescent Cove's extraterrestrial invaders. In many ways, *Home Alone* can be read as an optimistic answer to the Chiodo brothers' darkly comic vision. In Columbus' sunny worldview, latchkey kids are slapstick servants of the social order. The Chiodo brothers aren't nearly as optimistic. The Killer Klowns are latchkey kids gone wild.

Killer Klowns Konquer the World

The news isn't all bad, though. *Killer Klowns*, like *The Blob*, ends in triumph. But unlike Steve and Jane, who collaborate with adults in their victory over the Blob, the kids in *Killer Klowns* conquer their adversaries without adult assistance. *The Blob* celebrates the return to a social order that preserves the hierarchy of adult authority and teenage obedience. *Killer Klowns*, in keeping with the carnivalesque nature of its monsters, proposes an entirely new social order governed by an entirely new kind of adult.

Scripture instructs us to "put an end to childish ways" (*The Holy Bible*, New Revised Standard Version, 1 Corinthians 13:11). The adults in *The Blob* seem to have taken this wisdom to heart; they are school principals, cops, and grocery store owners. They are wearing jackets and ties when they show up at the police station to retrieve their errant teens. If they have any sense of whimsy, they keep it well hidden. If they harbor any subversive impulses, they have mastered them. *Killer Klowns* rejects the wisdom of the Scriptures. Instead of exchanging interstitial adolescence for unambiguous adulthood, its teenagers synthesize childhood, adolescence, and adulthood to produce a new order of being.

Here, too, the Terenzi brothers—the most immature characters the picture provides us—are key. They are ushered into the world of adult sexuality not by human partners but by female Klowns, a crucial distinction. The Dionysian Klowns personify unchecked teenage impulses. Their destructive actions are projections of the violent emotional turmoil that teens so often experience. The Terenzi brothers master that turmoil not by rejecting their teenage libidos for the childish comforts of ice cream and not by grasping after an adult sexuality that still eludes them, but by embracing their existing carnal appetites as personified by their interstitial Klown paramours.

This dynamic is also at work in the final defeat of the Klowns, when the Terenzi brothers save Mike, Debbie, and Dave from certain death. The ice-cream truck has a crucial role to play here, as well. The trio is surrounded by hostile Klowns in the circus-tent spaceship when the ice-cream truck plows through the wall, the Terenzi brothers at the wheel. Once again the brothers deploy the truck's PA system—not to pitch ice cream, but to give the ice-cream truck clown the voice of a Killer Klown "god" who directs his Klownish acolytes to stand down, allowing Mike and Debbie to escape. Here, too, the brothers synthesize multiple contradictory identities. By embracing the interstitial teenage selves embodied in Jojo the ice cream clown, they turn childhood temptation to adult moral ends.

These strands are woven together in the final images of the film, when *Killer Klowns* presents a new model of adulthood as a kind of permanent adolescence. Dave and the Terenzi brothers, presumed lost in the exploding Klown spaceship, come tumbling out of the sky in a Klown Kar, born anew. Dave emerges first. In defeating Klownzilla, the giant Klown King hidden in the bowels of the Klowns' spaceship, he has surrendered his pistol and badge, his final tokens of adult authority, to claim lasting teenage joys. The Terenzi brothers pop out a moment later, dizzy with whimsical delight. They're dripping ice cream, having taken shelter from the conflagration in the ice cream truck's freezer. They're clutching popsicles and sporting the lipstick kisses of their Klown paramours, both emblems of a newly forged identity that transcends interstitiality by drawing equally on childhood comforts and adult appetites.

The adults of the future, *Killer Klowns* suggests, will achieve their status not by putting an end to childish ways, but by embracing them, and carrying them on into the future. It is a percipient vision, for the teenagers of the '80s "grew up" during the decade of Pac-Man and MTV, when Van Halen was "Hot for Teacher" and Freddy Krueger haunted teenage dreams. By 1988, the generation gap had become a chasm, latchkey kids were the norm, and the youth culture augured by teen flicks such as *The Blob* had triumphed. It's not surprising that a *Killer Klowns* reboot is in the works at SyFy (Anderton). Its original adolescent audience is still out there, closing in on sixty. They dig the Marvel Cinematic Universe and the sweet, sweet sounds of Taylor Swift grooving in their earbuds. They're at the movie theater now, with an ice-cream cone in one hand and a ticket to the latest *Star Wars* movie in the other. They're planning a trip to the Top of the World after the show. Some pleasures never get old.

Works Cited

Anderton, Ethan. "New *Killer Klowns from Outer Space* and *Critters* Movies in the Works at SyFy." *SlashFilm*, October 23, 2018, www.slashfilm.com. Accessed January 18, 2020.

Bakhtin, Mikhail. *Rabelais and His World*. 1965. Trans. Helene Iswolsky. Indiana University Press, 1984.

Bala, Michael. "The Clown: An Archetypal Self-Journey." *Jung Journal: Culture & Psyche*, vol. 4, no. 1, 2010, pp. 50–71.
The Blob. Dir. Irvin S. Yeaworth, Jr. Perf. Steven McQueen, Aneta Corsaut, and Earl Rowe. Fairview Productions, Tonylyn Productions, and Valley Forge Films, 1958.
Booker, Keith M., and Keith Booker. *The Historical Dictionary of Science Fiction Cinema*. Scarecrow Press, 2010.
Carroll, Noël. "Horror and Humor." *The Journal of Aesthetics and Art Criticism*, vol. 57, no. 2, 1999, pp. 145–160.
_____. *The Philosophy of Horror, or Paradoxes of the Heart*. Routledge, 1990.
Cohen, Jeffrey Jerome. "Monster Culture (Seven Theses)." *Monster Theory: Reading Culture*. Ed. Jeffrey Jerome Cohen. University of Minnesota Press, 1996.
Davis, Janet M. *Circus Age: Culture and Society under the American Big Top*. The University of North Carolina Press, 2002.
Doherty, Thomas Patrick. *Teenagers and Teenpics: The Juvenilization of American Movies in The 1950s*. Temple University Press, 2002.
Driscoll, Catherine. *Teen Film: A Critical Introduction*. Berg, 2011.
Green, Jonathan. *The Vulgar Tongue: Green's History of Slang*. Oxford University Press, 2014.
Handelman, Don. "The Ritual-Clown: Attributes and Affinities." *Anthropos*, vol. 76, no. 3/4, 1981, pp. 321–370.
"Help for the Latchkey Kids." Editorial. *New York Times*, February 13, 1985, p. A26.
Hess, Judith. "Genre Films and the Status Quo." *Jump Cut: A Review of Contemporary Media*, no.1, 1974, www.ejumpcut.org. Accessed December 22, 2019.
The Holy Bible. New Revised Standard Version. HarperCollins, 2007.
Killer Klowns from Outer Space. Dir. Stephen and Charles Chiodo. Perf. Grant Cramer, Suzanne Snyder, and John Allen Nelson. Trans World Entertainment, 1988.
King, Stephen. *Danse Macabre*. 1981. Gallery Books, 2010.
"Latchkey Kid Is King in Marketing Realm: Clout Carries Over to Buying by Parents." *Chicago Tribune*, July 31, 1988. ProQuest. Accessed January 10, 2020.
"The Making of Killer Klowns." *Killer Klowns from Outer Space (Special Edition)*. Arrow Video, 2018. Blu-ray disc.
Mori, Masahiro. "The Uncanny Valley." 1970. Trans. Karl F. MacDorman and Norri Kageki. *IEEE Robotics and Automation Magazine*, June 2012, pp. 98–100.
Osgerby, Bill. "Full Throttle on the Highway to Hell: Mavericks, Machismo, and Mayhem in the American Biker Movie." *Underground U.S.A.: Filmmaking Beyond the Hollywood Canon*. Eds. Xavier Mendick and Steven Jay Schneider. Wallflower Press, 2002, pp. 123–139.
Peacock, Louise. *Serious Play: Modern Clown Performance*. Intellect Books, 2009.
Robinson, Bryan E., et al. "Taking Action for Latchkey Children and Their Families." *Family Relations*, vol. 35, no. 4, 1986, pp. 473–478.
Scahill, Andrew. "What Horror Films Reveal About Society's Fears." Interview by Oliver Ward. *CU Denver News*. October 31, 2019. www.news.ucdenver.edu. Accessed December 22, 2019.
Scream. Dir. Wes Craven. Perf. Neve Campbell, Courtney Cox, and David Arquette. Woods Entertainment, 1996.
Stott, Andrew McConnell Stott. "Clowns on the Verge of a Nervous Breakdown: Dickens, Coulrophobia, and the *Memoirs of Joseph Grimaldi*." *The Journal for Early Modern Cultural Studies*, vol. 12, no. 4, Fall 2012, pp. 3–25.
"Teenager, n." *OED Online*, Oxford University Press. December 2019. www.oed.com. Accessed January 11, 2020.
Towlson, Jon. *Subversive Horror Cinema: Countercultural Messages of Films from Frankenstein to the Present*. McFarland, 2014.
Wentworth, Harold, and Stuart Berg Flexner. *Dictionary of American Slang*, 2nd ed. Thomas Y. Crowell, 1975.
The Wild One. Dir. László Benedek. Perf. Marlon Brando, Mary Murphy, and Robert Keith. Stanley Kramer Productions, 1954.
Zucker, Wolfgang Max. "The Clown as the Lord of Disorder." *Theology Today*, vol. 24, no. 3, 1967, pp. 306–317.

Corpses, Rejects, Afterlives
Welcome to Zombieland
Jason V. Brock

There is no mistaking Rob Zombie's personal aesthetic.

His vision—and it *is* a vision, awash with unifying imagery and reference points over a span of more than three decades—has deep roots in the 1970s-era music and movies he was exposed to on AM radio, broadcast television, and in movie theaters as a youngster in his hometown of Haverhill, Massachusetts. Born on January 12, 1965, the man formerly known as Robert Bartleh Cummings absorbed these influences voraciously, eventually combining them with some unorthodox family experiences to articulate his interior realm in a potent synthesized expression that has few peers in modern entertainment spheres. That he has been able to—whether visually, sonically, filmically, or by other means—present his often brutal, sexual, and fantastic conceptions as envisioned, with minimal adulteration by corporate interests, and that these expressions have been met with generally positive critical reception and commercial success, is a testament to the appeal and scope of what Zombie has accomplished. He has transcended facile and clichéd interpretations as a jaded (and private—he prefers not to share much about his personal life) rocker having a go at vanity projects and has increasingly become a genuinely influential auteur with respect to both music and film in equal measure.

His earlier success as a musician and performer with his band White Zombie set the stage for Zombie's later cinematic efforts, beginning with his 2003 directorial debut *House of 1000 Corpses*. The storyline of *Corpses* is a bit contrived and doesn't always gel, but it does a decent job of presenting the core characters and their behaviors, even as it plays with tropes and ideas clearly influenced by horror classics from the '70s, mainly the grim Tobe Hooper effort *The Texas Chainsaw Massacre* (1974), Wes Craven's sordid retelling of the Sawney bean clan, *The Hills Have Eyes* (1977), and other slasher films proper. The result is competently directed, and has an appalling power, mainly driven by the intense subject matter and the strong performances of the leads, specifically Sheri Moon Zombie, the filmmaker's wife, as the sultry and insane Vera-Ellen "Baby Firefly" Wilson, Bill Moseley [who starred in *The Texas Chainsaw Massacre Part 2* (1986) as the demented Chop-Top] as the sadistic albino Otis B. Driftwood, and, especially, veteran character actor Sid Haig as the intimidating and charismatic clown leading the chaos, Captain Spaulding. Rounding out this ensemble of outsiders is the late 7'6" Matthew McGrory as the giant "Tiny" Firefly—a badly burned, mute sibling with a streak of empathy.

More than simply a rehash of borrowed themes and purloined visuals from Zombie's childhood enthusiasms, *Corpses* also acquaints its audience with a population of characters and settings pulled straight from his own life. As he has detailed in several interviews, Zombie and his younger brother (Michael David Cummings, known as Spider One, and the founder of the band Powerman 5000) had a dull upbringing in many respects in dour-sounding Haverhill. The exception to this was that their parents, Robert and Louise Cummings, were carnies for a time during the boys' youth—employed in traveling carnivals as he told Andrew Paul in *The Believer*: "That's what my parents would do, and our cousins and uncles. That's what everybody did for a living." Carnivals, of course, have a long and fascinating history, but, as Zombie has noted previously, the experiences they shared were by turns surreal, disturbing, and enthralling. After one particularly violent evening, the Cummings retired from the festival circuit permanently—though the people and events would leave an indelible mark on the impressionable youth later to become Rob Zombie:

> Everything's rigged. I think someone had lost a lot of money in one of the gambling tents, and they came back and lit one of the tents on fire, and just—whoosh—the whole midway was on fire. And then all the carnies ... everyone started pulling out their guns, and you heard shots. I was talking to this one guy—I don't remember his name anymore—and he was like, "You gotta get out of here!" And then someone ran up and hit him in the face with a hammer. Smashed his head open, and there was just blood everywhere. [*Shrugs*] You know? It was a riot. That's the last time [my parents] did it after that. (Paul)

Imagery and characters related to his time playing within the confines of the carnival grounds have been a staple of his musical and visual output ever since, and proven to be a rich foundation for his artistic manifestations. Indeed, the Firefly quartet represents a wayward and frantic group of characters who not only revel in serial murder and mayhem, but do so with a sense of gallows humor and panache that has the air of some fevered, dreadful carnival ingrained not in the present, but in the gritty past of the ghastly (and real) Ted Bundy-, John Wayne Gacy-, Charles

Manson-tainted horrors of their respective (and actual) 1970s spookshows, before morphing during the post–Internet 1990s into the twisted domain of celebrity-death-cult worship: murderabilia-drenched apologia for the morbidly curious, O.J. Simpson-ified masturbations flourishing thereafter online and by way of cable TV court "reality" shows and "ripped-from-the-headlines" package series about death and derangement, to include gory depictions lionizing killers and their pursuers and fictionalized in slick procedurals such as *Law & Order* or *CSI: Crime Scene Investigation*.

Zombie, to his credit, returned to a grimmer, more realistic mode of showing the horrors of psychopathy and its sometimes-lethal aftermath—perhaps rooted, again, in lived experience. Having seen violence firsthand in the carnival trade as a child—which he later contrasted with his otherwise relatively predictable upbringing in Massachusetts—even later, as a young man on his first day in New York City trying to find his own path (attending Parsons School of Design), he witnessed a murder: "'I was up in my room and I heard screaming, so I looked out of the window and saw someone being killed. Day one, and I was already involved in a murder case'" (McIver 13). It appears these raw situations inspired him to take his natural interests in the comforts of childhood pleasures (movies, music, TV, low-key upbringing) and his natural inclinations with respect to self-expression and imbuing realistic horror into the nonlinear proceedings of his fictional works, which are usually marked by the boring disrupted by the incredibly disturbing. It is a subversion of normality, the artistic equivalent to some people with borderline personality cutting themselves to "feel something." His approach further harkens back to the disturbing, almost documentarian feel of movies such as Craven's unnerving *The Last House on the Left* (1972) or George A. Romero's seminal classic *Night of the Living Dead* (1968). Adding to this are the bizarre allusions to clowns, The Marx Brothers, and the overall carnivalesque setting Zombie often provides as a context for unfolding action. Even his songs often have scraps of film dialogue or other "real" items interspersed within them, adding a "documentary" feeling to the output by making references to his youthful interests.

In particular, this film, while not exactly glorifying aberrant sexual obsessions (of the strange, deformed, or infirm, for example) and overt violence, does straddle a line between acceptable use of such things to render characterization and general good taste. It is antisocial in action, dialogue, and perhaps intention, seeming to desire an audience response somewhere between repulsion and eroticized deviance. The whole feel of the piece hangs together as a sort of waking nightmare, where the viewer and characters are bound together as hapless voyeurs in the insane three-ring circus atmosphere generated by the location of the roadside carnival run by

Spaulding and his family, and the grotesque possible motives hinted at by the on-screen madness. Clearly, Zombie used as starting points multiple frames of cultural reference in creating the entire scenario, including inferences (visually and sonically) to notorious serial murderer John Wayne Gacy (and his creepy alter-ego, Pogo the Clown), the artwork of Robert Williams, the horrors of the Edgar Allan Poe story "Hop-Frog," "clown sex" fetishism, his upbringing, and so on. Tobe Hooper again springs to mind, this time his underrated 1981 flick *The Funhouse*, about a sexually frustrated freak and his carny relations. Also, the eerie and disquieting Chuck Connors vehicle *Tourist Trap* (1979) about a weird man and his weird roadside attraction inhabited with automatons and masked figures. In addition, a strange irony is achieved by the sly names Zombie bestows on his main characters, several of which are Marx Brothers references according to the *Believer* interview (such as the characters of "Driftwood," "Spaulding," "Quale," et al): is this a signal that the whole film is really a bizarre "horror comedy," simply a quirk to add dimension to the premise, or just a wink to movies Zombie enjoys? Originally considered a one-off, Zombie would revisit the characters in the sequel a few years later.

If *House of 1000 Corpses* was a kind of twisted, adult version of Ray Bradbury's *Something Wicked This Way Comes* (1962), then its follow-up—2005's *The Devil's Rejects*—is more of an opera in scale than a novel. We return to the situational aftermath of *Corpses* and come to appreciate the enormity of the horrific enterprise. The four main characters are back, this time on the run from the law rather than lying-in-wait to ambush victims. Once again, Zombie's oddball fascination with the outsider "hillbilly cracker" elements of his aesthetic are fully displayed, calling to mind many Joe R. Lansdale characters, as though he is attempting to enhance the shock of *Deliverance* (1972) for modern sensibilities jaundiced by the horrors of 9/11 and the depravity of Daesh (aka ISIS), while infusing some indie-spirited Russ Meyer porno vibes. The lasting impression is one of a real story playing out in the dialogue and interactions, even as the characters themselves approach parody status with their melodramatic violence and decadence. Adding to this at-times disorienting imbalance between onscreen action and audience reality is Zombie's penchant (also shared by filmmaker Quentin Tarantino) for using actors he admired from his childhood reminiscences, tapping into a subtextual (almost subliminal) collective remembrance for filmgoers.

At any rate, Captain Spaulding and his deranged progeny (Haig's character is revealed to be the patriarch of the Fireflys) manage to find plenty of victims to exploit, and what ensues is often grueling and hard to watch, though the direction is superior this outing, the writing is sharp, and the acting generally exceptional. Perhaps that's what makes some of the action so nearly unendurable at times. Regardless, the film rivets the viewer, especially the portrayals by Bill Moseley; William Forsythe as the unhinged and sadistic Sheriff Wydell; and Sid Haig, once again, as the crazed ringmaster Captain Spaulding.

Though not without moments of levity, the drama is forceful and the stakes high as the action builds to an unforgettable and brilliant riff reminiscent of Sam Peckinpah's *The Wild Bunch* (1969), as the trio goes out in a silent, slow-motion "blaze of glory" to the strains of Lynyrd Skynyrd's epic "Free Bird." Never was Sid Haig more Canio from *Pagliacci* than in this moment. Even the final credits (an empty stretch of highway unspooling under the song "Seed of Memory" by Terry Reid) are liberating after all the violence and retribution on display, and both are masterful uses of music, à la Martin Scorsese. This is art, and the operatic power of the gestalt is undeniable.

Sid Haig's Captain Spaulding was supposed to have a greater role in the third installment of the franchise. While he is represented in the beginning of *3 from Hell* (2019), Haig was too ill to do much in the film—a fact that is evident in the little time he is onscreen. Haig died shortly after the film was released—unfortunately, on September 21, 2019—in the truest sense "crossing a border." That noted, his absence, while sharply felt, does not stop the movie from having its own impact and power despite that fact. As a result, the oft-repeated "Zombie zone" of Manson Family Values is disrupted without their very own "Charlie" around to lead everyone (or reign in their worst tendencies as the case may require to ensure survival). But, it seems, the children do always find their own way.

Bill Moseley and Sheri Moon Zombie return and give well-defined performances, replete with the rough edges and idiosyncrasies audiences have come to expect and appreciate with regard to their crazy characters. This work is smaller in scale and more intimate than either the "carnival atmosphere" of *Corpses* or the "operatic bombast" of *Rejects*; although the action is still bracing, and the drama still palpable, the effort is somewhat more subdued than the previous installments. A new personality—another relative (half-brother to Moseley's character) is introduced into the mix— and he does bring some edge and conviction to the grouping as personified by actor Richard Brake (playing Winslow "Foxy" Coltrane), the GG Allin to Moseley's Roky Erickson (the latter an obvious influence on Zombie's aesthetic). After catching the viewer up on the scenario, the story commences in earnest once "Baby Firefly" is freed from death row via devious means. After a brief aside in suburbia (where Zombie seems to be giving a nod to his vision corrupting the "normals" he had previously violated in his two John Carpenter-related remakes: 2007's *Halloween* and 2009's *Halloween II*), the action shifts, and, once again, as in the other movies, violence is used as a way of "crossing the border" into another phase of the characters' debauched lives.

Eventually, the trio of desperados decide to head south of the border, to Mexico. Once there, the film pivots into a kind of Fellini-esque-cum-Sergio-Leone Western. They are wanted, and the *narcos* have a score to settle. Full of nods to the Spaghetti Westerns of Eastwood and company, Zombie doesn't disappoint with the violence and tension. Instead of the clowns and circus/carnival trappings of the other two movies, this time those roles are filled by the "masked Mexican wrestler" motif—ably supplanting greasepaint with colorful head coverings and clown attire with suits more closely resembling costumes in construction—while the dingy town itself is populated with prostitutes rather than carnies, and a one-eyed dwarf taking the place of the giant (Tiny Firefly) from the prior offerings. The end of the film is open, suggesting more could be ahead for this rogue family. Are they *literally* in Hell? Or is Hell what one makes it? In retrospect, Rob Zombie has carved out quite a place with his vision.

While certainly not to everyone's taste, his Firefly Clan Trilogy (*House of 1000 Corpses, The Devil's Rejects, 3 from Hell*) are compelling and well-done. He also moves in similar territory with his film *31* (2016), which features debased characters (the worst of them in the guise of very wealthy aristocracy made up in traditional, exaggerated whiteface), as well as multiple referents to clowns and other freakish personae. Working with imagery, genres, and themes as diverse as noir, crime, Westerns, Tod Browning's influential 1932 picture *Freaks*, the surreality of Lynch's *Eraserhead* (1977) and *The Elephant Man* (1980), *Willy Wonka & the Chocolate Factory* (1971), and the disquieting ambiance of 1962's *Carnival of Souls*, in addition to dozens of definitive slasher, Giallo, and Universal horror films as points of reference, Zombie elevates the horror film experience, even when he misses the mark (as in the aforementioned *31*). By reaching into not only the past, but into his own internal preoccupations and anxieties to comment on a variety of phenomena—be it animal cruelty and the link to violence (Zombie is an ethical vegetarian), the exploitation of women, society's predilection with violent behaviors and offenders (including their parallels to vigilantes and so on), examinations of social status issues (in the form of metaphorical "freaks" such as giants, dwarves, albinos, and so on), abuse of institutional power (the police), the role of outsiders in culture, and a host of other concerns, including our attraction/repulsion to the macabre, dangerous, and evil—he goes places few filmmakers dare to.

It seems in Zombie's reckoning that the "true monsters" are humans and how they react under pressure, while the "freaks" generally possess an innate humanity, even compassion, that others lack. By flipping this script, he appears to be saying that "the final joke is on you"—so ignore this at one's peril. That he chooses to imagine this through ironic and often weird juxtapositions of over-the-top, operatic pandemonium and off-color humor to create a carnivalesque atmosphere of horror and self-reflection is a tribute to his talent—and to our own participation in these social injustices.

Works Cited

McIver, Joel. *Sinister Urge: The Life and Times of Rob Zombie*. Milwaukee: Backbeat Books, 2015.

Paul, Andrew. "An Interview with Rob Zombie." *The Believer*, November 20, 2017.

"Art for Art's Sake"

Art the Clown, Visuality, and the Cruelty of Allegoresis

Mattius Rischard

Modern popular cinematic narrative has all but eliminated the camera as a participant in the scene. We are conditioned to believe that the actors' gaze supports the realistic diegesis of a film when they look at each other or at any object in the scene, but never the camera. By extension, the suspension of disbelief involved in ignoring the camera or the audience behind it has also distanced the spectator to a safe degree of emotional remove from the social violence presented in cinematic aesthetics. The cinematic styles dominating popular visual culture have traditionally accustomed the viewer to a "realism" that mimics the structure of spying on private fantasies, although they are captured for mass viewing. Konstantin Stanislavski called this theatrical practice "public solitude" because it is rooted in the modern fetish for authenticity, for a display of characters' "real" selves that only come out when no one is watching (22). Why must the actors and the audience pretend there is no camera? Why is it dramatic convention since Diderot's time to maintain the "fourth wall" between the scene and the onlooker for its narrative to seem realistic or natural? Clearly it is a powerful and uncomfortable act for a subject in front of the camera to return the gaze of the audience: it disrupts the diegesis of narrative cinema and drama, causing the viewer to question their own role in the meaning and significance of visual culture. What does it mean for taboo images, such as violent scenes or pornographic films, to look back at the viewer? In the end, it is this mediated distance from art, from politics, from the sources of one's food, from community relations, and from the products of one's labor that distinguish global capitalism's pattern of cultural production—a pattern of institutionalized and commoditized expression and sensation also known as Modernity.

Modernity's aesthetic regime of sensibility in pop culture encourages both the democratized and hypermediated production and consumption of desire through its signifying imagery of satiation. This state of mediation in social relations has implications for power, as it can neutralize political concerns through aesthetics that formalize, abstract, and naturalize them. Simplified and easily relatable aesthetics make for stable signification in visual narratives, which comfort us with the familiarity of a mythology. To accommodate imagery that doesn't connote happiness and might even politicize the aesthetics through signifiers of pain or conflict brought on by the everyday violence, modernity's mythology presents a socially privileged structure of looking at it: what I term in this essay as the "Humanitarian/Sensationalist complex of visuality." The "countervisuality" that can undo this complex relies on tactics of defamiliarization or distanciation to structurally open the narrative aesthetics of Modernity's diegesis in the violence of drama and cinema to ethical and sociopolitical critique. I argue, similar to these structural choices both Roland Barthes and Walter Benjamin found in the filmmaker Eisenstein and the dramatist Brecht, that extra-diegetic "shocks" and "abjections" lead to defamiliarization in the grammar and structure of horror film narratology as well; but some horror films accomplish these structural critiques better than others. For instance, Art the Clown of *All Hallows' Eve* (played by Mike Giannelli) and the *Terrifier* (played by David Howard Thornton) series might stand higher in regards to extra-diegetic critique of the viewer's gaze towards violence than any other "scary clown" of contemporary horror (e.g. Pennywise, Joker, Killjoy, etc.), because Art disrupts the binary option between the compensatory Humanitarian/Sensationalist reactions delimited by depictions of violence and pain in traditional cinema. In this complex of visuality, such typical depictions are structurally removed to a safe degree from the gaze of a viewer to allow for the privileged pleasures of taboo sensationalism as a voyeur, or else dignification for feeling disgusted as a humanitarian witnessing simulated suffering.

Can the aestheticization of politics ever lead to the politicization of aesthetics? Walter Benjamin conceived of these cultural trends as opposing poles of artistic production, the former authoritarian and the latter revolutionary. Yet aesthetic juxtapositions of structure/content can effectively "shock" the spectator out of the diegetic fantasy, de-mystifying the underlying sociopolitical circumstances at work "in the background" of traditional dramatic narrative by gesturing simultaneously to the beautiful and the grotesque in the same "amoral" Art. No popular trope fits this mechanism better than the sadistic clown. Contemporary visualizations of the sadistic clown combine cultural anxieties regarding globalism, disaffection, alienation, automation, and a-historicism with earlier carnivalesque aesthetic elements and the engaged viewing practices of Brechtian theater, where the audience is invited to participate in the social commentary held up to them in the performance. As Kristeva has shown in *The Powers of Horror*, horror cinema itself—a flourishing cultural industry for visualizing evil clowns—is open to these radical ruptures of meaning (abjection) and "*signifiance*" (meanings made possible through the "loss" of a singular meaning) over the abstract mythologizing of a hegemonic narrative, precisely because horror demands that a viewer attend to that which has been "cast off" or "thrown out" of the conscious mind and sequestered into unconscious domains reserved for the grotesque, the excretory, and the primitive. For instance, Art (the Clown) functions by dramatizing the power of social privilege as relying on both the omnipotence of the voyeur and enclosure of those exposed to violence for reproducing their exploitation while concealing this exploitative practice within the naïve "ecology" of the decaying environs recorded for the audience. Despite his sparse and brutal narrative function (he has no backstory, no proper name, no clear motivation), he operates through a sadistic form of poetry that inscribes the demarcation between being and nothingness in a set of taboo performances as an allegory for the pain of isolation and fractured identity brought on by Modernity itself. At the same time, this allegoresis can be considered as amoral abstraction, like the economic processes and social relations giving rise to the morally and physically decrepit pretext enabling his horrid transgressions.

Identification with the killer clown as a critic of the visuality complex compensating for the Modernity mythos can lead a viewer to a perspective of resistance, yet psychologizing the clown by means of representing a schizoid interiority (as in Jack Nicholson's, Heath Ledger's and Joaquin Phoenix's portrayals of the Joker) produces an identification-projection with the fetishized actor-face, as Barthes shows in his critique of the Actors' Studio and Marlon Brando (74–75). This fetishism for the actor's interiority limits the sociopolitical critique through a structure of meaning that annihilates the viewing subjectivity unless they are already sufficiently distanced from the ideology that invites such a practice. An entire industry of directorial commentary, actor interviews, and film trailers is based upon this fetishizing practice. On the other hand, simply alienating or villainizing a clown to the point of abjection and monstrosity (i.e., Killjoy, Pennywise, etc.) cannot open up the critique of Modernity if it retains the same structure of framing meaning through identification with the "heroes" of modern society who destroy the beast. To both condemn Modernity and demand that the spectator take responsibility for their complicity in passive identification with the cruelties latent in allegorizing "the pursuit of happiness," and bourgeois "sentiment," the structure of meaning in the film must break the diegesis that keeps on mythologizing violence against the body. Laura Mulvey has psychoanalytically defined this problem in "Visual Pleasure and Narrative Cinema," when she claims that "the mass of mainstream film, and the conventions within which it has consciously evolved, portray a hermetically sealed world which unwinds magically, indifferent to the presence of the audience, producing for them a sense of separation and playing on their voyeuristic phantasy" (24–5). In the clown genre, Art functions by reaching out and gripping the masses of pacified consumers acting out their fantasies like peeping toms to counter, or perhaps even brutally castrate the scopophilia facilitated by the indifferent actors, the invisible camera, and the darkened auditorium or living room.

A mass of spectators is manufactured through a structure of feeling conditioned by visual stimulus that creates a common aesthetic pattern to which a community can relate and identify itself. This unifying aesthetics makes for stable signification in visual narratives that are shareable and relatable. Perhaps this aggregative aesthetic phenomenon is why some of the most authoritative cinematic producers of the twentieth century, such as Walt Disney and Leni Riefenstahl, occupied such powerful positions in the Hollywood and Nazi culture industries. Riefenstahl wrote of Disney's fascination with the dreamlike aesthetic of her fascist stylizations in *Olympia* (1938), the documentary series propagandizing Aryan athleticism at the 1936 Berlin XI Olympiad; while Disney himself, unable to view a screening of *Olympia* in Riefenstahl's private theater for fear of anti–Nazi sentiment in the States, personally hosted Riefenstahl for a tour of Disney Studios in the month following Kristallnacht (see Graham 433). Art Babbitt (a prominent Disney animator) testified to seeing Disney and his lawyer often attend meetings of the German American Bund in the 1930s, and Riefenstahl herself commented in Steven Bach's biography *Leni* (2007) that it was "gratifying to learn how thoroughly proper Americans [i.e., Walt Disney] distance themselves from the smear campaigns of the Jews" (Bach 179). Both producers were highly successful in the business of stabilizing national myths through the pleasure of aesthetics; they both relied on audiences willing to make themselves complicit in a willful naivety towards the violence of the social conditions enabling such patriarchal utopias, as Susan Sontag has demonstrated in the aesthetic effects of Riefenstahl's *Triumph of the Will* (see her chapter "Fascinating Fascism"). These ways of looking at images created modern audiences who were ready to consume a compensatory fantasy of intensely romanticized identification-projection, prepared to turn life into pure formal fetish.

The clown, as a symbol of happiness, is not supposed to express sadness; as a symbol, it is supposed to stabilize the fulfillment of happiness through the consumption of whatever product it is advertised with.

Otherwise, it is no longer providing the positive cultural myth that comforts the viewer with its repetition-compulsion. The commodified clown, as a semiotic accomplice to capital, is constructed as an intensely empathetic sadomasochist. He represents the poison that prompts the pain of industrialized being, and the only one with the medicine to ease the suffering associated with the carnival of contemporary culture. He has become what Derrida called a *pharmakos* for globalization and its isolating mental affect in all its dangerous psychic intensities (Derrida translated the Greek *pharmakon* as simultaneously meaning a "poison" and a "remedy" to the functioning of the Athenian city-state, where a *pharmakos* is the individual who corporeally serves this purpose as a "scapegoat"; see Derrida 61). The corporatized appropriation of clown aesthetics in the service of productive power inhibits the clown's politically sanctioned ability to satirize that authoritarian power in the historic tradition of medieval fools and jesters because the bodily indulgence that was the Rabelaisian signature of the carnivalesque has been harnessed to the state through mass consumer industries and ideologies. Clowns have lost a bit of their critical "teeth," as it were, because they have to cater to a universe of overwhelmingly middle-class consumers, rather than mediating between a mass of historical producers (peasants, slaves, freemen) and a tiny culture of consumers (aristocrats, kings, patrons). Most contemporary jesters still capable of social satire through their mimesis of dissatisfaction with the status quo—e.g., sad, antisocial clowns—are confined to the genres of horror and standup comedy in the aesthetics of mainstream visual culture, or else lurking on the margins of criminalized Juggalo and Joker-type iconography as the discursive response to the "clownishness" of modern mythologies that compensate for a political economy so violent that it must be understood as a cruel joke.

Roland Barthes was rightly skeptical of mythic, or vaguely connotative meanings attached to commodified signs, especially in the contemporary regime of image-based cultural media, where layers of meaning get appropriated, quoted, and cited in the instant service of a cultural mythology. According to Barthes' *Mythologies* (1957), "The Photographic Message" (1961) and "The Rhetoric of the Image" (1964), connotative meanings are mythic in nature precisely because the "literal" or "commonsense" meaning of an image in its fetishized state, distanced from the object(s) it has captured in time, leads to the powerful illusion that it has a purely literal (i.e., denotative) and universal meaning. The symbolic connotations that seem literally "obvious" to individual interpreters are naturalized, because their reading has been culturally conditioned to ignore the levels of meaning being structurally appropriated in the narrative sign conveyed to them. In reality, when subjects first learn the obvious denotations of things represented in signs, they are actually being positioned within hegemonic ideology by learning all the dominant connotations at the same time. One might even assume that all "denotations" are just the most commonly assumed interpretations of a sign under a given ideology that overdetermines its meaning. In this sense, all negotiation of meaning in a hyper-mediated visual culture must involve some sort of allegoresis, or instantaneous imposition of myths over the mass of semiotic connotations available in the wash of pop cultural imagery.

Textual allegory and cinematic photography are ethically dangerous enterprises for the same reason: they annihilate the responsibility of interpretation for the reader, and facilitate a passive, authoritative hermeneutic practice, i.e., the imposition of an ideological *mythos*. Walter Benjamin argued against both the facile allegoresis of the privileged, interpellated gaze and its related social phenomenon—the aestheticization of politics, or the transformation of real social tensions into merely abstracted formalities independent from any ethical concerns: "This is the heart of the allegorical way of seeing[....] The greater the significance, the greater the subjection to death, because death digs most deeply the jagged line of demarcation between physical nature and significance" (*The Origin of German Tragic Drama* 166). Nothing makes something connote (signify) a beautifully mythic importance more than someone enduring pain or death for it. As artistic devices, cinema and non-visual variants of allegory attempt to transform objects such as ruins, mutilated corpses, tombs, and the unsettling ambiguity of objects bearing the temporal trace of pain into a preferred sequence of symbols, a sensible narrative of visually "pregnant moments," in the parlance of Barthes. At the same time, Benjamin warns that authoritarian Modernism as an aesthetic style (typified by the Fascist Riefenstahl in Germany and the Futurist Marinetti in Italy) had translated the purposefully amoral nineteenth-century *L'art pour l'art* philosophy (i.e., "art for art's sake") into a violently militant, nationalist *mythos* that purposefully ignored its own political implications for social oppression. In Marinetti's turn-of-the-century "Futurist Manifesto," notice especially principles seven and nine:

> Beauty exists only in struggle. There is no masterpiece that has not an aggressive character. Poetry must be a violent assault on the forces of the unknown, to force them to bow before man. [...] We want to glorify war—the only cure for the world—and militarism, patriotism, the destructive gesture of the anarchists, the beautiful ideas which kill, and contempt for women [41–2].

Benjamin attributes a fitting slogan to Marinetti's Futurists—*fiat ars—pereat mundus* ("let art be created, though the world perishes")—in the epilogue to the essay *The Work of Art in the Age of Mechanical Reproduction*

(1935), where he discusses this link between fascism and art by concluding that as long as fascism expects war "to supply the artistic gratification of a sense of perception that has been changed by technology," then fascism is the "consummation," of "*L'art pour l'art*" (244). Agreeing with Benjamin, but emphasizing the role of propaganda's audience rather than its producer, Barthes also demonstrates that the ideological (i.e., mythic) connotations we allegorize onto images are merely our ethical imposition of cultural reasoning and values onto the cognitive perceptions of signs, because "connotation drawn from knowledge is always a reassuring force—man likes signs and likes them clear" (29) to avoid the discomforts of ambiguity in an image. The attempt to stabilize meaning through aesthetic choices in the grammar of the photographic image or the narratological language of cinematic allegory facilitate the "identification-projection" (27) associated with privileged viewing practices and attempt to hide the artificially constructed "fissure" in visual signs that create potentially contradictory or paradoxical meanings (i.e., "third meanings" or "obtuse meanings" beyond denotation and connotation), as well as conceal the "sutures" holding the intended meanings together (Barthes 58–9).

In the context of Western capitalism, global imperialism, and neoliberal democracy, I have been terming the mythology that dominates popular ways of looking "Modernity." Defined historically as material developments in social relations and a corresponding cultural rejection of tradition for the sake of productive disciplinary power, the industrial period propped up by Modernity places an ideological prioritization on individualism, freedom, and formal (i.e., rhetorical) equality, invests faith in the secularism of inevitable social, scientific, technological progress, rationalization and professionalization, encourages a movement from agrarian community toward capitalist urbanity, laboring for a market economy, as well as the development of the nation-state, representative democracy, and a heterotopia of public institutions such as schools, prisons, hospitals, and militarized police (Foucault, 170–7). This institutionalized worldview enables a kind of semiotic economy dislodged from the exigencies of politics or material production, discursively compelling the exchange value of things by equating their conspicuous consumption with happiness; in short, the ideology functions to uphold a global market by loading objects with the value of cultural (mythic) signifiers, i.e., by representing the value of commodities in some form of media.

As a representation of value acquired by association with the consumption of happiness, a clown is a perfect signifier for connoting the "fun" to be had with a spurious modern commodity because the clown structurally functions as the artistic embodiment of a facial expression. What is a clown but a hyperbolic mimesis of the human face? An exaggeration of its ability to signify the meaning of an emotion? Yet if all the face can signify is happiness, then the smile has opened itself up to *signifiance*—a semiotic phenomenon of one sign deferring meaning through the "successive reshapings and reweavings of the web of language" (Kristeva 225) that renders the signifier as an infinite differential, denoting nothing and everything at the same time. In the case of the clown's smile—specifically a *murderous* clown's smile—it has lost the ability to signify any single feeling and gained the ability to signify many concepts simultaneously (i.e., an ambiguously floating signifier in direct tension with the actions of the body it is attached to). Based on this phenomenon, both an ahistoric emptiness and a richness of potential critique is characteristic in the paradox of the killer clown: it is a functional model for the arbitrary nature of facial signification itself, especially once we consider the subjects behind the generic faces we encounter in a contemporary urban environment have been crushed into abject submission to modernity, interpellated to the point of rendering an individual subjectivity irrelevant to the body's social analysis. Such is the (de)individualizing effect of disciplinary techniques on the docile, obedient subject of modern institutional "micro-power," which takes as its political project "the conduct of conduct," or the production of a self-policing individual, with little-to-no sense of "self" left to surveille, according to Foucault (26–9). Effectively, the psyche or soul of the individual has become "the effect and instrument of a political anatomy; the soul is the prison of the body" (30).

Even if one were to consider the effects of Modernity on the state of this individual subject before thinking through the radical schism between its compelled bodily gestures and signification, look no further than the psychological studies of smile mask syndrome (SMS) or *honne/tatemae*, which were coined in the post-war period in East Asian countries as a product of globalized Western sociocultural and economic influence on the individual. SMS was coined as an explanation for the symptoms that university students exhibited during counseling in Makoto Natsume's practice, who noticed that a number of them had spent so much time faking their smiles that they were unaware that they were smiling even while relating stressful or upsetting experiences to him (Dong Chun Shin 87). Japanese author Tomomi Fujiwara notes that the demand for a common smile in the workplace emerged in Japan by the 1980s, and blames the cultural changes wrought by the Tokyo Disneyland, opened in 1983, for popularizing the demand for an obligatory grin for the customer (see Lewis's article for an interview with Tomomi Fujiwara). In South Korea, a similar phenomenon was observed when Yoon-Do-rahm compared the current society, which is full of "smile-masks," to a clown show: both are characterized by plentiful, yet empty and fake significations of happiness (Sun-You Lee 8–9).

Honne and *tatemae* (Japanese for "true sound" and "public façade") entered the lexicon after World War II as a result of the conflict of these imported corporate practices of bodily signification (Doi 35). Similar concepts exist in the Arabic terms *zahir* (ظاهر) and *batin* (باطن)—the latter being an inner private self that interprets the world through desire and the former a social self that "manifests" in a public face (see *The Oxford Dictionary of Islam*). In Western psychoanalysis, where the repression of anti-social desires into the unconscious is a concept at least as old as Freud, Donald Winnicott used "true self" to describe a subjectivity based on spontaneous authentic experience and a feeling of being alive, i.e., having a real self. The "false self," by contrast, Winnicott saw as a defensive façade, which, in extreme cases, could leave its holders lacking spontaneity and feeling emptied-out behind a mere appearance of being real, which becomes the basis for a narcissistic personality (140–57).

It seems that, across the nations with ways of articulating a self-discipline to culturally accommodate the mythology and ethics of Modernity, they share the common characteristic of a collectively imposed social relation that lead to the production of subjects who cannot reconcile the demands for a public face with their interior experiences and desires, nor can they accept the imposition of a strict ideological divide between private and public ways of being. These schizoid subjects are products of the repeated psychological splitting of the ideal self-image as soon as it encounters a discrepancy between real and ideal conditions created by modern technologies of power. Fredric Jameson has demonstrated how our hypermediated representations of reality construct this schizophrenic experience, smashing our sense of time and place in the process of interpreting and ordering what we see: "both in our relationship to public History and in the new forms of our private temporality, whose 'schizophrenic' structure (following Lacan) will determine new types of syntax or syntagmatic relationships in the more temporal arts" such as cinema (6). With the loss of historicity, the present is experienced by the schizophrenic subject "with heightened intensity, bearing a mysterious charge of affect" (28), which can be "described in the negative terms of anxiety and loss of reality, but which one could just as well imagine in the positive terms of euphoria, a high, an intoxicatory or hallucinogenic intensity" (28–9). Being lost in the multitude of alienating fictions of contemporary photography and imagery, the modern subject has no space to critique the construction of representation, only to conform their interpretations of that which they look at with the mythology (i.e. the collection of beliefs and values bound up in narrative) that co-constructs the media in the never-ending search for emotional "intensities" compensating for the depthlessness of image-worlds. The cultural logic of late capitalism leads to an aesthetic regime demanding ego-dystonic and schizoid responses at every turn to understand what is demanded by the status quo.

The complex of visuality, or the set of historically and culturally determined hermeneutic options available to the viewer within an aesthetic regime, that Modernity has enabled in its middle-class appeal since at least the eighteenth century, has been one of refined "sensibility," which takes the dualistic form of Humanitarian/Sensationalist responses to the sensations produced by an image. Karen Halttunen has explained the link between the cult of sensibility, Humanitarianism, and what she terms "the Pornography of Pain" in British and American popular imagery. The author conducts a critical discursive analysis of early capitalist thought, visuality, and the aesthetic responses acculturated to middle-class political ethos: "Adam Smith, who learned from Hume and Hutcheson to treat ethics as a matter of sentiment, sentiment as a matter of sympathy, and sympathy as a matter of spectatorship. Smith's 'man of virtue' feels sympathy by first seeing the sufferings of another, either in reality or in his mind's eye, and then exercising his imagination in an effort to enter into those sufferings." (307). Humanitarian sentiment moving the public to social justice activism served as an ethical justification for publicizing images of suffering, such as the circulation of *Uncle Tom's Cabin* among Abolitionists; but Halttunen points out that "the convention of spectatorial sympathy at the core of the eighteenth-century literature of sensibility was deeply ambivalent in its treatment of the pain and suffering of other sentient beings" (308). This ambivalence is exaggerated and parodied in the Sensationalist response to the same kind of torture and eroticism in Gothic Romances, and *Uncle Tom's Cabin* itself: Freud has documented that "in my patients' *milieu* it was almost always the same books whose contents gave a new stimulus to the beating-phantasies" including *Uncle Tom's Cabin* (180). The satire inherent in Sensationalist aesthetic responses rested on the fact that Humanitarian deployment of violent imagery is privileged by its mediated distance from actual violence: "Although spectatorial sympathy claimed to demolish social distance, it actually rested on social distance—a distance reinforced, in sentimental art, by the interposition of written text, stage, or canvas between the virtuous spectator and the (imaginary) suffering victim." (Halttunen 309). While ostentatiously promoting a moral imperative to stop the violence depicted, the violent imagery was employed in practice for the voyeur's satisfaction with their own repulsion; an aestheticization of politically sensitive concepts, rather than a politicization of aesthetic formality.

If a smile can be painted on someone who is actually very angry or sad, the clown is not just demonstrating as straightforward a lesson as "people can be dangerous because they conceal their actual intentions." While this meaning might be ascribed to the social demand for power to identify interiority through exterior signs after the middle-class moral panics brought on by the John Wayne Gacy clown-murders, the fad of Pennywise the evil clown as a distinctly suburban villain, the urban myths around clown-like hooligans using the Halloween season to terrorize the nuclear family's trick-or-treat tradition, the public gang injunctions against the Juggalo "clown-gangster" movement, and the clown makeup ban at the US *Joker* (2019) premiere, these connotations negate the historical role attributed to the semiotic practices of carnivalesque jesters in performance. The bourgeois, psychic crises with clowns, according to Tim Adam's account in *The Guardian,* manifest as "Coulrophobia, a word only coined in the 1980s," which

> took hold after the 1990 film of Stephen King's novel *It*, featuring the sadistic clown Pennywise, who preyed on children (King's novel borrowed some elements from the real-life story of serial killer John Wayne Gacy, who had performed as Pogo the Clown). The stereotype has subsequently been mined by numerous low-budget films, and lately fuelled by a series of terrifying YouTube clips of ghoulish clown "pranks" in underground carparks and on deserted roads.

In addition, the National Gang Intelligence Center's reports still track the criminal activities of the clown-faced Juggalos as a loose organization of cultural practices affiliated with vandalism, drug use, trespassing, and petty theft. *USA Today* columnist Bill Keveney writes "Landmark Theatres bans costumes, as well as masks, face paint, for 'Joker' screenings" based on the fear of mass shootings and public disorder fomented by the premiere. These panics are rooted in the clown's aesthetic fulfilling the structural function of the "fissure/suture" outlined by Roland Barthes (58): by providing us with a painted mask—i.e., a sign of a facial expression rather than a face in itself—the murderous clown highlights the fissures between inner ideals and socially compelled behavior/signification, as well as the frustrations with public demands for an artificial suturing of the inner face and the outer face. From the standpoint of signification and performance, the question becomes: who is really in control of signifying our affect and intentions to others? Are we all just postmodern "clowns" in the sense that we paint on the face demanded for an urbanized routine by institutions and their subjects? That our lived realities have been subordinated to aesthetic form in order to maintain and compensate for the *mythos* of Modernity? Applied in the current instance of clowns-as-signifiers, if the individual is losing the ability to signify anything but the aesthetically naïve pursuit of happiness, like a clown, *is there anything truly left inside the subject to signify?*

Art, unlike so many other modern clowns driving cinematic narratives, remains a silent pantomime across his films. Without entering the world of speech, he cannot be understood as having any human motives or being bound by any cinematic laws of realism. He is purely an aesthetic inscription, an ambiguous signifier; as such, there is little to no plot beyond him stalking young women, homeless folk, and workingmen through decrepit warehouses, service tunnels, and defunct gas stations. Protagonists develop, but never last beyond half of any film before Art shifts focus to new prey. The thinly-spread plotlines guide the viewer's focus away from traditional expectations of narrative to the fragmented meanings of individual acts of violence, and the spectators' role in engaging with them. In this way, Art's function is more structurally similar to the killers in *Funny Games* (2007) than other modern clown films, in that the villains' common purpose for manufacturing their murder-porn is to censure the audience for enduring it by returning their voyeurism. In *Funny Games,* only Paul (Michael Pitt) is capable of speaking with the camera—winking at it and rewinding it to invite our participation. After he and Peter (Brady Corbet) have taken a family hostage, Paul turns to the camera and asks the audience whether they will bet on the family's survival. After the mother Anna (Naomi Watts) seizes a gun and shoots Peter, Paul uses a remote to "rewind" the diegesis and disarm her, placing us firmly in the position of the voyeur with the power to control the fantasy. Paul also occasionally references horror film scriptwriting to match his actions with parodied storylines. The movie ends on Paul grinning directly at the camera, just like Art in *All Hallows' Eve*. Both murderous depictions consciously parody the notion of violence as an aesthetic without ethical limitations, i.e., "art for art's sake," and demand the audience to question their looking practice in response.

Given its historical usage, the "art for art's sake" authoritarian formalism is a distinctly privileged social tradition. In "Black African Aesthetics," Leopold Senghor argues that "art is functional" and that "in black Africa, 'art for art's sake' does not exist" (28–9). Chinua Achebe asserts that "art for art's sake is just another piece of deodorised [sic] dog shit" (19). Mao Zedong said, "There is in fact no such thing as art for art's sake, art that stands above classes, art that is detached from or independent of politics" (86). Nietzsche also points out:

> When the purpose of moral preaching and of improving man has been excluded from art, it still does not follow by any means that art is altogether purposeless, aimless, senseless—in short, *l'art pour l'art,* a worm chewing its own tail. [...] what does all art do? does it not praise? glorify? choose? prefer? With all this it strengthens or weakens certain valuations [24].

Against Modernity's subtle valuations supporting a violent voyeurism, Art the Clown claims the right to look back at the naïve gaze of the middle-class voyeur in a tradition of "countervisuality" that questions the dialectic Humanitarian/Sensationalist complex of visuality supported through socially privileged and hyper-mediated looking practices. "It is the performative claim of a right to look where none technically exists that puts a countervisuality into play," according to visual cultures scholarship: "[l]ike visuality, it interfaces 'formal' and 'historical' aspects. The 'right' in the right to look contests first the 'right' to property in another person by insisting on the irreducible autonomy of all persons, prior to all law" (Mirzoeff 478). To control for unproductive viewing practices justified by an "art for art's sake" aesthetic regime filled with pornographies of pain, Art holds the viewer to account for their liberal sentimentalism. The extradiegetic gaze makes him unique from killer clowns like Killjoy, Pennywise, and Joker, who don't resolve the identification-projection problem, but instead encourage us to be heroes who kill our fear or sympathize with the brutality of modern being (although they have their moments of third meaning/*signifiance*) rather than critique its sociopathic forms of visual sign-making and its performative motivation located in mass viewing/reading practices—a horror necessary for the contemplation of the exploitation, rather than an egotistic fear/desire towards the pain of a subject with which the audience can project themselves onto the medium.

Benjamin's understanding of extradiegetic "shock" (*Understanding Brecht*, xiii) coincides with Barthes' reading of Brechtian theater and Eisenstein's cinematic montage as producing socially conscious *Gestus*, which is a useful structure for thinking through Art's horrific mimesis. The critics acknowledge "rhetorical forms may be gestural, which is why it is pointless to criticize Eisenstein's art (as also that of Brecht) for being 'formalizing' or 'aesthetic': form, aesthetic, rhetoric can be socially responsible if they are handled with deliberation" (Barthes 74). Essentially, both authors see the defamiliarization of social rituals functionally rejecting bourgeois "realism" and highlighting the "fissure/suture" of theatrical disguises as a way of undercutting Western mythmaking and its fetish for interiority. The postmodern clown, as a fissure/suture for meaning, is an uncanny reminder of a simpler time before the traumas of growing up, a carnivalesque revenge upon the "serious" authority, a commentary on the cruel amorality of aesthetic fetishism, a critical performance of sadomasochistic/voyeuristic viewership, and an expression of happiness that undoes its own signification (*signifiance*). That is, it calls attention to its own artificiality, prompting the onlooker to question its "naturalness" or authenticity, and to focus on the very manufacturing of a smile in performing/signifying "happiness" to others.

As a clown-mime, Art's visuality is emphasized over his verbal enunciation. His Brechtian *Gestus* is always social (since we cannot understand him as an individual), highlighting where *our* gaze goes (rather than fetishizing *his* gaze) while he is performing profane acts for the viewer. Barthes saw the same use value in Brecht and Eisenstein's dramatic capabilities of distanciation, alienation, and estrangement through the defamiliarizing Gestus—i.e., de-individuating the image to render it a social structure capable of critique. Through the *rôle* of the mime-as-artist, Art's slayings involve an unnerving combination of sadism and performativity. This contradiction makes him a perfect vehicle for the paradoxes of horror (as) entertainment. According to Anton Bitel, an Oxford-based critic and member of the London Film Critics' Circle: "If all this Art-ful nastiness is a subtext-free thrill-and-kill ride which openly advertises the sheer senselessness and gratuity of all its on-screen cat-and-mouse deaths by numbers, it is also an unapologetically 'pure' genre entry, confronting—and amusing—us with all the sinister masked vicariousness of the Halloween spirit." Art is also liberating the means of production that police the aesthetic regime of "tastefulness" for viewers from the constraints of Hollywood firms; he is free from the politics that limit the production of truly horrific films and minimize the self-reflexivity of looking, given that *Terrifier* and the upcoming *Terrifier 2* were completely crowdfunded (the sequel has exceeded its fundraising goals by 430 percent). As director Damien Leone has put it on the *Movies and Mania* blog: "the inmates are running the asylum" when it comes to narratological and aesthetic decision-making. Strangely, this freedom of Art from the politics restraining the means of cinematic production helps the film work to critique the amoral philosophy of "art for art's sake," as well as the perverse social distance instantiated by the binary Humanitarian/Sensationalist visuality complex facilitating our looking at the horrific in order to authenticate ourselves by shrinking away or deriving pleasure from it.

Art makes a progression from a meta- to an extradiegetic presence across the films *All Hallows' Eve* and *Terrifier*. In other words, he appears first in a film-within-a-film, doubly removed as he performs his tortures, before the layers of diegetic distance begin to collapse. The initial structure keeps representation at a safe remove, until Art "escapes" the frames of diegesis and starts knocking on the television screen itself, as if demanding entry into our world. *All Hallows' Eve* is a horror anthology frame narrative with Art as the recurring villain. A babysitter in a suburban household on Halloween comes across a nondescript VHS tape containing three abduction-murders in one of the children's candy bags. The tape contains everything taboo to the repressive bourgeois visuality complex: graphic torture, sadomasochistic eroticism, Satanic ritual, predatory masculinity, and cannibalism—none of which are resolved or castrated by any narratological condemnation or just punishment. The elder sibling reacts with a properly

Humanitarian sensibility, consistent with her feminine, middle-class status, by shrinking away and screaming in disgust. The younger boy engages in an equally appropriate Sensationalist response, consistent with a privileged masculine voyeurism, by luridly staring at the ambiguous eroticism of pain, and smiling. While the babysitter initially stops the series of Art's short films, she is unexplainably seduced back into watching the rest of them alone, as if desiring to master her own abject impulses to look away or become aroused. Sontag explains in *On Photography* this middle-class practice of overcoming the anxiety of relating to abject imagery via Diane Arbus, who typifies "the kind of art popular among sophisticated urban people right now: art that is a self-willed test of hardness. Her photographs offer an occasion to demonstrate that life's horror can be faced without squeamishness" (32). These structures of photographic signification feature

> a leading tendency of high art in capitalist countries: to suppress, or at least reduce, moral and sensory queasiness. Much of modern art is devoted to lowering the threshold of what is terrible. By getting us used to what, formerly, we could not bear to see or hear, because it was too shocking, painful, or embarrassing, art changes morals—that body of psychic custom and public sanctions that draws a vague boundary between what is emotionally and spontaneously intolerable and what is not [33].

This kind of photography—and the visuality complex it invites for the aesthetic cult of sensibility viewing it—demonstrates how the privileged Humanitarian/Sensationalist response to imagery structures an apathetic self-annihilation that makes one naïvely irresponsible for anything but their own wellbeing: "The photographs make a compassionate response feel irrelevant. The point is not to be upset, to be able to confront the horrible with equanimity. But this look that is not (mainly) compassionate is a special, modern ethical construction: not hardhearted, certainly not cynical, but simply (or falsely) naïve" (33). Such willful ignorance to the social tensions underlying aesthetic statements effectively frees the subject from any ethical considerations in their formulation of taste.

Art punishes the viewer who looks to be repulsed, the voyeur who peeps to be aroused, and the spectator who stares to become callous. He denies their power to distance themselves from the scene via the diegesis. Strangely enough, in claiming the autonomy of a right to look back at the audience and approach them, to escape the narrative frame of the short film into canvas paintings of himself, then into the babysitter's world, and then into our own, he alienates us from the ability to identify too closely with the diegetic characters. He keeps us from the voyeurism to which most horror cinema accustoms the subject, typically enabling them to project themselves like gods into a mediated representation of pain and pleasure without implicating their own gaze in the performance.

Terrifier takes Art's estranging powers of radical defamiliarization as a given tactic of the prior film, freeing him up to consciously perform his heinous acts for the audience as a way of further defamiliarizing the middle-class Humanitarian/Sensationalist visuality complex from its structural support in the diegesis. His ethical critique of "art for art's sake" now furthers its form of brutal satire: narrative largely falls to the wayside as Art (the clown) becomes a direct mimesis of Art (aesthetics), equating cultural production with amoral gestures at meaning-making through violent representations—i.e., a cruel allegoresis that is free of ethics. He mimics taking selfies with a body he has cut in half simply for the purpose of photographing the performance. He collapses in a fit of silent laughter when his prey finds her friend's bullet-ridden corpse done up as a circus sideshow, and we behold the carnage along with her. Art quietly dances through a decrepit warehouse, naked except for a woman's scalp and a bodysuit made from her skin. He rides around a loading bay on a tiny tricycle, innocently honking his toy horn while grinning into the shadows where his prey and the camera are located with a bloody, carnivorous grimace, full of rotting gums and sharp teeth. Rather than simply killing a homeless woman, he steals her doll and "mothers" it in a service passage until she finds him. He invites her to cradle him as he cradles the doll, luring her gaze before eating her face. He inscribes the word "ART" in feces on the bathroom wall of a pizzeria before killing the cashier charged with cleaning it up, just as he carved the words "PIG" and "SLUT" into the amputated trunk of a woman sutured back together so that she could survive long enough to read herself in a mirror at the end of *All Hallows' Eve*. He transforms his lone survivor at the end of *Terrifier* into a macabre, faceless sculpture before being shot by the police. When she is released from the hospital, only to be mocked on late-night talk shows for her mutilated countenance, she murders a television personality herself by gouging the celebrity's eyes out. Art, always more than human, later emerges from a body bag by returning the gaze of the audience and smiling as he strangles the coroner.

We are led to wonder: who are these silent performances and inscriptions for? The ambiguity of spectatorship's role in the structure of making meaning lies at the core of Art's horror. When Art is inscribed simply for Art's sake, when the politics of a violent gesture become mere aesthetics, and that amoral formality is naïvely mediated to be commodified by the modern consumer, the way we look at cruelty falls back into the unproductive structure of the Humanitarian/Sensationalist visuality complex. This viewing practice seeks to compensate for, rather than remedy or critique, the brutalities of maintaining social distance, hierarchies, and inequalities. As such, it must be countered and, thereby, broken through the autonomous and terrifying gaze of Art on full display.

Works Cited

Achebe, Chinua. *Morning Yet on Creation Day*. Heinemann Educational Press, 1975.
Adams, Tim. "Send Out the Clowns: Why Are They Losing Popularity?" *The Guardian*, June 7, 2015.
All Hallow's Eve. Dir. Damien Leone. Image Entertainment, 2013.
Bach, Steven. *Leni: The Life and Work of Leni Riefenstahl*. A.A. Knopf, 2007.
Barthes, Roland. *Image, Music, Text*. Trans. Stephen Heath. Fontana Press, 1977.
Benjamin, Walter. *The Origin of German Tragic Drama*. Verso, 1985.
_____. *Understanding Brecht*. Verso, 1998.
_____. "The Work of Art in the Age of Mechanical Reproduction." *Illuminations*. Ed. Hannah Arendt. Trans. Harry Zohn. Shocken, 1968, pp. 217–51.
Bitel, Anton. "FrightFest Halloween All-Dayer 2017: Seven Flavours of Fear." *Sight & Sound*, BFI, November 10, 2017.
Derrida, Jacques. "Plato's Pharmacy." *Dissemination*. Trans. Barbara Johnson. Continuum, 1981, pp. 61–172.
Doi, Takeo. *The Anatomy of Self: The Individual Versus Society*. Trans. Mark A. Harbison. Kodansha International, 1986.
Foucault, Michel. *Discipline and Punish: The Birth of the Prison*, 2 ed. Vintage Books, 1995.
Freud, Sigmund. "'A Child is Being Beaten': A Contribution to the Study of the Origin of Sexual Perversions." *The Standard Edition of the Complete Psychological Works of Sigmund Freud, Volume XVII (1917–1919): An Infantile Neurosis and Other Works*. Psychoanalytic Electronic Publishing, 2017, pp. 175–204.
Funny Games. Dir. Michael Haneke. Warner Independent Pictures, 2007.
Graham, Cooper C. "*Olympia* in America, 1938: Leni Riefenstahl, Hollywood, and the Kristallnacht." *Historical Journal of Film, Radio and Television*, vol. 13, no. 4, 1993, pp. 433–450.
Jameson, Fredric. *Postmodernism, or, the Cultural Logic of Late Capitalism*. Duke University Press, 1991.
"Juggalos: Emerging Gang Trends and Criminal Activity." *National Gang Intelligence Center*, February 15, 2011.
Keveney, Bill. "Landmark Theatres Bans Costumes, as Well as Masks, Face Paint, for *Joker* Screenings." *USA Today*, September 26, 2019.
Kristeva, Julia. "L'engendrement de la formule/The engendering of the formula." *Semeiotike: Recherches pour une sémanalyse/Semiotics: Research for a Semanalysis*. Seuil, 1969, pp. 217–310.
Lee, Sun-you. "The Depressing Truth Behind a Smile." *The Hanyang Journal*, vol. 316, 2012, pp. 8–9.
Lewis, Leo. "Smiling Can Seriously Damage Your Health." *The Times*, February 9, 2008.
Marinetti, Filippo Tommaso. "The Futurist Manifesto." *Le Figaro*, vol. 20, 1909, pp. 39–44.
Mirzoeff, Nicholas. "The Right to Look." *Critical Inquiry*, vol. 37, no. 3, 2011, pp. 473–96.
Mulvey, Laura. "Visual Pleasure and Narrative Cinema." *The Sexual Subject: A Screen Reader in Sexuality*. Routledge, 1992, pp. 22–34.
Nietzsche, Friedrich. "Skirmishes of an Untimely Man." *Twilight of the Idols*. Leipzig, 1889.
The Oxford Dictionary of Islam. Ed. John Esposito. Oxford University Press, 2003.
Senghor, Léopold Sédar, and Elaine P. Halperin. "African-Negro Aesthetics." *Diogenes*, vol. 4, no. 16, 1956, pp. 23–38.
Shin, Dong Chun. "Emotional Labor and Human Rights Protection in the Case of Airlines." *The Korean Journal of Air & Space Law and Policy*, vol. 29, no. 2, 2014, pp. 87–108.
Sontag, Susan. "Fascinating Fascism." *Under the Sign of Saturn*. Farrar, Straus & Giroux, 1980, pp. 73–105.
_____. *On Photography*. Farrar, Straus & Giroux, 1977.
Stanislavski, Constantin. "Direction and Acting." *Acting: a Handbook of the Stanislavski Method*. Crown Publishers, 1947, pp. 22–32.
Terrifier. Dir. Damien Leone. Epic Pictures Group, 2018.
"*Terrifier 2*—USA, 2020—First Pic of Art the Clown on Set." *Movies & Mania*, October 25, 2019.

Winnicott, Donald. "Ego Distortion in Terms of True and False Self." *The Maturational Process and the Facilitating Environment: Studies in the Theory of Emotional Development.* International Universities Press, 1960, pp. 140–57.

Zedong, Mao. "Talks at the Yenan Forum on Literature and Art." *Selected Works of Mao Tse-tung,* vol. 3, 1967, pp. 69–98.

Clowns, Bogeymen, and the Anxiety of Strangers
Analyzing the Cautionary Elements of Jon Watts' Clown *(2014)*

Debaditya Mukhopadhyay

Unlike most other scary clowns, the antagonist of Jon Watts' *Clown* (2014) has only one specific aim. This clown (called Clöyne) does not keep killing random people just for the sake of it. Instead, it is shown to have a specific trait of abducting children to feed on them, which makes it resemble a folkloric bogeyman figure. Rather than simply being an interesting creative choice, such resemblance, as I will explain in the following sections, marks a notable development of the scary clown genre as a whole for two main reasons. Firstly, it shows this genre bringing the child-devourer supernatural clown back. Second, it highlights this clown figure's connection with contemporary American society's anxieties regarding strangers and the dangers they pose to children more prominently than its earlier appearances. I will explain these aspects by analyzing the figure of this film's demoniacal entity called Clöyne through the lens of folklore. Before that, I will outline the genealogy of this scary clown by referring to its usage in Stephen King's *It*, which arguably was the first instance of scary clown narrative featuring an antagonist gorging on children.

Pennywise: The Scary Clown Meets the Bogeyman

Though the monster of King's novel is ultimately shown to be an alien and during the last face-off between the monster and the Losers' Club, its original form is said to look like "a nightmare Spider" (1053), it does have a notable connection with bogeymen. I will outline this connection by drawing upon textual references and King's own acknowledgment of Pennywise's links with trolls (a recurrently used bogeyman figure). As described in George Beahm's account of the novel's genesis, King had clearly acknowledged the "troll under the bridge" of the famous story "The Three Billy Goats Gruff" as his takeoff point for this novel (258). Additionally, as explained by Cory R. Goehring, "The Three Billy Goats Gruff" actually "makes an appearance" in King's novel itself when "young Ben overhears story hour" (20). Most importantly, the novel's antagonist bears a striking resemblance to the bogeyman figure for its shapeshifting abilities and luring of children.

In her study of the folkloric roots of Freddy Kreuger, Karra Shimabukuro observes that the definitive feature of bogeymen is that: "Bogeys can become anything" (48). In the light of this argument King's alien monster appears to be a bogeyman of sorts because it is shown to keep changing its form in accordance with the fear of its targets. Moreover, the monster's method of luring children by offering them what they like most, too, connects this monster with bogeymen; in order to bring out this link, at this point, I would refer to Marina Warner's views regarding the bogeyman figure.

Warner, in the prologue of her study on bogeyman figures gives an idea about the way male bogeyman figures abduct and slaughter children using the story of Zagreus. Warner's account of the myth shows how the stranger bogeyman wins a child's trust by taking forms that children love. Zagreus was the son of Zeus and he knew that "he should not take anything from strangers, and certainly not eat anything they press on him" (1) but as soon as the Titans take a form that children like, Zagreus fails to resist their temptation and gets devoured by them. Garb of the clown is shown to function in a similar manner in King's novel. Just like Zagreus, child victims of this monster mistake the stranger to be a friend, despite knowing how risky it is to do so, because the alien uses its clown avatar as bait. As shown in the iconic death scene of Georgie, when the monster appears in the colorful costume of the clown, it wins children's trust effortlessly.

As explained by Warner, the Titans from the story of Zagreus or any other antagonist who lure children, thus, function as bogeymen. Viewed in the light of such observations, the alien monster of King's novel indeed becomes a modern variant of the bogeyman figure but apart from that this connection makes a notable impact on the figure of the scary clown as well. Though King's novel and its adaptations are basically about an alien, they do not really exhibit the horrors of an alien antagonist like the *Alien* or *Predator* franchise. Instead, they introduce a new kind of scary clown—a clown that eats children. A few notable examples of scary clown films, like *The Clown Murders* (1976), *Blood Harvest* (1987), and *Clownhouse* (1989) did exist prior to the release of the first adaptation of King's novel in 1990, but none of them featured a child-devouring clown. Naturally when this TV series by ABC network showed a scary clown feeding on children, it immediately caught the public imagination.

In this way, King's Pennywise became "the most memorable scary clown in visual media" (Radford 67). It introduced the scary clown as a present-day bogeyman and as a large number of viewers became engrossed in the tale of Pennywise onscreen, this fusion of the two found its way into the collective imagination. Despite the novelty and popularity, the child-devouring clown, as well as its folkloric connections, never really found its way into the scary clown genre. Instead, it gradually went into oblivion with the release of new scary clown films. In the next two sections, I will explain the reasons behind this development by showing how King's novel itself and scary clown films releasing after the TV series of 1990 obfuscated Pennywise's connections with bogeymen.

Obfuscation of the Connection in It *and Its Adaptations*

To begin with, the novel did not show the scary clown attacking children exclusively. Instead, Pennywise the Dancing Clown is seen eating the grown-up Adrian Mellon both in the novel and the film *It: Chapter Two* (2019). Rather than solely demonstrating the vulnerability of children (as in the majority of bogeyman stories), the ending of *It* endorses the power of childhood innocence. As suggested by Tony Magistrale, the five surviving members of the Losers' Club manage to defeat the monster only because deep inside they always remained "children maintaining the mutual bond of love" (109). While King's novel and its film versions initiated the obscuring of the clown figure's links with the bogeyman, the subsequent scary clown films furthered it.

Disappearing Connection from the Genre

Since Pennywise gained popularity onscreen, nearly every scary clown film started utilizing the aforementioned link, but the problem is they did it in such a convoluted manner that the connection with the bogeyman started disappearing. Although these films showed psychopaths, serial-killers, and evil entities from other worlds killing one victim after another by exploiting the time-honored tradition of viewing the clown as a ludicrous figure, just like King did in *It*, none of the clowns in these films resembled the bogeyman figure quite like Pennywise. None deceive their victims, nor are they supernatural beings that gorge on children.

The majority of the scary-clown films made following the release of *It* (1990) utilize the clown figure's connection with the bogeyman figure to a significant extent, but none of them gave a proper expression to this crucial connection. As a result, a plethora of films showing clowns as scary appeared, but none of them explained why they were scary. The audience simply accepted scary clowns to be a staple figure of horror without wondering why exactly they were doing so. This universal acceptance of the scary clown may be understood from a scene in *The Cabin in the Woods* (2012), where clowns are shown to be enlisted with all other classic horror antagonists including vampires, werewolves, and zombies. Scary clowns of these films ceased to have any special interest in attacking or devouring children in particular. The psychotic serial killers of films like the *Camp Blood* (1999–2020) series or *Fear of Clowns* (2004–07), and so on, are shown to kill at random.

Among the supernatural scary clowns, only the troop of clowns from *Killer Klowns from Outer Space* (1988) is shown to be interested in eating humans. Other supernatural clowns like Killjoy or Mr. Jingles (the antagonist of the 2006 slasher film *Mr. Jingles* and its 2009 remake *Jingles the Clown*) do not attack children. The exception to this is the clown of *Hellbreeder* (2004), who is shown gorging on children, but even this film does not further the exploration of the link between the scary clown and bogeyman. Instead, it tries to appear scary by means of exploiting the popularity of the scary clown figure in and of itself. Watts' film marks a significant departure from this trend by reinstating the scary clown as a devourer of children and offering a backstory that marks a resurfacing of the scary clown's connection with the bogeyman.

Clown: Reconnecting the Scary Clown with Bogeymen

When Kent McCoy meets Herbert Karlsson to understand why he was being unable to remove the clown costume he wore for his son Jack's birthday, instead of talking about the procedure Karlsson starts an intriguing account of the clown figure in general. He tells Kent: "The original clown, he was not funny at all" and shows him a diary that describes this "original clown" to be a creature of Nordic regions that "lived up in the mountains, with a skin white as snow and the red nose, blistered by the cold." According to Karlsson, as well as the diary he shows, over time this creature and its method of luring children using an odd physical appearance gave birth to the figure of the clown. This ancient creature originally called

"Clöyne," had a "white face and red nose," just like the ones used by present day clowns "to make people laugh" and "entertain children." The Nordic origin, as well as the physical features of the Clöyne bears a resemblance to traditional trolls, who, according to Alda Sigmundsdóttir's book *Icelandic Folk Legends*, are said to be "Icelandic oicotype of a folk character designed to frighten children—a local version of the bogeyman" who live "inside caves or mountains"(14).

The film's cautionary element informs the audience that people might be entertained by the "white face and red nose" of a clown, but when they do so they remain ignorant of the actual purpose the alluring face of the Clöyne served. Though neither the makers nor the reviewers of the film declared this backstory to be authentic, it certainly is more than a baseless scary legend. By using this account of Clöyne, the film becomes the first amongst scary clown flicks to advance a theory about the very figure of the clown originating from a child-luring monster that resembles the troll or other similar bogeyman figures, thereby, marking a resurfacing of the link between the clown and the bogeyman.

Reasons Behind the Connection's Return

But why does *Clown* make room for such a resurfacing? A significant answer may be found, by tracing how this film reflects a particular kind of anxiety that became prevalent among the American population during previous eras. Richard Louv describes this anxiety as the "Bogeyman Syndrome" (126). According to him, "since [the] 1980s, fear of strangers—and beyond that a generalized, unfocused fear—has come to outrank the fear of traffic" (124) amongst the American adults who started finding bogeyman everywhere. An echo of Louv's observations can be found in Mary Ann Stokes' 2009 essay where she explains this severe anxiety about the strangers in "[the] modern urban community" to be mostly a social construct and refers to the phenomenon as "Stranger Danger." Stokes defines "Stranger Danger" as "a buzzword developed over the past decade in education and media [... which] can be viewed as the modern embodiment of the 'wicked witch' or 'bogeyman'" (7), thereby, highlighting how a return of the bogeyman figure in the contemporary collective imagination grew from the dread of strangers.

Watts' film notably engages with such anxieties. The figure of Clöyne is used in a metonymical way in this film. The Clöyne functions mostly as a deceiver. It deceives its host human at first and once it manages to take over the host's body and mind, it captures children by pretending to be their best friend or acquaintance. Kent McCoy, possessed by the Clöyne, is shown to recurrently lure children by pretending to be a friendly or helpless person.

Even when Kent kills Colton by invading his house, it is implied that the monster manages to kill him only because Colton does not run immediately from him, thinking he was being visited by someone he knew. The McCoys try their best to stop the Clöyne by having Kent chained in their basement, but its deceiving abilities help him to break free from that as well. At first, it lures Jack by introducing itself as Dummo and promising to be his best friend. It gains Jack's trust by saying things like "You know you can always talk to Dummo" and uses Jack to escape from the chains.

What might be the reason for the film to use the figure of a clown to embody these apprehensions regarding strangers? Can this be a result of real-life incidents involving clowns? As suggested by Benjamin Radford, even during "the heyday" of clown panic, "no hard evidence was ever found that the clowns even existed" and more importantly: "no children were actually harmed or abducted" (5).

Why then does this idea of scary clowns persist in popular culture? Perhaps it is because traditional bogeymen have increasingly been found to lose their fearfulness among children in the twentieth century and later. Maybe clowns have displaced diabolical and religious figures in the collective unconscious as sources of evil and mayhem. Or perhaps the horrors of terrorism and pandemics are just too grimly real, and figures traditionally associated with merriment have become fantasy analogues for such daily, grinding realities. As shown by Marina Warner, "The twentieth-century approach to medieval drollery" is marked by the tendency to "cutif[y] or infantili[ze]" monster figures (299). On the other hand, clowns appeared to be a fitting option for filling the gap left by these customary bogeyman figures because of their usual association with the figure of the wayward transgressor. In short, the clown's figure has increasingly become a major source of alarm because the collective imagination is seeking a new form for its fear of strangers and since the clown has habitually been viewed as an epitome of strangeness and disruptive behavior, it has become a perfect embodiment of such anxiety.

Cultural Memories of the Trickster and Its Role in Connecting the Clown with Bogeyman

Using Joseph Durwin's observations in the essay "Coulrophobia and the Trickster," some of the developments mentioned above may be traced back to the cultural memories of the trickster. Such stories show the trickster, as well as its various manifestations (the court jester, et al.), to be wild and formidable beings. For example, clowns in the form of jesters or other participants of "ritual clowning" have always been licensed to be unruly and even gross. Furthermore, Durwin informs that despite being an epitome of misrule, a majority of Native North American tribes held these tricksters in great esteem and entrusted them with the protection of their people (5). In his conclusion, Durwin explains the transformation of the clown from its ancient roots as a sacred Shaman to its modern iteration as a petty entertainer by calling it a "demystification of the unknown" (19), and ascribes the fear of clowns to be a result of the partially retained cultural memories of the "sacred clown"(19).

Interestingly, though Durwin outlines the clown's recurrent appearances as an unmanageable character across time and civilizations, his conclusion does not relate this tradition of imagining the clown to be an unruly deceiver while explaining the possible sources of coulrophobia. Building on Durwin's findings, one finds that the fear of clowns is not just the fear of the sacred shamanic clown, but it is also the fear of the wild deceiver thought to have unknown capabilities. In other words, it seems possible to derive an important insight regarding the basis of the fear of clowns by taking into account the shared cultural memories of clowns as tricksters with meta-human abilities, beings who are dangerous chiefly be*cause* of their unpredictable nature. Usually they have been imagined as transgressors who can commit horrific acts without any hesitation and, hence, this inherent potential permits them to emerge as an ideal replacement for the traditional bogeyman.

Conclusion

While Stephen King's Pennywise could be credited as an impactful early instance of imagining the clown as bogeyman in modern pop-culture terms, Watts' Clöyne should be considered a proper furthering of this trend. Mark Dery opined that Millennials started endowing clowns with villainous features in part because they searched for a "societal scapegoat" for venting fears much like the witch-hunters of the Middle Ages who sought relief from their fear of plagues by killing witches (66). It is worth reflecting that, no matter the zeitgeist, no matter the presiding culture or its associated traumas, human fears—and their concomitant coping strategies—will never cease to reflect its past, will never stop evolving, and will never abandon tried and true iconography, be it the devil, godheads, or evil clowns.

Works Cited

Beahm, George. *The Stephen King Companion: Four Decades of Fear from the Master of Horror*. New York: Thomas Dunne Books, 2015.

The Cabin in the Woods. Dir. Drew Goddard. Perf. Kristen Connolly, Chris Hemsworth, Anna Hutchison, Fran Kranz, Jesse Williams, Richard Jenkins, and Bradley Whitford. Lionsgate, 2014.
Clown. Dir. Jon Watts. Perf. Laura Allen, Andy Powers, and Peter Stormare. Cross Creek Pictures, 2016.
Dery, Mark. *The Pyrotechnic Insanitarium: American Culture on the Brink.* New York: Grove Press, 2016.
Durwin, Joseph. "Coulrophobia and the Trickster." *Trickster's Way,* vol. 3, issue 1, 2004, Article 4, 1–22.
Goehring, Cory R. "Seven Children and *It*: Stephen King's *It* as Children's Story." *The Many Lives of It: Essays on the Stephen King Horror Franchise.* Ed. Ron Riekki. Jefferson, NC: McFarland, 2020, pp. 18–31.
It: Chapter Two. Dir. Andy Muschietti. Perf. Jessica Chastain, James McAvoy, and Bill Hader. New Line Cinema, 2019.
King, Stephen. *It.* New York: Simon & Schuster, Inc., 1986.
Louv, Richard. *Last Child in the Woods: Saving our Children from Nature-Deficit Disorder.* New York: Algonquin Books, 2005.
Magistrale, Tony. *Landscape of Fear: Stephen King's American Gothic.* Ohio: Bowling Green State University Popular Press, 1988.
Radford, Benjamin. *Bad Clowns.* Albuquerque: University of New Mexico Press, 2016.
_____. "Creepy Clowns Stalk UK Children? Reality and Folklore." *Skeptical Inquirer,* vol. 40, issue 2, March/April 2016, pp. 5–6.
Shimabukuro, Karra. "The Bogeyman of Your Nightmares: Freddy Krueger's Folkloric Roots." *Studies in Popular Culture,* vol. 36, no. 2, Spring 2014, pp. 45–65.
Sigmundsdóttir, Alda. *Icelandic Folk Legends: Tales of Apparitions, Outlaws and Things Unseen.* Reykjavík: Little Books Publishing, 2016.
Stokes, Mary Anne. "Stranger Danger: Child Protection and Parental Fears in the Risk Society." *Amsterdam Social Science,* vol.1, issue 3, 2009, pp. 6–24.
Warner, Marina. *No Go the Bogeyman: Scaring, Lulling and Making Mock.* New York: Farrar, Straus & Giroux, 1999.

Out of the White (Terror) and into the Black (Presence)

Difference as Monstrous in Stephen King's It: Chapter Two

Kim Hester Williams

> "from that moment I declared
> everlasting war against the species,
> and, more than all, against him who had formed me,
> and sent me forth to this insupportable misery."
> —Mary Shelley, *Frankenstein*

> "We went into the black together."
> —Stephen King, *It*

Introduction: Difference. Made Monstrous.

When confronted with the image of the clown, we are faced with a difference that provokes fear and, in many cases, as I have experienced with my own children, loathing. What is the source of this reaction to the figure of the clown? Is it, pun intended, the common fear that is often provoked by the stark make-up, exaggerated facial features, energetic and proliferating gestures, and distorted voice of the clown? How can we account for the terror-stricken response so often provoked by the very sight and presence of a clown? I argue that not only does the clown represent that which is so transparently different from us. It represents our fear of difference, as manifested in American racialized culture—embodied as a living nightmare, and as a self-reflexive racial haunting. A historical overview concerning the fear of clowns reveals the role racialization has played in the image of the clown as a stark visual representation of exaggerated and imaginative difference. For example, in addition to clowns serving as sources of entertainment as early as the eighteenth century in England, they egregiously and, apropos to my discussion, reemerge in the American blackface minstrel shows of the nineteenth century. The proliferation of racial performance using the trope of "clowning" continued, infamously, in twentieth- and twenty-first-century theatre, film, and with popular figures such as Disney's flagship character, Mickey Mouse.

In the 2019 film *Joker*, the clown as marginalized menace is exploited to its full extent when we learn the backstory of one of Batman's nemeses. Namely, we learn that Arthur Fleck, a disaffected young "white" man who will later be self-transformed into "The Joker," has suffered great trauma as the victim of a society that has categorically rejected and alienated him. He is rendered powerless against this assault which, I suggest, functions as a racial paradox. Historically, socially, and politically, Arthur's whiteness and masculinity should prevail. He should be at the top of the hierarchical, hegemonic food chain. He should be revered or at the very least in full control—of everything and everyone. This is what Arthur imagines in his fantasies of fame and romance with his Black female neighbor, Sophie Dumond, which elicits a parallel white male character's psychosis of power and control in Octavia Butler's speculative novel *Kindred*. Rufus, the "white" young boy later turned slave master, violently enforces his will onto his love interest, Alice, an enslaved Black woman, after she rebuffs him. Rufus tries to do the same to Dana, the Black female protagonist and hero of the novel, who has been thrust back into the American slave past—from the 1970s—to "save" Rufus and Alice, both of whom and together, are her ancestors—thus, the title, *Kindred*.

The constant rejection and abuse Arthur, in *Joker*, experiences throughout the first two-thirds of the film, results in his forced isolation and exacerbated mental illness provoking a state of emotional chaos that, like Mary Shelley's creature in *Frankenstein*, he eventually and fully unleashes onto his enemies, particularly and directly onto all those who have tortured or mocked him. Arthur summarily destroys those who have attempted to destroy him. Once he fully realizes and embraces his monstrous emotions and actions, he becomes The Joker, at once—in his public debut—fully dawning the costume of the clown, most notably for the purposes of this essay, the white masking and red lips that function metaphorically as a symbolic representation of the terror of whiteness. Again, it is worth noting the historical relationship of "clowning" and blackface performance. In the introduction to *Inside the Minstrel Mask: Readings in Nineteenth-Century Blackface Minstrelsy*, the editors explain that

> Quite strikingly, many minstrel performers began their careers in the circus, perhaps even developing American blackface out of clowning (whose present

mask in any case is clearly indebted to blackface), and continually found under the big top a vital arena of minstrel performance. Clowning is an uncanny kind of activity, *scariest when it is most cheerful, unsettling to an audience even as it unmasks the pretentious ringmaster,*" 12 [italics mine].

This prompts a crucial question about what is perhaps the most recognizable and influential "scary clown" trope: Stephen King's *It*. Precisely, what is the real horror of King's *It* narrative? What and who, exactly, is *It*? While the shapeshifting, monstrous clown in Stephen King's masterful novel and the adapted cinematic versions remains somewhat mysterious and opaque, what is clear is that Stephen King paints a vivid, unequivocal portrait of white suburbia in the 1950s that is echoed in Reagan-era 1980s and foretold in 1930s depression-era America represented by the small town of Derry, Maine, with its history of prolific death: "In the year 1930, for instance—the year the Black Spot burned—there were better than one hundred and seventy child disappearances in Derry—and you must remember that these are only the disappearances which were reported to the police and thus documented. *Nothing surprising about it*" (King 160) as expressed by the Chief of Police to the Black male pivotal character and narrator, Michael Hanlon.

While Derry, Maine, can be read as one of the central characters of the horror that is *It*, Mike Hanlon, the lone African-American member of the "Losers' Club," is simultaneously the documenter—largely through narration—and, importantly, the one most aware of *It*'s implicit as well as explicit horror. More pointedly, he is intimately familiar with the horror of whiteness. As with previous speculative narratives by King that portray 1930s depression-era America, for example in *The Green Mile* (1996), King expounds on the intersection of America's racist history and practices (e.g. the racism inherent in American jurisprudence and the corresponding prison industrial system), the economic "possessive investment in whiteness," (Lipsitz) and white masculinity—in crisis. Yet and still, as George Lipsitz argues, "Whiteness is everywhere in American culture, but it is very hard to see" (Lipsitz 369). Given the slippery signifier of whiteness, King must make its terror transparent—as scary as it is experienced by its most vulnerable and unsuspecting victims.

In Part I of the novel, "The Shadow Before," in the opening chapter of the section titled, "Derry: The First Interlude," readers are made aware that Mike (Michael Hanlon) has been keeping notes for a manuscript he has been working on titled, "Derry: An Unauthorized Town History" (King 147). Mike's notes lay the foundation for the story of *It* as he reveals throughout the novel what he has discovered about the history, or rather the haunting, of Derry. He begins his manuscript notes with the underlying and crucial question, "Can an entire city be haunted?" (King 147). We might ask, in turn, can an entire nation be haunted? Indeed, the haunting in Derry is not the typical ghostly figure or the dead soul wandering the earth. It is the "feeding place" where an original party of English white settlers, "numbered about three hundred" (King 155) were granted, or bestowed, the land that is (now) Derry and where, in the year of 1741, every person in that "Derry Township just disappeared" (King 155). As documented in Mike's manuscript, they were there in June of that year, "about three hundred and forty souls—but come October they were gone" (King 155). Although one account attributes the disappearance to an Indian massacre, Mike explains there is "no basis" for such a conclusion and instead insists that "More likely, someone's stove just got too hot and the house went up in flames" (King 155). In fact, there is no explanation, documentation, or understanding provided to or by Mike for this disappearance. They were simply there one day and gone the next, "Without a trace" (King 155). Neither the disappearance nor Indian massacres are discussed. Nothing in the town is "discussed," certainly not the history of violence that plagues and haunts Derry—and that haunts the US given it is clear there were Indigenous occupants in the eighteenth century and there were, as well, massacres in which white settlers perished and scores of Indigenous people were slaughtered. Still, "there is a curtain of quiet which cloaks much of what has happened here" (King 156).

As Mike tells Bill in *It: Chapter Two*, "You see, memory's the thing," after which he explains to Bill that he "had to know how it all started" (*It: Chapter Two*). Mike then shows Bill an early eighteenth-century Shokopiwah artifact with Indigenous carvings that begin to animate as they stare at it. Mike explains, "They [Native Americans] helped me on my journey. They showed me things. A vision" (*It: Chapter Two*). Mike has spiked Bill's water with a hallucinogenic drug so that he also can "see" and experience what Mike was told when he was transported back in time to listen to the Indigenous community's knowledge of, and how to expel, It. It was the current Indigenous community, notably who lived just outside Derry, who helped Mike understand that "all living things must abide by the laws or the shape they inhabit" (*It: Chapter Two*). If we understand Stephen King's *It* story—akin to many of his stories—in relation to American identity and lived racial trauma resulting from a long history of settler colonial relations—and whiteness—it becomes clear that the monstrous clown has taken the form of racial fear and anxiety—difference as (white) terror. It is this metonymous "shape" of racial difference that must be defeated. Through an Indigenous vantage point of clairvoyance, Mike is able to see *It* arrive and later to realize that they must attack the very shape, falseness, and expansiveness of *It* to defeat the monstrous clown, the manifestation of all their fears, anxieties, and trauma—the trauma of difference.

The latest visual installment of King's "scary clown" story, the film sequel, *It: Chapter Two* (2019), provides a visual representation of the history of racial trauma as well as the key to expunging its horror. Unlike the prior popular film, *It* (2017), *It: Chapter Two* foregrounds Mike Hanlon's narrative and, concurrently, King's racial narrative, that is, his discourse on whiteness as terror. At the beginning of *It: Chapter Two*, shortly after the opening sounds of children laughing and singing eerily, we are shown images of Beverly Marsh floating with eyes wide and no pupils. It is, after all, about seeing and not seeing. Subsequently, the scene shifts to the flashback of her, as a teenager, explaining her "visions" of each of the Losers' Club members as adults—a crucial scene from the earlier *It* narrative where, at the end of the film, Bill Denbrough insists they all take a blood oath to "come back" if It ever does: "Swear it. Swear if it isn't dead, if it ever comes back, we'll come back too" (*It*, 2017).

Yet, in *It: Chapter Two*, as in the novel, it is Mike Hanlon who calls them back to Derry. Mike has never left the town of Derry, much like Black people in America can never seem to escape racism. He is both fixed in and by the town and its racial past—again, much like a microcosm of American history. In fact, no one in America can escape *It*, namely, America's haunting racial past; however, Mike, more than any other character, is both attuned to and entrapped by it and so it is Mike who must discover the key to ridding both himself, his "Loser Club" friends, and Derry (America) from it—forever. As he narrates in the opening scene, after the flashback, "Memory, it's a funny thing. People want to believe they are what they choose to remember. The good stuff. The moments. The places. The people we all hold on to. But sometimes, sometimes, we are what we wish we could forget" (*It: Chapter Two*, 2019).

Mike's words provide the voiceover narration and backdrop to several key opening images in the film: a large statue replica of Paul Bunyan, the famous mythical giant American lumberjack from the late nineteenth and early twentieth century, bright pristine city buildings juxtaposed to a dark, empty school hallway with lockers backlit, abandoned city factories, and an alleyway locating a building that, as we later discover, is the site of an infamous 1930 arson fire in which dozens of African Americans were killed purposefully by a white supremacist group in cahoots with local law enforcement, followed by the camera panning a brick wall peppered with flyers about missing children. The most visible image from the flyers is the picture of a young "white" girl that immediately calls attention to the death of innocence. It is clear from these opening visual markers that Derry is plagued by a history of difference and trauma.

"Much of what happened" in Derry is a chronicle of the aftermath of settler colonialism, slavery, and the socioeconomic ravages of U.S. empire.

We learn from Mike's manuscript that several other "unexplained" incidents have occurred in Derry's history including the brutal dismemberment of a crew of lumberjacks in 1879 (harkening back, paradoxically, to the image of Paul Bunyan who comes alive toward the end of the film, as the monster clown It, possesses the statue); a domestic violence incident in 1851 when John Marson, "killed his entire family with poison and then, sitting in the middle of the circle he had made with their corpses, he gobbled an entire 'white-nightshade' mushroom" (King 159); and the 1906 Easter Sunday Kitchener Ironworks explosion that killed 102 people, eighty-eight of whom were children. Additionally, although *It: Chapter Two* never shows the full story, Mike's father, Will Hanlon, told him about the 1930 Black Spot fire in which a nightclub frequented by mostly Black patrons, including Black military servicemen like Mike's father, and some white patrons, was set on fire by the local Legion of White Decency, described by Will to Mike as, "the Northerners' version of the Ku Klux Klan" (King 452). This catalogue of terror remains mysterious given the lack of details documented within the town's archives; however, Will Hanlon, Mike's father, offers a living testament and first-hand witness account to the Black Spot incident of racial terror inflicted upon the African-American residents of Derry and all patrons, black and white, who were present at the Black Spot on a Saturday night in 1930.

It is worth noting that King is careful not to inundate the reader with racial tropes or stereotypes throughout the novel. Nevertheless, unlike the 2017 and 2019 film adaptations, he devotes a significant amount of time and space describing the events of 1930, including the Black Spot fire. Although we are not made privy to the details concerning the massacres that occurred in eighteenth-century colonial America, readers are made well aware, especially with the visual representation of Indigenous people in *It: Chapter Two*, of the racism proliferated in American history and society, particularly in the Jim Crow era but not limited to the southern states. The "n-word" flows freely in the novel, experienced by Will most often in his capacity as an Army soldier. We are also made aware of the relationship between race and class oppression when Will tells his son Mike that the Legion of White Decency:

> weren't worried about niggers raping white women or taking jobs that should have belonged to white men, because there weren't any niggers to speak of up here. In Lewiston they were worried about tramps and hobos and that something called "the bonus army" would join up with something they called "the Communist riffraff army," by which they meant any man who was out of work. The Legion of Decency used to send these fellows out of town just as fast as they came in. Sometimes they stuffed poison ivy down the backs of their pants. Sometimes they set their shirts on fire [King 452].

While he employs racial coding sparingly and meticulously, unlike the overdetermined racial tropes in *The Green Mile*, yet and still, very much like *The Green Mile*, King places a magical negro figure (Hester-Williams) at the center of the *It* narrative—and narration. This is forcefully transparent in the *It: Chapter Two* sequel. Michael Hanlon doesn't possess any "magical" powers per se; however, he is the narrator whose adult occupation as a librarian inculcates extraordinary powers of knowledge, interpretation, and insight as he recounts the tale of It and works throughout the film to keep his friends united against It. To be sure, Mike possesses a critical lens that is an essential tool used by King to express the horrors of whiteness.

Consequently, it is no coincidence, or attempt to be clever, that King chooses the form of a shapeshifting clown as the monster du jour. Described in the first chapter, "The face of the clown in the stormdrain was white, there were funny tufts of red hair on either side of his bald head, and there was a big clown-smile painted over his mouth" (King 13). At first glance, King's *It* combines the connotative symbolism of innocence and whiteness, masked by the image of his monster clown. At the beginning of the novel, we are introduced to two "white" male children in the first chapter, "After the Flood," Bill Denbrough and his younger brother, George (nicknamed Georgie to reinforce his youthfulness). It is Georgie who first encounters the clown modeled after the children's show referenced in the opening chapter, Howdy Doody, as well as the classic clown circus figure, Bozo, and the iconic clown, Ronald McDonald, representing the paragon of mega-fast-food chains, McDonald's, that was founded on April 15, 1955, in San Bernardino, California. These are the images that immediately come to six-year-old George Denbrough when face to face with Pennywise, the monster clown. The seemingly innocent, playful yet perplexing clown, and its corresponding hegemonic racial signifiers, will continue to haunt Derry with an inescapable sphere of influence—and terror—that expands beyond the town and the various decades depicted in the novel to our own present era.

The Flood

> "it was never explained."
> —Stephen King, *It*

Water and fire appear throughout the narrative as harbingers of death and demise. The town of Derry is ravaged again and again with both "natural" and man-made disasters. Lurking beneath the literal surface is the evil of historical denial in the form of Pennywise, the dancing monstrous clown whose sharpened teeth lie constantly in wait to devour its victims. Symbolic also is the first depiction of death by Pennywise, the death of Georgie Denbrough and the death of innocence—of youth and ignorance, as intimately experienced by Georgie's older brother, Bill Denbrough. The representation of whiteness here is important. In *It: Chapter Two*, we are made aware of the haunting that plagues Bill because of the death of his brother. Pennywise, the ferocious clown shape shifts to represent to Bill both whiteness and the trauma of memory that he must expunge. Bill confronts *It*, in the form of his deceased little brother, first reasoning and then insisting, "it wasn't your fault […] you were a good brother" (*It: Chapter Two*). This, as with much of the film, serves symbolically as a foil to white toxic masculinity and a way for characters like Bill, to articulate—beyond the inarticulateness represented by his stutter—a way beyond the stronghold of enforced white masculinity. Bill Denbrough is sorry for what happened to Georgie. But he knows that there is more to this memory and to Georgie's (and his own) trauma and suffering. There is more to the terror of *It*.

The novel awakens us to the horror of suddenly being made aware of an inescapable racial past—and present. The unmistakable figure of the clown will not let us forget or ignore the (racial) past and its horror. In this regard, Pennywise represents America's past as its racial subconscious. In the strictest Freudian sense, he is the unconscious materialized. Pennywise is a manifestation of the *American* dream and its nightmare. Pennywise is both the dream and the nightmare of race that continues to haunt America. The dream is false because it is a dream of white supremacy which is, simultaneously, a nightmare. Moreover, the nightmare extends to the ultimate terror of whiteness as it relentlessly threatens and subverts the dream of freedom and democracy—for everyone, including "white" people.

> "It always comes back, you see. It."
> —Stephen King, *It*

Stephen King's *It* locates anxieties about whiteness, or the tenuousness of whiteness, at the site of the symbolic power of blackness, represented forcefully and explicitly through the figure of Michael Hanlon. It is not only the character Michael Hanlon that provides the symbolic power of blackness in the novel and the film sequel, *It: Chapter Two*. Black figuration is omnipresent throughout the *It* story and its film adaptations. For example, in the novel the use of black vernacular to describe and employ one of Richie Tozier's "dozen different voices," where we are told that Richie, "was speaking in what he called his Nigger Jim Voice" (King 303). It is significant that King inserts this reference to the classic Mark Twain novel, *Huckleberry Finn*, where there is a constellation of white masculinity, racial violence in the form of slavery—embodied in the character of Jim, and economic degradation—embodied in the form of Huck. Taking this allusion into full account, one can clearly see that King means for readers to consider how toxic white masculinity and resistance to white, masculinist hegemony manifest as terror—It, again, in the form of the monstrous clown.

Such visual and rhetorical racial figuration represents a perceived transformative association with the Black body. The crisis of whiteness and racial terror often figures centrally in Stephen King's stories, for example, notably in *Different Seasons* (e.g., "The Shawshank Redemption"), *The Green Mile*, and *It*. These stories serve as ruminations on the failure of American democracy and, relatedly, as commentary on the "structures of feeling" (Williams 47) of whiteness—as terror. That is, *It* is symbolically and simultaneously whiteness manifested and the horror (shape) of whiteness. Conversely, the uses of black figuration, as with the use of the Black narrator in *It* and the film adaptation, *It: Chapter Two*, contribute to the belief in a post-racial triumph over institutional and structural racism. Yet, these uses of the symbolic power of blackness also reveal a rupture and an implicit critique of racial hegemony, namely the supposed "neutrality" yet paradoxical superiority of whiteness (Dyer). As an imaginative representation of "whiteness," the racial narrative in *It* reinforces the ongoing "spectacle of race" (Markovitz) and the notion of American exceptionalism (i.e., overcoming whiteness by simply reducing its shape) that disregard the material realities of American empire and racism. Nevertheless, King's *It* does reveal the instability of whiteness and its opposition to the democratic principles of social and economic equality, made ever so elusive by the "psychological wages of whiteness" (DuBois).

Michael Hanlon: "In the Wake" and into the Black

"Out of the blue and into the black"
—Neil Young, quoted in Stephen King's *It*

How do we "reason" the history of racial hegemony, economic dispossession, and the anthropocenic exploitation, proliferation, and commodification of ongoing Black death—again, racial terror and our constant living and trying to survive "in the wake" (Sharpe). As Christina Sharpe's insightful metaphor informs, the lived experiences of Black people in the Diaspora are akin to a perpetual "slave ship hold," especially in settler colonial societies where legalized slavery was practiced for centuries and where the extralegal killing of Black people has persisted from Reconstruction and Jim Crow to the current twenty-first-century era of Black Lives Matter.

What are we to do to reconcile the ensuing racial violence—that is, the absence, invisibility, and paradoxical hypervisibility that makes the racial subject prone to even greater violence and, it seems, more frequent death? King's immense story demands a great deal of attention from the reader—1,153 pages of attention to be exact. Much of that attention in the early chapters is devoted to difference and to race, a theme that the film versions only provide in obscured moments such as the advice Mike receives after his failure to perform the routine farm function of killing a sheep. His grandfather explains, "There are two places you can be in this world. You can be out here like us, or you can be in there, like them. You waste time hemming and hawing and someone else is going to make that choice for you. Except you won't know it until you feel that bolt between your eyes" (*It*, 2017). It is clear in this early scene that the film adaptation, *It*, and its sequel rely on "difference," no less on the most transparent difference represented by Mike Hanlon and Pennywise. While film audiences are never made fully aware of the history of racial oppression and violence that is the source of the burned and screaming bodies trying to escape what we later learn is a fire caused by racial terror, the vision of burned arms reaching out to Mike throughout both films represent the urgency of his—and our—desire to permanently get rid of It, that is, white terror.

In King's weighty, interweaving stories, Black characters—namely, Will and Mike Hanlon—are located pivotally. Their presence and voices demand that our attention be directed to the links between race, or racialization to be more precise, and violence. At one point, Will Hanlon describes his determination and fortitude against racist subjection when an Army Sergeant (Wilson) forces him to repeatedly dig and then un-dig a hole in the ground in response to what Sergeant Wilson perceived as a "smart nigger [...] in hack with me" (King 447). In response to Wilson's attempt to punish, physically exhaust, and "break" him, Hanlon recounts to his son Mike that, "I decided I wasn't going to give up until I fell unconscious or dropped dead. I had my dander up" (King 449). This passage is reminiscent of the chapter in Frederick Douglass' *Narrative* (1845) where Douglass physically resists and defeats the Methodist "slave-breaker" Edward Covey, in a "lengthy fistfight" after which, he informs the reader that, "You have seen how a man was made a slave; you shall see how a slave was made a man" (Douglass 65–66).

In addition, this *It* chapter is pivotal because it is the moment where Mike finally learns about the details of the infamous Black Spot fire. He had been asking his dad to tell him what happened, but both Will and Mike's mother decided Mike was too young to hear about it. They were doing what many Black parents in the age of Jim Crow did: share just enough information to keep their Black children safe, but not too much information that might debilitate them in mind and spirit. Mike's persistence is rewarded when—on February 20, 1985, as we learn from Mike's diary notes—Will decides, in the absence of his wife, to tell Mike the entire story of the Black Spot fire. He prefaces the story with the aforementioned history of the Legion of White Decency in Derry followed by the housing discrimination he and other African-American residents experienced leading up to the residents being ostracized from the white "clubs" only to create their own club in an abandoned "old requisition shed" (King 465). As it happens, and as has been so often the case throughout the history of racial oppression, the Black residents ended up not only creating a decent space to gather and have a good time, but also they created a popular hangout so successful that white patrons began to frequent their club, first deridingly and then more affectionately, referred to as the Black Spot. Will and his friend Ev McCaslin promptly put up a sign that said, "THE BLACK SPOT and just below COMPANY E AND GUESTS" (King 466). A Dixieland combo played "bodacious" on the weekend at the club and soon white soldiers from the base began to visit, and then, "more and more of them turned up as time went on" (King 467).

The problem at that point, according to Will, is that when the club became so popular as to attract white patrons in significant numbers, he and the other Black soldiers running the club and Black patrons, "forgot to be careful" (King 467). Black and white promiscuous spaces and solidarity is dangerous, perhaps the most dangerous and threatening to white supremacist ideology and racial hegemony. As told by Will, "the Legion of Decency ended it" (King 469). They torched the building on a Saturday night when "the joint was jumping, going round and round" (King 469). In great and gory detail, Will describes the mayhem that ensues, the trampling of bodies including his own, the burning of flesh, and the wailing and piercing screams of victims. Will witnesses the horror of the "last dozen or so that made it out (who) were on fire" (King 476), but it was clear that they would not survive. Will explains to his Black son Mike that, "*They* were the real ghosts we saw that night, nothing but shimmers shaped like men and women in that fire" (King 476). The final corpse that Will witnesses clinging, unsuccessfully, to life was a Black woman who was "burnin like a candle" and whose eyelids were on fire (King 476).

Ominously, Will also remembers seeing a bird on the scene, a bird he describes as "sixty feet from wingtip to wingtip. It was the size of a Japanese Zero" (King 477). The bird was chasing after the white men in the white sheets who were fleeing the scene of their crime. It had grabbed one of the men "by the sheet" as it "hovered" above. Will explains that the bird, "It didn't hover, [….] It floated. It floated. There were big bunches of balloons tied to each wing, and it floated" (King 477). Shortly afterward, while in the library further researching the town's history, Mike falls asleep with his head in his notebook. He wakes up to find there are tracks and that he has had company the night before. Something had come to him in the night and "then simply disappeared" (King 478). It left a single balloon with a picture of his face, "the eyes gone, blood running down from the ragged sockets, a scream distorting the mouth on the balloon's thin and bulging rubber skin" (King 478). In the film depiction of this scene, *It: Chapter Two*, we see and hear Mike scream, which is echoed throughout the library. The echoes reach us beyond the screen and the pages of *It*. We experience and feel the horror that is the real monster of *It*: the racial terror and trauma of difference.

Conclusion: It Always Comes Back

> "That's the one that haunts *me*."
> —Stephen King, *It*

The horror and, in fact, the haunting in both the *It* novel and *It: Chapter Two* film, centers on our collective anxieties about masculinity and whiteness. Crucially, *It* also portrays a crisis of being, belonging, and of humanism. This coinciding horror and crisis of being is not only caused by hegemonic gendered and racial constructs of "otherness," anti-blackness, and white supremacy. Rather, what audiences bear witness to in Stephen King's *It* is what we witness to writ large in hegemonic societies with a history of racial terror, like the United States. Racialization and difference as terror is deeply engrained in our culture and body politic. The horror represented visually and rhetorically by *It* is, in fact, a symptom of the "deep ambivalences" and anxieties about the historical and present dialogic "avowals and disavowals" (Kim) of racial circulation—and difference. *It* is also about the denial of economic and environmental degradation perpetuated by racial circulation within the "racial state" (Goldberg). One definition of circulation is movement to, from, or around something, with the common example given of the "circulation" of fluid in a closed system. The fluid circulating (and percolating) in Derry, Maine, is its hegemonic racial past and the "closed system" within its constant movement of racialism, homophobia, and toxic white masculinity that permeates the town but that is also hidden—underground—in the sewers and in the physical form of the white clown, Pennywise. First encountered by Georgie in the sewer, Pennywise represents the pushing down, the denial, of Derry's racial past, of its patriarchal and hegemonic present that is both visible and invisible, both real and imagined.

Returning to the *It: Chapter Two* film, once Mike and the Losers' Club discover the secret to destroying the killer clown—namely, once they discover that It's power is their own fear—the film, as in the novel, takes a dramatic turn and the "Losers" cease to be the hunted and become the hunters. They are able to quite literally diminish the size and force of It by confronting and then exorcising their individual and collective fear. They begin to embrace, not only their true identities; they embrace their connection and love for one another—beyond difference. This is a pivotal and decisive moment, one of both healing and growth. Not insignificantly, Mike chooses Bill Denbrough to reveal the town's painful racial history of settler colonial genocide. When Bill takes the powerful elixir and, like Dana in Octavia Butler's novel *Kindred*, is thrust back into America's traumatic, violent racial past, he becomes more forcefully united with Mike's determination to kill It. Likewise, all of the "Losers" begin to understand that they must "make small" the threat that Pennywise, the evil clown, represents. As dramatically and visually portrayed in *It: Chapter Two*, the "Losers" quite literally take another oath and join hands. They now fully realize that to survive, to save themselves and Derry, they must make whiteness small and they must destroy It—together.

To better understand the conclusion of the novel and the film sequel, we should consider the first encounter with the monstrous clown, that material and psychic manifestation of whiteness that we are introduced to in the first chapters of the novel and the opening scene of the 2017 film. The novel begins with a major signpost of white masculinity in chapter eleven of Part 1, "After the Flood (1957)" when a gay couple, Adrian Mellon and Don Hagarty, are noticed by a group of young "white" men incensed that the two men are holding hands and "giggling like a couple of girls" (King 21), followed by what is described as a brief kiss. One of the men, John "Webby" Garton, immediately expresses disgust exclaiming, "Oh, man, I'm gonna barf" (King 21). Hagarty's partner, Adrian, is wearing a paper hat "with a great big flower sticking up from the top and nodding in every direction" (22). The hat which says, "I 'Heart' Derry," infuriates Webby and insults his masculine civic pride. After Webby insists that Adrian take off the hat, in a similar mode of resistance displayed by Will Hanlon, Adrian makes a sexual innuendo comment directed at Webby, which ultimately results in his being the second fatality in the novel. Akin to the brutal beating and murder of Adrian and the Legion of White Decency's torching of black bodies in The Black Spot club in 1930, we might turn to the violent declaration and enforcement of whiteness through the deliberate running over and killing of Heather Heyer by a white nationalist protester in Charlottesville, Virginia, in 2017. White masculinist extralegal—and often, for non-white people, legal—policing covets and functions by notions of racial purity.

Its rules are intensely enforced and buffered by the strictures of white heteronormativity. As Megan Burke explains, "paying attention to the way a racialized heterogendered system structures and becomes a justification for action—discloses that our contemporary gender schemas are profoundly entangled in old white supremacist myths of rape and commitments to disempowered white womanhood" (Burke 2).

Race, as we know, is not a biological fact. Neither are gender roles. These are assigned, imagined, and re-imagined fictions of our lived experience. As the philosopher Sylvia Wynter expressed:

> The problem of the Human is thus not identity-based per se but in the *enunciations* of what it means to be Human—enunciations that are concocted and circulated by those who most convincingly (and powerfully) imagine the "right" or "noble" or "moral" characteristics of Human and in this project their *own* image-experience of the Human into the sphere of Universal Humanness [Mignolo 108].

We are left, then, with the question: can these categories of difference ever be disavowed? Is there no end to the hegemonic forces that drive racial and gender oppression and the subjugation of the majority of all those in the path of its death parade? Will there continue to be "closed systems" where the only fluidity that occurs is in the shapeshifting racial terror of whiteness. I am reminded of Jordan Peele's horror film, *Us* (2019), in which a Jesus-like homeless figure, a battered "white" male figure, looms on both ends of the narrative projecting his haunting, knowing smile, much like the wide, sharpened teeth displayed by Pennywise before consuming his victims. The ghosts and the monsters smile knowingly because they understand that they are tethered—and they know that we, too, as Jordan Peele and Stephen King have so poignantly portrayed, are also tethered. We are *It* and *It* is *US* (US pun most definitely intended). We represent the 99 percent who, in fact, do know, regardless of our fantasies of ignorance and innocence, the true (white) terror of difference. Given its biopolitical proclivities and strategic resilience, we might reconsider the view of King's narrator, Mike Hanlon: "But knowing where to look—and *when* to look—goes a long way toward solving the problem. *It* always comes back, you see" (King 151).

Works Cited

Bean, Annemarie et al. *Inside the Minstrel Mask: Readings in Nineteenth-Century Blackface Minstrelsy*. Wesleyan University Press, 1996.
Burke, Megan. *When Time Warps: The Lived Experience of Gender, Race, and Sexual Violence*. University of Minnesota Press, 2019.
Butler, Octavia. *Kindred*. Beacon, 1979.

Douglass, Frederick. *Narrative of the Life of Frederick Douglass, an American Slave. Written by Himself*. Anti-Slavery Office, 1845, pp. 65–66.
Dubois, W.E.B. *Black Reconstruction: Toward a History of the Part Which Black Folk Played in the Attempt to Reconstruct Democracy in America, 1860–1880*. Routledge, 2017.
Dyer, Richard. *White*. Routledge, 1997.
Goldberg, David Theo. *The Threat of Race: Reflections on Racial Neoliberalism*. Wiley-Blackwell, 2009.
Hester Williams, Kim D. "Neoslaves: Slavery, Freedom, and African American Apotheosis in *Candyman*, *The Matrix*, and *The Green Mile*." *Genders*, no. 40, 2004, pp. 3–43.
Kim, Claire Jean. *Dangerous Crossings: Race, Species, and Nature in a Multicultural Age*. Cambridge University Press, 2015.
Lipsitz, George. *How Racism Takes Place*. Temple University Press, 2011.
_____. *The Possessive Investment in Whiteness: How White People Profit from Identity Politics*. Temple University Press, 2018.
_____. "The Possessive Investment in Whiteness: Racialized Social Democracy and the 'White' Problem in American Studies." *American Quarterly*, vol. 47, no. 3, 1995, pp. 369-387.
Markovitz, Jonathan. *Racial Spectacles: Explorations in Media, Race, and Justice*. Routledge, 2011.
Mignolo, Walter D. "Sylvia Wynter: What Does It Mean to be Human?" *Sylvia Wynter: On Being Human as Praxis*. Ed. Katherine McKittrick. Duke University Press, 2015, p. 108.
Sharpe, Christina. *In the Wake: On Blackness and Being*. Duke University Press, 2016.
Williams, Raymond. *The Long Revolution*. Greenwood, 1975.

PART TWO

Real-Life Clown Horror

The Return of the Killer Clowns
A Field Guide to Surviving the Zombie Clown Apocalypse

Jennifer K. Cox

From time to time, local papers reel in readers with headlines shouting about the unusual, uncanny, or downright unsettling details of stories about criminally inclined clowns; slowly, similar eerie appearances accumulate until they eventually form a national wave of reported "killer clown" sightings. While some of these past events offered a reliable newspaper gimmick with which to pique curiosity, present-day audiences may have become inured to the intended shock of using clowns to sell stories with lurid or macabre elements. Though the incongruous pairing of clowns and crime remains a popular horror trope, it has outgrown its original sense of surprise. Such headlines rarely deliver stories of any substance, although the clown's figure may seize audience attention long enough to make a mundane bid for commercial gains. For example, in his 2016 study, *Bad Clowns*, Benjamin Radford describes how UK filmmaker Alex Powell posted images of himself on social media dressed as a clown to hype his book's publication (102). Aside from the current paragraph, this chapter title makes no direct reference to the Northampton Clown's 2013 memoir, *Zombie Clown Apocalypse*. While this essay focuses neither on Powell's anecdote, nor on similar news stories about clown sightings, sinister or otherwise, the public acceptance of such stories points to a larger cultural issue of the increasing recurrence of clown figures as signals of unarticulated anxiety. More specifically, this essay examines the significance of changes to the clown's recurring resurrections in new versions and adaptations for film and television.

Radford enumerates various additional clown sightings in 2014, including a Staten Island Clown, several more in California, and a full-blown "clown panic" in France (99–107, passim). I suggest this significant uptick in recent real-life clown sightings—along with too many "phantom clown" sightings to list—is the manifestation of a contemporary urban mythology of clowns. Popular culture perpetuates a figure constructed by contemporary folklore that includes personal anecdotes and rumors of killer clowns, and then reinforced with inherently unverifiable online accounts. Current iterations of the clown mythos, fostered by film and literature as cultural texts, continue to grow in complexity and scope since the figure first appeared.

Lowell Swortzell, NYU professor of educational theater, places the first recorded clown performance at about 2270 BC (8). The longevity of the clown's mythology seems particularly relevant at the time of this publication (2020), when audiences have seen a reboot of the Disney classic *Dumbo* (2019); a new incarnation of Pennywise, and a *Joker* (2019) dramatically different from earlier portrayals as Batman's nemesis. Additional popular texts with clowns, circuses, and carnivals include Jordan Peele's *Us* (2019), *The First Purge* (2018), *Hell Fest* (2018), *Fantastic Beasts: The Crimes of Grindelwald* (2018), *The Greatest Showman* (2017), the FX anthology series, *American Horror Story* (2014–2019), The Amazon series *Carnival Row* (2019), and the Netflix series *Stranger Things* (2016–2019). These examples are by no means intended to serve as a comprehensive list, particularly when one considers the conspicuous absence of an entire subgenre of "clown horror"; however, in terms of mainstream popular appeal, these texts offer some of the most visible examples of clown figures that, as Swortzell notes, suggest "the clown's role as commentator and social critic persists today as a universal element of world theater" (8).

Historically in the US, clowns have a long tradition as children's entertainers; though appearances change with time and cultural context, contemporary audiences recognize clowns as symbolic figures that play a familiar comedic role. Since the days of ancient Greece, audiences have been conditioned to laugh when clowns appear. Swortzell comments on the clowns' appearance when he notes, "the clowns of ancient comedy realized that exaggeration and incongruity played a large part in humor. They consequently made it their business to create larger-than-life characters rather than merely lifelike ones" (16). The same elements of exaggeration appear in the oversized shoes and prosthetic rubber noses of modern-day clowns. During a PBS special on "The Circus," Dominique Jando points out the diversionary function of most circus clowns in between acts: "After these extraordinary aerial performers, they send in the clowns and everything comes back to Earth" (2018). Their distinctive features and outlandish antics draw the audience's attention to themselves, and away from stagehands setting up for the next act, to preserve the grander illusion of performance. In addition to a lengthy association with early nineteenth-century American circuses—billed as "Sunday-school shows" for their family-friendly format, Swortzell describes clowning in many indigenous cultures as a "skillful dramatic commentary that illustrates and interprets laws and rituals [the clown] appears to ridicule" (8). Since contemporary audiences may never experience live circus performances that compare to the height of the shows' Gilded Age popularity in the US, they may also lack a clear frame of reference for the clown's undeniably positive historical persona.

More recent incarnations have updated the clown's characteristic comedic behavior and historical function to fit a contemporary urban mythology. Instead of recognizing the clown's traditional appearance as appropriate to children's entertainment, contemporary folklore reconstructs this appearance—a white face accented by sharp contrasts of brightly pigmented eyes, nose, and mouth—as a symbol of evil. John H. Towsen comments on this salient visual presentation, noting "Their very appearance makes it clear that clowns are separate creatures altogether, that then never really can belong [… they are] always intruders, and almost always impostors" (246–247). While their faces may recall a complexion like death's pallor, Eli Simon explains that the clown's white-face is designed "[t]o exaggerate facial features so that emotions, thoughts, discoveries, and inspirations can be clearly discerned throughout stadium-sized arenas […] the battle to capture an audience's imagination can be won or lost with the face" (105). Though many religious traditions use white to signify characteristics of innocence and purity, other cultural traditions associate the color more closely with death: in pale graveclothes, the stark bones of the human skull, and Gothic tropes of damsels in billowing white gowns.

The white greasepaint, called "clown white," highlights the performers' features on stage; however, the visual elements can also be read as a death's head, with over-emphasized eyes and mouths as faculties of visual and oral consumption. Donald McManus confirms these themes in citing director Dario Fo as a critic who associates the clown with class struggle: "'Clowns, like minstrels and 'comics,' always deal with the same problem—hunger, be it hunger for food, for sex, or even for dignity, for identity, for power'" (16). In fairness, the clown's uncanny appearance does reflect a historically ambiguous role. As Charles Bucknell notes, characters like the devil and the allegorical figure of Vice—a clown who embodied the Seven Deadly Sins—provided the comic relief in medieval morality plays (156). Despite this association, as allegorical figures, both the medieval clown and the devil were conduits for laughter rather than terror, emphasizing a carnivalesque sense of ambivalence.

In contemporary pop culture, men dressed as clowns present figures of terrifying reversal. Though their benign appearance has long signified mute pantomimes who epitomize harmless country bumpkins or ethereal artists, the same characters now serve as a recognizable trope in horror narratives: the figure of the Killer Clown. This horrific reversal relies on the same comic principle of incongruity that leverages audience expectations only to produce the opposite emotional affect. In his article, "Horror and Humor," Noël Carroll describes the similarity of these functions as follows:

> the basis of comic amusement is *incongruity*—the bringing together of disparate or contrasting ideas or concepts. Comic teams, for example, are often composed of a tall, thin character and a short, fat one. And European clown performances are frequently comprised of [sic] an immaculately clean, sartorially fastidious white clown—the epitome of orderliness and civilization—and an unruly, disheveled, hairy, and smudged clown—the lord of disorder and mischief [153].

Carroll elaborates on how the same mismatched elements that make audiences laugh are also the transgressive properties inherent in Hollywood monsters; while monsters represent an immediate physical threat to protagonists, he specifies that, "we [the audience …] are disgusted by the monster. We find it loathsome and impure" (150). In this context, the notion of impurity goes beyond a werewolf with muddy paws. The dirt itself adds another layer of impurity, but more importantly Carroll points out, "Things that are interstitial—that cross the boundaries of the deep categories of a culture's conceptual scheme—are primary candidates for impurity" (152). The werewolf is impure because it crosses the human-animal boundary; its muddy paws merely emphasize the blurring of these categorical boundaries.

Many of the same traits in classic Hollywood monsters—exaggerated size, categorical transgression—can also be found in traditional clown costuming. In addition, the nonverbal sound of laughter clowns elicit from an audience parallels the nonverbal sound of screaming that monsters generally produce. Carroll adds to these points of contact beyond mere parallels, and defines the clown figure as a full-fledged monster: "It is a fantastic being, one possessed of an alternate biology, a biology that can withstand blows to the head by hammers and bricks that would be deadly for any mere human, and the clown can sustain falls that would result in serious injury for the rest of us" (155). Ultimately, context determines whether interstitial figures such as monsters or clowns deserve a belly laugh or a blood-curdling scream; however, popular urban legends have overshadowed the clown's role as mythical trickster and provincial simpleton of oral and theatrical tradition to foster a new paradigm of sinister otherworldly predators.

Andrew McConnell Stott would position Canio, the clown from Leoncavallo's *I Pagliacci* as the "original" killer clown, describing how "At the end of the nineteenth century, a new figure emerged from the ashes of the harlequinade—a clown intent not on laughter, but on awful, bloody revenge" (3). While this popular 1892 opera does portray a murder by a man dressed as a clown, his use of the phrase "killer clown" only aligns in meaning atomistically; in other words, Canio is a killer, and is also dressed like a clown;

however, I apply the meaning of "killer clown" as a compound phrase, in which the words are linked semantically. As George Lakoff explains, "It is often the case that the meanings of compounds are not compositional; that is, the meaning of the whole cannot be predicted from the meanings of the parts and the way they are put together" (147). This essay addresses killer clowns in the compound sense of the phrase: the figures under examination are not killers who happen to be dressed as clowns; they are clowns who use their uncanny, theatrical appearances *in order* to kill. To apply this compound meaning to *I Pagliacci* risks an anachronistic reading of the operatic text.

A similar operatic pathos, though infused with more of Grand Guignol horror, made national headlines in the early 1970s with the arrest of real-world "killer clown," John Wayne Gacy. Radford notes, however, that "His occasional forays as a clown had nothing to do with his serial killing, nor did he kill anyone while in costume [...] nonetheless it cemented his gruesome reputation as a killer clown" (113). Although Gacy did not use his theatrical persona to commit murder, he made no attempts to correct media stories that used the phrase "killer clown" to capitalize on its sensational contradiction. While the historically positive association of clowns and children has not been completely erased, pop-culture texts reinforce the "killer" half of the compound phrase, imparting a specific meaning in the context of horror narratives. The clown's previous characteristics of amiable ambiguity and ingenuous comic pratfalls have been overshadowed by the now-familiar horror trope. Iconic film roles reinforce disturbing clown qualities in horror narratives like Stephen King's *It* (1986), the murderous marionette in *Poltergeist* (1982), or the horror-comedy *Killer Klowns from Outer Space* (1988).

Scholars like Radford and (to a lesser degree) Stott, highlight the rise of coulrophobia's popularity as a folk theory. As Stott notes, "although not listed in either *Webster's* or the *Oxford English Dictionary*, [coulrophobia] is widely known as a fear of clowns" (5). Radford offers what little clarification exists, acknowledging that "Coulrophobia, as such, is essentially nonexistent in the medical and psychological literature. A handful of professional journal articles mention it in passing, but by far the great bulk of references are to newspaper and magazine articles" (34). If *coulrophobia* is not listed as a clinical term, it is because people do not fear clowns *per se*, but develop phobias after a particularly traumatic incident, according to the American Psychiatric Association's criteria for phobias (APA 2014, 200, qtd. in Radford 35). In addition to traumatic experiences, Radford notes the "indirect ways that such a phobia can be created: both by seeing other people menaced by clowns, and what's rather stiltingly referred to as 'informational transmission,' and which could include seeing scary clowns in movies"

(36). The increase of killer-clown figures in horror movies, however, does not suggest a parallel increase in cases of coulrophobia (such as they are); after all, horror audiences are supposed to be afraid of threatening clowns like Pennywise or Killjoy. What the popularity of coulrophobia—as a folk theory—*does* suggest is that the cumulative reinforcement of killer clowns via urban legends, horror tropes, and rumors has shifted our cultural recognition from seeing the clown as a simple fool to seeing him as an embodied foreshadowing of a grisly murder.

Based on the social and historical context of their creation, horror stories often reveal some of the anxieties circulating within a specific culture. For example, literary analyses of classic ghost stories and Gothic tales like *The Turn of the Screw* (1898), or *The Haunting of Hill House* (1959) often cast hauntings as a Freudian return of the repressed, and other genre scholars read alien invasion stories—like Jack Finney's *The Body Snatchers* (1955)—as the worst-case scenarios arising from the nuclear anxiety of the atomic age. While these are certainly not the only possible interpretations, they do set up an interesting prism through which to examine the return of the killer clown in contemporary horror narratives. Some might read this trending figure as a symbol of our inherently destructive entertainment sources, but each narrative lends its own degree of contextual nuance. Film and television have resurrected these particular characters to the widest selection of audiences in the recent past—they serve as illustrative examples primarily due to their popular appeal and the recency of their reappearances in cultural texts. After debuting in season four of the FX anthology series *American Horror Story: Freak Show* (2014), Twisty the Clown reappears in season seven, *Cult* (2017). Even more recently, two feature films opened within a month of each other, returning Pennywise (4 Sep) and the Joker (4 Oct) to the silver screen in the last quarter of 2019.

When one considers how pop culture keeps resurrecting clowns in new versions and adaptations, this unsettling character becomes even more puzzling. While a comprehensive list of killer clowns in literature, comics, and film is beyond the scope of this paper, I will focus on three of the most popular clowns as symbols of cultural anxiety in their most recent re-imaginings: Pennywise as a symbol of childhood anxieties; the Joker as a symbol of anxiety about injustice and anarchy; and Twisty as symbolic of anxieties about disability.

Pennywise the Dancing Clown: Childhood

Tony Magistrale describes the significant imagery for the monster known as It as the "masterful choice of a carnival clown as a unifying symbol for various creatures representing the monster It. Pennywise the Dancing Clown (Tim Curry) purports himself as a character created for the amusement of children" (185). Curry's performance in the 1990 miniseries recalls classic comic gags of performers like Jimmy Durante; his dry one-liners evoke a sense of nostalgic whimsy just before a shocking reversal. As Magistrale observes, "Pennywise's dark sense of humor, always bordering on the obscene (it is impossible to separate this character's grotesque humor from his terror), is lost on the children he seduces" (186). As an era populated by infamous serial killers was ending, 1990s American culture saw groups like the Parents Music Resource Center (PMRC, co-founded by Tipper Gore) organize to protect children from the questionable influences of mass entertainment. Radford points out with some irony that a "key reason that evil clown Pennywise is so widely known is that *It* was seen in nearly 18 million households, including by children and teenagers. If *It* had been a PG- or R-rated theatrical release, its audience would have been cut by two-thirds" (67). Both recent cinematic remakes received R ratings, but that does not seem to have negatively impacted audience numbers.

As Stephen King describes during "Author of Fear" on the "Special Features" disc for *It* (2017), healthy human psyches have a hard time rationalizing the monstrous acts of killers like John Wayne Gacy or Ted Bundy, who may have killed as many as seventy women. Using Pennywise as a stand-in for the real-life killers releases viewers from the compulsion to make sense of the antagonist's actions. We feel no empathy for a non-human monster; It, no matter the form, is a deep pit of consumption, a hunter who feeds on childhood fears at the peak of fruition. While the monster of the 1990 series relied on comic bits to seduce the Losers, the 2017 and 2019 films lean into the clown's unpredictability to produce horror.

The character's shift in appearance reflects his changing tactics: Curry's clown, in minimal makeup, wears a colorful costume reminiscent of TV icon Bozo, with a fringe of red hair above an expansive white brow, some blue on his eyelids, and a classic red rubber nose. In 2017, Bill Skarsgård's Pennywise wears a Victorian-era ruffled costume in what starts as an almost monochrome white, as if to emphasize his character is the blank screen onto which the Losers project their deepest fears. By the time audiences see *It: Chapter Two* in 2019, the clown's white costume, like his face paint, shows more signs of wear and neglect. The lace-up tunic and leggings go from dingy gray to torn shreds of indecipherable color. His costume, like his minimal makeup, is punctuated by dashes of red pom-poms, like drops of blood. Instead of exaggerating the natural curve of his mouth, Skarsgård's Pennywise extends his grin in red lines blended upward into his eyes, like a parody of Pierrot, the sad French clown. Instead of a rubber nose, only the end of the actor's natural nose is painted red.

Another special feature called "Pennywise Lives!" includes interviews with Skarsgård and director Andy Muschietti, who recounts discussing his plans to give Pennywise a walled eye with digital effects, but was surprised that Skarsgård's physical control made digital edits unnecessary. The actor describes how he creates the clown's extreme strabismus: "I said, Oh, I can do that. I've always had a kind of lazy eye, and I can kinda like, make it *go*." He demonstrates his talent for the camera, letting his left eye drift slowly to the far outer corner while his right eye maintains contact (2017). If Curry's clown relies on "Gotcha!" for scares, Skarsgård creates a more physically erratic and unsettling character. The actor explains how his portrayal reflects the ambiguous nature of the monster: It is not really a clown, but something else *pretending* to be a clown because he associates them with children, so there are "glitches" in his movements, as if to glimpse what's behind the costume (2017).

In both versions, the clown's liminal status parallels that of the Losers, who cling to the last stages of childhood as they prepare to become young adults. Like his pre-teen prey, clowns are also liminal figures: they (often) resemble adults in size, but their actions communicate a childlike perception of the world. Such incongruous behavior has long been established as an expectation for clowns, as Towsen notes: "Many of the most enduring clowns [...] were fascinating contradictions, combining naïveté and ingenuity" (67).

The 2017 screenplay further emphasizes the displaced status of the Losers, but updates social norms of the 1990 miniseries by twenty-seven years. By narrative logic, the monster's hibernation cycle would have ended by 2017 and a new hunting cycle begun. Such strategic release dates leverage the power of nostalgia for many Generation X viewers, who first saw the killer clown on TV as children, and might also see the newer films as adults. The Losers form a separate community of outcasts; they're still located in Derry, but clearly not part of it—and rely on one another to reinforce their choices. As Erin Mercer points out, "The cyclical return [...] is connected with recurring personal and communal horrors of history" (318). This interpretation might also reflect a sense of fragmented cultural identity after a polarized 2016 political season. Following the presidential election, man-on-the-street interviews reflected how many people expressed that they didn't recognize their own country any more. In similar fashion, the adult Losers must work hard to remember their childhood home of Derry, because they, too, have forgotten the site of so much trauma.

The Joker: Injustice/Anarchy

In an interesting connection, an establishing shot of Derry's main thoroughfare in *It* shows the Losers pass the Paramount theater, which has *Batman* (1989), with Jack Nicholson as the Joker, listed as one of the movies on the marquee. A figure like the Joker, who has been around for eighty years now, is more closely connected to crime than childhood. Different iterations of his character have tended to resemble gangsters like Al Capone, who murdered rival gang members in the Prohibition-era St. Valentine's Day Massacre. *The Dark Knight* (2008) features a similar scene in which Gotham's most notorious gangsters gather and discover the Joker has been robbing them all—and hilarity ensues as the Joker randomly executes fellow criminals.

The Joker's character is fueled by his fundamental opposition to Batman's character traits: where Batman seeks order, the Joker creates chaos. While Batman refuses to cross the line and kill his enemies, the Joker does not hesitate to kill any character for any reason. Except for Batman: he just wants to "play" with Batman. His unusual appearance (according to comics lore) results from a toxic chemical bath, and his grotesque facial scars have competing origin stories; audiences understand that he uses this appearance to create fear among criminals and citizens alike. As Cynthia Barounis points out, "The disfigured face serves as evidence of a ruined subjectivity, indicating an origin story whose horrors account for the perverse behaviors of the present" (317). He lacks the same acquisitional goals as other villains, but seems to subvert power dynamics to prevent others from assuming they have power over him.

Though Cesar Romero (1966) and Jack Nicholson play Batman's nemesis with a sense of camp-like whimsy, Heath Ledger's unhinged performance in *The Dark Knight* earned the actor a posthumous Oscar. Barounis suggests Ledger's Joker employs an aesthetic she describes as "disability camp" (305), and that "what is most compelling about the Joker's camp spectacles is precisely their tendency to combine outrage with outrageousness, and their willingness to take humor and its politics seriously" (305–306). His eccentric appearance, erratic behavior, and memorable tagline, "Why so serious?" indicate that director Christopher Nolan's film attempts a more cerebral cultural critique than merely one-upping the previous Joker's performance.

The anarchic villain pushes back at the irony of a masked vigilante who's hailed as a hero for catching bad guys in masks. Throughout the film, Barounis notes, "the Joker devises a set of brutal schemes throughout the film in an attempt to coerce Batman into unmasking himself and making his identity known" (311). The film's abundant use of costumes and disguises interrogates the moral and legal (and sartorial) boundaries that define abstract concepts like justice, or even the self, a point the Joker illustrates when he pleads, "Will the real Batman please stand up?" (2008).

When he replaces Gotham's Finest with his own henchmen in police uniforms, and later dresses innocent hostages in clown masks to disguise them as criminals, the Joker employs the same anonymity afforded by costuming to his own advantage. His actions complicate the boundaries of identity, shuffling the outer markers of civilians, criminals, police officers, and heroes like a con man orchestrating a game of Three-card Monte. When Ledger's character, dressed as a nurse, blows up a local hospital, he further illustrates the subversive power of camp. Barounis references Susan Sontag's essay ("Notes on Camp," 1984) in defining "the camp sensibility as the 'dandy's love of the unnatural: of artifice and exaggeration'[....] In reducing objects and identities to their surface qualities, the camp aesthetic shatters deep meaning and the integrity of symbols and revels in the power of artificiality" (309). Viewers recognize Batman as a hero steeped in his own symbolism and gadgetry, as does the Joker. The difference is that the Joker places no faith in the "brand" that separates his hero identity from the rest of Bruce Wayne's life. In one of the film's early scenes, a group of vigilantes inspired by Batman dress in DIY Batsuits; when an imitator is apprehended, he asks the real Batman, "What's the difference between you and me?" The classist overtone in Batman's answer "I'm not wearing hockey pads," is cringeworthy. As Barounis points out, "In the end, Batman's vigilantism has less to do with populist democratic revolt than with corporate exceptionalism" (315).

Mentor-slash-quartermaster Lucius Fox (Morgan Freeman) recognizes the futility of pursuing a criminal who sees chaos as his ultimate goal. Yet Batman's dogged pursuit involves accessing information from Gotham's cell phone users to find the Joker. Fox resigns over this blatant violation of privacy disguised as protection. He advises his billionaire boss, "Some men aren't looking for anything logical, like money [...] they can't be bought, bullied, reasoned, or negotiated with. Some men just want to watch the world burn" (2008). Ultimately, when combined with the Joker's actions, Batman's overreach forces viewers to question his code: at what point will the ends (saving citizens) justify the means, even if that means killing the Joker?

Overall, the film seeks to define some guiding principles for deciding how to act decently in indecent times. Different characters illustrate the various benchmarks society uses to measure value like fairness or justice. Batman relies on his own moral sense of right and wrong; District Attorney Harvey Dent (Gotham's "White Knight") retreats to the blind chance of a coin flip after he's disillusioned with the legal system and disfigured by a freak accident. The Joker sees chaos as an egalitarian force when he states, "It's not about money—it's about sending a message: everything burns" (2008). His anarchic perspective, however, does nothing to reaffirm nature's stubborn vitality in the face of mankind's made-up laws; instead, Ledger's Joker defies mankind's social constructions, and also perverts nature's laws with his defiance. In a deviation from his characteristic black-or-white moral perspective,

Batman agrees to play "the Dark Knight," a villain designed to preserve Dent's (posthumous) heroic commitment to justice in the eyes of Gotham's citizens.

Joaquin Phoenix's take on the character in *Joker* (2019) has earned awards from the Golden Globes, the Screen Actors Guild, the British Academy of Film and Television Arts (BAFTA), and the Academy of Motion Picture Arts and Sciences (the Oscars). Instead of taking up the mantle of crime boss, Phoenix's titular character embodies a *description* rather than a *title*, as evidenced by the missing definite article. He's not *The* Joker, he's just *a* joker, one of many struggling Gotham citizens perceived as clowns by the powers that be. His portrayal ignores comic lore, including the famous facial scars and Batman himself. Instead, Phoenix presents the mentally ill Arthur Fleck as a character sketch: he's just another working clown who lives with his mom and dreams of becoming a comedian.

Rather than serve as foil for Batman's crime-fighting efforts, this Joker highlights the inadequacies of a social and political system that fails him, as city-wide budget cuts reduce services for the working class. His illness presents in a paradoxical manner that confounds those around him: in moments of stress or physical confrontation, he bursts into fits of inorganic, forced laughter that borders painfully on panicked tears. His mother (played by Frances Conroy) sympathizes, perhaps because she has bequeathed her own instabilities to her son. Her devotion to former employer Thomas Wayne leads Arthur to suspect a biological connection where none exists, but Phoenix performs with such pathos it's hard not to be disappointed for the clown who falls through the cracks of a broken society.

Michileen Martin notes that some of the film's strongest inspiration originates in Robert De Niro's performances in *Taxi Driver* (1976) and *The King of Comedy* (1982), which Phoenix reflects by reframing his character's madness independent of Batman rather than playing him as another codependent, criminally insane archenemy (looper.com). *The New Yorker*'s Richard Brody criticizes director Todd Phillips for pulling political punches and pandering to Republican critics, whitewashing historical references to the Central Park Five and subway shooter Bernie Goetz, among others (Brody n.p.). Phoenix's struggling artist realigns the erstwhile crime boss with Romantic portrayals of sad, "moony" French Pierrots. As Helen Borowitz notes, "literary works [used] the clown as a symbol of the creative artist, often ignored by an unresponsive public" (23).

Twisty the Clown: Disability

Though perhaps not as well-known as Pennywise or the Joker, Twisty the Clown also returns from the dead in the FX anthology series *American*

Horror Story (*AHS*). Prior to the *Joker*'s release, actor John Carroll Lynch's performance made Twisty the only "real" clown in this selection, by which I mean the character earns a living performing as a clown. In contrast, Ledger's Joker and Pennywise engineer clown identities to disguise their crimes. Although Twisty doesn't *start* as a killer, Radford cites Seth Abramovich in the *Hollywood Reporter,* as he recounts how communities like Clowns of America International reacted negatively to the show's sensationalized depiction of clowns (Abramovich 2014, qtd. in Radford 76).

In *AHS* season four, *Freak Show,* Lynch's character Twisty appears sporadically to menace the townspeople of 1950s Jupiter, Florida, with bloody murder. He emerges from the trees as a teen girl (Bonnie) on a picnic date smooths the blanket, mentally preparing to "go all the way" when her boyfriend (Troy) returns from the car. The clown's sudden, disheveled appearance startles Bonnie, but she greets him nervously and accepts the proffered paper flower bouquet. Twisty's pantomime performance allows the audience to read his visual rhetoric and acknowledge the clear threat his appearance signals: an oversized, plastic grin edged in dirt and blood covers the bottom half of his face; smeared clown makeup remains on the upper half, and a bald cap with ragged edges like torn flesh sits atop his head, framed by three stiff tufts of indeterminately colored hair.

Alarmed by the intrusion, Troy gruffly demands, "Who the hell are you?" The clown merely resumes his pantomime, pulling three juggling pins from his bag before using the last to knock both teens unconscious. Bonnie wakes to the squelching sounds of Twisty stabbing Troy with garden shears, and the camera recedes as she screams. The horrific clown disappears for a while, as does Bonnie, and absent any suspects, the townspeople waste no time in blaming his crimes on Fraulein Elsa's Cabinet of Curiosities, the freak show just outside town limits. Viewers glimpse Twisty on the show's periphery, but he is not part of the freak show proper, although their storylines overlap in various ways.

Twisty harbors a deep hatred for little people, whom he derogatorily refers to as *freaks*, though he extends the term to all carnival workers. He reveals his backstory at the insistence of Edward Mordrake, a spectral figure described by carnival lore as a two-faced Grim Reaper who appears on Halloween to drag a soul back to hell. An English nobleman born in the 1800s, legend describes how an unusual deformity gave Mordrake two faces, like the Roman god Janus, but the incessant whisper of anterior back-channeling drove him mad. After repeatedly failing to kill his "demon twin," Mordrake escaped the asylum to join a freak show; one Halloween he snapped, and murdered his entire troupe before hanging himself. Now, superstitious carnies refuse to perform on Halloween for fear of summoning Edward Mordrake "and his demon half-face" (2014). Actor Wes Bentley plays the ominous Mordrake, summoned by a forbidden performance, per folkloric law. The genteel ghost functions as an expository device, visiting several characters in search of one whose story will reveal them as "Corrupted. Diseased. Perfect in [their] monstrous imperfection[....] One more *pure freak* to add to our unhappy number" (2014). When initial interrogations fail to find a soul sufficiently befouled to sate the demon's appetite, Mordrake seeks to sample the killer clown's darkest moments.

The mentally challenged Twisty describes his role as the "special children's clown" in a circus during the '40s. He loved his work and considered himself an expert at making children laugh. Jealous of his position, some fellow clowns (little people), exploited Twisty's simple nature to drive him away from the circus. Their off-color innuendos and threats to report him for child abuse frightened Twisty; despite his innocence he fled, but he never forgave the freaks. The show uses historical comedy tropes that align with what Beth Haller describes as "destructive disability humor," an early phase of humor which regularly "included 'freak shows' and the use of mentally disabled people as representative fools" (170, qtd. in Barounis 306). Twisty's exaggerated revulsion at the little people working with him as "freaks" seems to interrogate both stereotypes of disabled bodies as comedic objects.

Mordrake sympathizes with the clown's loss, and Twisty's tale of despair continues with a gun in his mouth. The bullet that failed to kill him destroyed his lower jaw, leaving him with a grisly disfigurement and a severe speech impediment. He bemoans his accident, "I thought: I'm so dumb, I can't even kill myself" (2014). Historically, clowns put great effort into performances to appear stupid, as Towsen notes, "the clown usually will exert a tremendous amount of misguided energy and, more often than not, accomplish very little. His methods are as inappropriate as his failure is predictable" (206). On stage, the bigger the pratfalls, the bigger the laughs, but this clown's life is unintentionally tragic.

With a partial mask to disguise his missing jaw, he resolves to regain his identity the only way he knows how: by replacing his audience so he can resume his work. As Rosemarie Garland-Thomson notes, "American individualism is most clearly manifest in the conviction that economic autonomy results from hard work and virtue, while poverty stems from indolence and moral inferiority" (47). The portrayal of a man losing his livelihood to unforeseen circumstances communicates deep cultural anxieties about physical and professional vulnerabilities, especially during times of economic fluctuation. For this reason, some viewers might (briefly) find Twisty not *entirely be*yond sympathy. Initially, Mordrake seems to accept the clown's justification, acknowledging he is "misunderstood." The demon twin, however, seeks a darker shame beyond Twisty's tragic circumstances, implied by the simple imperative: "Tell me about the children."

A near-hysterical note of self-righteous anger stains the clown's reply as he emphatically explains: "I saved them … from the freaks! From the evil, mean *freaks*!" (2014). Even deeper than self-pity, his long-held hatred of freaks is what drives him to kill. This rationalization fails to connect until viewers see Twisty in a recent flashback, loitering at the freak show's entrance and attempting to sell an anemic bunch of balloons to nervous ticketholders. The spieler at the gate encourages them to ignore the "kooky" guy in the grubby costume and buy their balloons inside. Twisty's earnest grunts turn to muted screams of rage as he turns, unblinking, and departs; he connects this exclusion from the current freak show to past incidents that drove him from the circus. In his mind, the freaks are stealing his audience, *again*, and his overgrown sense of indignation compels him to *save* them—by kidnapping them. The word *save* assumes an additional connotation of storage when he imprisons kidnapped victims in an old school bus, where he performs his (terrifying) "funny show" for his captive audience of "rescued" children.

The erstwhile clown's underdeveloped sense of right and wrong—which he oversimplifies as *nice* and *mean*—also allows him to equate the act of murder with *saving* children from their parents by labeling parental actions like bedtime or denial of unlimited candy as *mean* rather than *responsible*. He concludes his defense with a happy sigh, "I'm a good clown," that renders Mordrake speechless. Instead of seeking commonality with differently abled performers, the downward spiral after his accident only amplified his hatred of all freaks; rather than take responsibility for his actions, he blamed them for his loss and chose to take revenge, painted as "justice." Mordrake initiates Twisty (with a dagger) into his dubious "coterie," and the clown's physically restored shade joins them as a "brother" on their return trip to hell. Twisty's inability to understand his actions in appropriate moral, ethical, and legal contexts—as not just wrong, but criminal—represents a darkness deep enough to sate the demon's thirst. His hatred of freaks adds another layer of disability to his character: he's blinded to the possibility that *freak* might also serve as any positive kind of self-description.

The body horror of Twisty's graphic injury reinforces viewers' fears of mortality, and echoes stereotypical associations of disability and monstrosity. As Thomson notes, "The 'invalid' body is impotence made manifest" (42). Twisty's maimed jaw obviously impairs his speech, but also likely causes great pain, and difficulty eating. His hidden injury becomes a present absence, similar to the invisibility of his diminished intellect; both conditions haunt viewers with their own physical and intellectual vulnerabilities, as the possibility of severe injury lurks within every moment. Commenting on the semiotics of masks, Frank Proschan cites Claude Lévi-Strauss:

"Like a myth, a mask denies as much as it affirms. It is not made solely from what it says or thinks it is saying, but of what it excludes" (144, qtd. in Proschan 23). Though Twisty hides his wound with a false toothy grin, viewers are keyed to anticipate the horror of the clown's real smile behind the gruesome, ragged edges of his mask.

Though *Freak Show* establishes Twisty as a distinctive killer clown in popular culture, he returns as a caricature of his original role in season seven, *Cult*. Swortzell points out how caricatures exaggerate a character's simplified features, and that "the clowns of ancient comedy realized that exaggeration and incongruity played a large part in humor" (16). The same element of incongruity also plays a part in horror stories, with differing levels of perceived danger. This season opens as two viewing parties watch the 2016 presidential election results. Both look on in disbelief, but for different reasons, thereby establishing a recent timeframe and the major oppositional figures. After the opening credits, the show transports viewers to a summer lakeside setting where two young lovers bypass food for foreplay—until one sits up, certain she hears someone watching their private picnic.

The scene replays Twisty's debut from *Freak Show*, except it updates some details for modern audiences and places greater emphasis on the clown's status as an established legend. Like all good urban legends, Twisty materializes when his name is invoked. His sudden arrival still panics the lovers, but in this version, the man pulls a gun from his backpack and fires at the intruder. The disheveled jester calmly absorbs the ineffective shots, then pulls a set of garden shears from his bag and stabs him. The woman dials 911 as she flees, screaming, but the operator's voice betrays her hiding spot. The last viewers see of her is a close-up of a severed (pierced) tongue next to a smart phone as the dispatcher bleats, "Hello?" Removing his mask as he picks up the phone, the clown lisps wetly: "Wrong number" (2017). As the scene ends, Twisty's features harden into the stylized pen-and-ink lines of a comic-book panel: his legend is fodder for a modern-day penny dreadful in the hands of an eight-year-old boy.

The comic-book portrayal of Twisty's original scenes depicts his actions in an oversimplified and exaggerated mode, much like a caricature. As an urban legend, the veracity of the events has been replaced by repetition, repeated by friends of friends via word-of-mouth for almost a century. While Twisty only appears in a few scenes, his legend has grown into mythological proportions, thanks to current trends in popular horror fiction. Viewers of past seasons know that the girl (Bonnie) survived Twisty's interruption of her picnic, but the comic-book telling alters details to amplify the effect of horror. Both Twisty's urban legend and his mass-produced action figure function according to the same principles: simplification plus amplification. Each storytelling mode simplifies the details to compensate for an attention span too short for truth complicated by details and nuance; the legend and the toy smooth out the rough edges, making the story easy to digest. The same modes also amplify those caricatures as truth, boosting power via repetition, shocking imagery, auditory volume, or reported testimonials. In this manner, the show depicts how people use various story modes—as urban legends, manifestos, secrets, conspiracies, or subreddit threads—disabling audiences with paralyzing fear in order to destabilize power.

The show's blue-haired alt-right antagonist (Kai) echoes these sentiments when he declares that people love fear, as it absolves them of responsibility to think critically or take meaningful action as participating members of society. The show illustrates how individuals who surrender power to cult leaders like Charles Manson or Jim Jones (among other notable narcissists and demagogues) through fear—of disappointment, or eternal hellfire—disguises the uneven exchange of personal freedom for promises of security, regardless of whether the cult in question refers to a small community group or a democratic republic.

Kai and his supporters leverage the clown's powerful mythology by disguising themselves in grotesque, hypersexualized clown masks to trigger specific cultural anxieties. Creators Ryan Murphy and Brad Falchuk lean into the popularity of coulrophobia, which, as a culturally manufactured anxiety, symbolizes the over-sensitivity and paralyzing political correctness the show parodies. They also feature sensational images known to trigger fears like trypophobia (fear of irregular patterns, like tiny holes), agoraphobia (fear of feeling trapped), and feretrophobia (fear of being buried alive). Combined with these clinical fears are cultural topics commonly found in sensitivity training workshops, including homophobia, xenophobia, gynophobia, rape culture, trigger warnings, and safe spaces. As a sensationalized form of entertainment, *Cult* simplifies all of these concepts under the general category of fear, and then exaggerates this simplicity. Employing such over-simplification throughout the season's episodes emphasizes some missing elements of critical thinking, such as the importance of influential details and contexts; taking more than one critical perspective into consideration; resisting the temptation to be ruled by emotion; as well as making informed individual choices rather than surrendering to peer pressure (or "groupthink").

The commercialized comic-book version of Twisty—and his action figure—coupled with the season's overarching parody of the 2016 presidential election campaign, make the clown a figure that triggers disabling levels of fear and anxiety. His likenesses also signify cultural states of anarchy and absurdity that create an underlying sense of horror. While the action figure might also echo symbols of childhood, the story emphasizes the doll's status as a physical object. Mass-produced and widely available, the character's role in this season is reduced to a commercialized plastic identity, but still serves as a tool that is deployed to disable victims with fear. Ultimately, this season examines a variety of caricatures to highlight how the quality of visibility, particularly as social media presence, has displaced what once counted as truth.

Conclusion

The Killer Clown's frequent appearance (and reappearance) in contemporary cinematic texts might be read as a signal of a growing cultural anxiety about the power of unexplained mythology. Though the clown's history extends backwards as far as ancient Egypt, US audiences have a distinctly American perception of clowns, beginning at roughly the same time as the nation itself. The phenomenal success of Gilded Age circuses grew with the expansion of the railroad, and again with historical figures like P.T. Barnum, John Bailey, and the Ringling Bros. Americans paint these captains of a burgeoning amusement industry with the same mythological palette used to re-mythologize clowns. While European audiences can trace the history of some clown figures to medieval mystery plays and Italian comedies, American culture has limited exposure to carnival cultures and practices that were once part of the (Catholic) Church's unofficial culture. Instead, US audiences cite the circus and the (Stephen) King as notable forces in the mythology of clowns. Prior to Barnum, however, American audiences lack a cultural benchmark for this popular figure; we understand the mythology, but the details fade.

Fortunately, as Towsen points out, "clowns can and do emerge spontaneously out of their own native cultures, in the process reinventing ancient forms of comedy" (64). In other words, *they always come back*, so perhaps we should have expected zombie clowns. When comedic characters cross over into horror, however, it seems to signal a significant cultural change. The characters that caused so much laughter at pies in the face and baseball bewilderment now haunt our nightmares.

Such contradictions might indicate cultural anxiety around entertainment in general, as western society becomes increasingly fixated on "productivity." With technological advancements that erase boundaries between work hours and free time, many professionals remain on duty, accessible by cell phone, e-mail, or any number of social media platforms at all hours. Recent reactions to the global coronavirus pandemic have merely amplified this erasure of boundaries. We fear the backlog of e-mails, work, and communication that inevitably accrue when we allow ourselves the luxury of leisure time. We fear falling behind in work, punish ourselves, and police others for not taking things "seriously" enough. Unlike typical clown performances, we work hard to ensure our success because failure is not funny, but it's often difficult to discern between work and play.

The connection between clowns and childhood seems obvious enough, but each new killer clown figure brings up a variety of possibilities for interpretation. The clown's traditional performance function—as a visual distraction from background movement (while changing scenes between acts)—parallels the social media and "false news" stories that distract people from more important events on the political stage. Clowns only distract audiences from the stagehands as they set up the next spectacle; however, when absurdity and exaggeration become the new "normal," distinguishing between satire and horror presents audiences with a formidable challenge. In such contexts, clowns might signal anxiety about who's really behind the mask. We might be relieved to discover a "normal" human alter ego under the greasepaint and garish costume; finding out the clown costume is real, and doesn't come off, would be terrifying.

Characters like the Joker and Twisty (as resurrected caricature) help illustrate these functions in greater detail, distracting authorities from their own ulterior motives. In addition to their powers of obfuscation, both Twisty and the Joker share a physically enforced grin as the result of an injury; this detail of disability imparts a sense of "toxic positivity" that pervades US productivity culture (Lukin n.p.). Professional settings often force us to "grin and bear it," stunting natural emotional responses to keep a straight (professional) face until we reach a location with sufficient privacy; alone, we are finally permitted to act like humans who experience real, ugly, human emotions. The same toxic positivity appears in any setting where negative, excessive, or otherwise unacceptable emotions regularly get smothered in order to perform our expected social roles. The standard greeting, "How are you?" demands a bland, positive reply; people would be horrified if someone offered a personal detail, instead of "Fine." Such scripts serve as formalities to sustain the simulation of community.

Perhaps we have forgotten what clowns were for in the first place. Nostalgic places and childhood entertainments like the circus, that once provided comfort or a joyful temporary escape, have slowly decayed, enriching the subconscious soil in which our nightmares take root. The clowns once associated with jolly, wholesome childhood fun have turned into terrifying figures that deny audiences the warm refuge of nostalgia as they threaten to devour us whole. Instead, we are ourselves consumed with greed, with ambition, with documenting the spectacle of our lives on social media—and the marker denoting "accomplishment" gets pushed back further with every revolution. Perhaps clowns really signal a sense of anxiety that accompanies the realization that we can never go back to the "good old days," and perhaps more importantly, they make us question just how good those days were to begin with.

Works Cited

Abramovich, Seth. "Professional Clown Club Attacks *American Horror Story* Over Murderous Character." *Hollywood Reporter*, October 15, 2014. hollywoodreporter.com.

American Horror Story: Cult: The Complete Seventh Season. Created by Ryan Murphy and Brad Falchuk. Perf. John Carroll Lynch. Twentieth Century Fox, 2017.

American Horror Story: Freak Show: The Complete Fourth Season. Created by Ryan Murphy and Brad Falchuk. Perf. John Carroll Lynch. Twentieth Century Fox, 2014.

Barounis, Cynthia. "'Why so serious?' Cripping Camp Performance in Christopher Nolan's *The Dark Knight*," *Journal of Literary and Cultural Disability Studies*, vol. 7, no. 3, 2013, pp. 305–320. doi: 10.3828/jlcds.2013.26.

Borowitz, Helen O. "Painted Smiles: Sad Clowns in French Art and Literature," *The Bulletin of the Cleveland Museum of Art*, vol. 71, no. 1, 1984, pp. 23–35. www.jstor.org/stable/251598 45. Accessed November 5, 2018.

Brody, Richard. October 3, 2019. www.newyorker.com. Accessed December 21, 2019.

Bucknell, Peter A. *Entertainment and Ritual: 600 to 1600*. Stainer and Bell, 1979.

Carroll, Noël. "Horror and Humor." *Journal of Aesthetics and Art Criticism*, vol. 57, no. 2, Spring 1999, pp.145–157.

The Dark Knight, Dir. Christopher Nolan. Perf. Heath Ledger. Warner Brothers, 2008.

"Edward Mordrake Part 2," *American Horror Story: Freak Show: The Complete Fourth Season*. Created by Ryan Murphy and Brad Falchuk. Perf. John Carroll Lynch and Wes Bentley. Twentieth Century Fox, 2014. DVD.

Garland-Thomson, Rosemarie. *Extraordinary Bodies: Figuring Physical Disability in American Culture and Literature*. Columbia University Press, 1997.

Hansen, Regina. "Stephen King's *IT* and *Dreamcatcher* on Screen: Hegemonic White Masculinity and Nostalgia for Underdog Boyhood." *Science Fiction Film and Television*, vol. 10, no. 2, 2017, pp. 161–176. muse.jhu.edu/article/664060.

It. Dir. Andy Muschetti. Perf. Bill Skarsgård. Warner Brothers, 2017.

It: Chapter Two. Dir. Andy Muschetti. Perf. Bill Skarsgård. Warner Brothers, 2019.

Jando, Dominique. "The Circus," Documentary. Public Broadcasting Service, pbs.org, 2018.

King, Stephen. "Author of Fear," *It*, Special Features DVD. Warner Brothers, 2017.

Lakoff, George. *Women, Fire, and Dangerous Things: What Categories Reveal About the Mind*. University of Chicago Press, 1987.

Lukin, Konstantin. "Toxic Positivity: Don't Always Look on the Bright Side." August 1, 2019. psychologytoday.com.

Magistrale, Tony. *Hollywood's Stephen King*. Palgrave Macmillan, 2003.

Martin, Micheleen. "How Joaquin Phoenix transformed into the Joker." *Looper*. www.looper.com. Accessed December 21, 2019.

McManus, Donald. *No Kidding! Clown as Protagonist in Twentieth-Century Theater*. University of Delaware Press, 2003.

Mercer, Erin. "The Difference Between World and Want: Adulthood & the Horrors of History in Stephen King's *IT*," *The Journal of Popular Culture*, vol. 52, no. 2, 2019, pp. 315–329.

Miska, Brad. bloody-disgusting.com. Accessed December 21, 2019.

Muschietti, Andy, and Skarsgård, Bill. "Pennywise Lives!" *It*, Special Features DVD. Warner Brothers, 2017.

Proschan, Frank. "The Semiotic Study of Puppets, Masks, and Performing Objects." *Semiotica*, vol. 47, no.1, 1983, pp. 3–44.

Radford, Benjamin. *Bad Clowns*. University of New Mexico Press, 2016.

Simon, Eli. *The Art of Clowning: More Paths to Your Inner Clown*. Palgrave Macmillan, 2012.

Stott, Andrew McConnell. "Clowns on the Verge of a Nervous Breakdown: Dickens, Coulrophobia, and the *Memoirs of Joseph Grimaldi*," *The Journal for Early Modern Cultural Studies*, vol. 12, no. 4, 2012, pp. 3–25.

Swortzell, Lowell. *Here Come the Clowns*. The Viking Press, 1978.

Towsen, John H. *Clowns*. Hawthorn Books, 1976.

The Transcendental Anonymity and Moral Ambiguity of Phantom Clowns

Joanna Parypinski

Introduction

On the night of August 20, 2016, two anonymous callers in Greenville County, South Carolina, reported to police "a suspicious person dressed in circus clown clothing and white face paint trying to entice children to follow him into the woods" (Field). When a deputy went to the Fleetwood Manor apartment complex to follow up on the calls, a woman told him that her son had seen "several clowns in the woods 'whispering and making strange noises'" while another resident claimed to have seen a clown with a "blinking nose" standing near a dumpster at two-thirty in the morning on August 21 (Field). This was the start of a panic that would sweep the nation in late 2016. Within four months, more than 44 states had reports of creepy clown sightings (Dwilson). A list of reports by state, posted on Heavy.com in December of 2016, shows the proliferation of sightings as well as commonalities, such as death threats against students and teachers. There were menacing text messages in Arizona; an Instagram account called "mozzytheclown" threatening California schools; unverified video of a clown dancing in a parking lot in Massachusetts—and that's just the tip of the iceberg (Dwilson). Some reports crossed state lines: a Facebook and Twitter account called "Aint Clowning Around" targeted students and teachers in multiple states (Wright). This wasn't the first time that phantom clowns had terrorized the US. A similar incident occurred in 1981, but in 2016 the hysteria was able to spread rapid-fire across the internet, creating a viral folklore in the form of replicated videos, images, and tweets.

This clown hysteria spread through technology in such a way that the folkloric reproduction transcended the spontaneous reality of clowns appearing in physical locations. Through this process, the phantom clown story has achieved a kind of "transcendental anonymity," a term snidely coined by Michel Foucault in his speech "What Is an Author?" yet one with merit here: anonymous, in that the digital texts created from this phenomenon have no one clear authorial source; and transcendental, in that this lack of author-function allows the material to transcend the individual and take on a greater power of its own. While Foucault suggests the "transcendental" is merely another way of sanctifying the author in his or her anonymity, the term "transcendental" as it applies to the clown hysteria suggests instead the power to transcend the original trappings of the author-function entirely. The phantom clown narrative is a folk story with no identifiable source, or with a highly deindividuated source, collectively compiled, shared, and owned by the masses. It is not so much a series of strange events that have occurred, but a series of tweets and posts working together to create a multimodal folkloric narrative.

The phantom clown phenomenon largely exists in the collaborative stories shared and the pixels of digital images, more than it exists in physical reality. Like fairy tales and urban legends, the power of the sightings is not in the lived experience but the vicarious experience, the possibilities conjured through storytelling. It is the *possibility* of threat that engenders fear, particularly in contemporary American society when physical threats to safety are less abundant than they were in ages past, when our ancestors told stories around the fire with the dark of the uncharted forest encroaching on their backs. Indeed, in most cases, clowns pose no real threat to physical safety in the way that a hungry bear might; rather, the threat lies on a less tangible plane. In our modern milieu, phantom clowns present primarily a moral threat: that of the evil, anonymous stranger corrupting or harming the innocent. By representing this moral threat, phantom clowns become folk devils threatening society's desire to keep children safe from harm. In both 1981 and 2016, phantom clowns served their folkloric function to dismantle the status quo, and in doing so they spoke to growing fears of moral ambiguity in the modern era.

Phantom Clowns, 1981 and 2016

Loren Coleman first coined the term "Phantom Clowns" in his 1983 book *Mysterious America* after tracking the spread of a clown epidemic that began in Boston in 1981. Police had received reports that men wearing clown outfits were driving around in vans, luring children with candy: an image (sans the clown costume) that ought to be familiar to anyone aware of the "Stranger Danger" fears prevalent in the '80s. These reports came out in newspapers and local televised news. Curiously, despite the proliferation of such reports, no adult civilians or police officers ever saw the clowns. Coleman said, "There were no arrests, no photographs, no evidence and no abductions" (qtd. in Balsamini). Many chalked up the mysterious clown sightings to children's imaginations. And yet, how could children across the country all collectively make up the same exact story? "That was the mystery," said Coleman. "How do people in different parts of the country have the same experience? There was no internet or wire stories or national stories about this phenomenon" (qtd. in Balsamini). These weren't the only disturbing reports related to children circulating in the '80s. Around 1983, there was a surge of reports "alleging that [children] had been sexually abused as part of the ritual of secret, Satanic cults, which included torture, cannibalism, and human sacrifice" (Cohen xvii). Stanley Cohen wrote in his book, *Folk Devils and Moral Panics*, about moral panics involving a fear of corruption or injury to children, including the Stranger Danger fear and the Satanic Panic. Moral panics are periods of intense fear that involve exaggerated threats to societal values, with the threat usually stemming from a "folk devil" or perceived evil-doer (Bartholomew). Coleman himself found a correlation between the "folkloric" nature of Satanic child abuse allegations and the folkloric elements of the clown panic, both of which threatened children's safety and innocence.

At the time, scary clowns were very much in the public consciousness, with two key culprits. The first is John Wayne Gacy, who assaulted and killed over thirty young boys in the 1970s in the Chicago area (and who sometimes dressed as "Pogo the Clown"). Gacy was arrested for the murders in 1978, and his lurid 1980 trial was widely followed at the time. It was the first instance of a "real" killer clown, a figure that was already frightening moviegoers thanks to John Carpenter's *Halloween* (1978). In the opening scene, a young Michael Myers, dressed as a clown, stabs his sister to death with a butcher knife. This opening set the stage for the iconic slasher movie and its series of sequels. *Halloween* was a wildly popular box-office hit, grossing forty-seven million dollars in the U.S., which comes out to about $169 million in today's dollars (Roffman). Between the origin of cinema's most infamous serial killer and the true-crime horror of John Wayne Gacy, killer clowns were already prevalent in America's psyche by 1981, when phantom clowns emerged to terrorize the country's youth. This phenomenon had a lasting impact, notably in the recurrence of 2016.

The similarities between the 1981 and 2016 clown sightings are unavoidable. In both instances, children reported the threats and sightings, and there was a lack of firm documentation to prove their claims. In both instances, the phenomenon spread from the East Coast across the

United States. But in 2016, the phantom clown phenomenon had something else that helped it spread: the internet. After the first sightings were reported, the stories went viral. One example was a viral Facebook post by Caden Parmelee from September 2016, which included a video of a clown standing in tall grass on the side of a road in Florida, at night. In the video, the car stops to film the clown, which stands unmoving, watching the car. A voice can be heard saying "What the hell is that, dude?" When the clown begins moving toward the car, the same voices says, "Let's get the hell out" before the video cuts off (Toledo). The strangeness of the video, along with its spontaneous filming, lends authenticity to the confused and frightened reaction of the person in the car. Other such videos proliferated, most with similar experiences: a clown is spotted, and when it begins to move closer, the person recording becomes frightened and hurries away.

With other videos following this same structure, the clowns were a largely unrealized threat—after all, the videos never showed a clown actually reaching the person filming and hurting them—yet still these viral posts had real-world consequences. In Alabama, multiple schools were put on lockdown as a result of the Flomo Klown scare, in which "children had been messaged online by a Facebook user named 'Flomo Klown,' who allegedly made a threat against the student's school using gun emoji" (Biunno). Several people were arrested for the scare, which started on the Flomo Klown's Facebook page that said "I kill people for a living." Though the scare largely occurred via these internet messages, the very real and present fear of a potential school shooting—there were thirty-five school shootings in 2016 alone ("10 years")—clearly had ramifications beyond the digital world. While several were arrested, many more occurrences of phantom clowns continued to go unexplained. The potential illegality of these threats likely made their anonymity all the more imperative. Yet this anonymity also has an uncanny effect. When a face and name can be put to the culprit behind the mask, it doesn't seem so alarming; it is when the many anonymous clowns can appear anywhere, at any time, that the panic spreads. And in this case, the uncertainty is compounded by how the phantom clowns exhibit both small-scale and large-scale anonymity: on a smaller scale, the individual disguises his or her identity by donning the clown outfit; on a larger scale, the phenomenon as a whole represents a transcendental anonymity, a collection of individual experiences all represented by one common symbol—the clown.

People who hadn't themselves encountered a single clown began to fear the possibility of clowns coming to get *them*, in their town; because if it happened *there*, why not *here*? Through the internet, the clown sightings took on a life of their own and came to exist in the digital realm in the larger-than-life way of folklore and urban legends. The problem with this is the lack of verifiable documentation. Despite images and videos circulating across social media, who could say whether these were real or hoaxes? Some of those claiming to have experienced clown sightings could be lying to get attention, and no one on the internet would be the wiser. But why would someone lie about such a peculiar experience? Loren Coleman discusses this idea in his book *The Copycat Effect*, which explores the way the media can influence certain trends and cause "clusters" of behaviors: "Suicide clusters, school shootings, terrorist attacks and phantom clowns are all driven from one incident to another by the media reporting on them" (qtd. in Giaimo). Notice that these are all negative behaviors; Coleman also suggests that this copycat effect tends to compound and feed off of negative news.

Yet clowning, in particular, is such an eminently strange, almost inexplicable behavior; what would compel someone to dress in a clown outfit and go out scaring people? According to social psychologist Craig D. Parks, "The spreading of unusual behaviors is more common at times when there is a lot of tension, conflict and anxiety" (qtd. in Clarridge). This would seem to suggest that such behavioral clusters might be more prevalent during times of social, moral, or political upheaval. The connection between politics and moral threats has been noted by Loren Coleman, who suggests that election years, when we have political fatigue and turmoil, tend to correspond with surges in the phantom clown phenomenon (Giaimo). Parks elaborates on a similar assessment of how deviant behavior often follows political turmoil: "You may have people who don't like the way the world is going, who feel that their economic situation is not improving or are very upset about the high-tension presidential race[....] All things being equal, that could incline them toward deviant behaviors" (qtd. in Clarridge). Twenty sixteen was indeed a high-tension presidential race, and much of the anti–Trump or anti–Clinton sentiment stemmed from a sense of moral righteousness: the surety that one's own side was morally correct, and that the other side was morally wrong. The focus on morality made it a particularly divisive year, so it is interesting that this is precisely when the phantom clowns erupted back onto the media landscape. And it spread like a social contagion. Parks also points out the changing nature of social contagion in the internet era, claiming that "[a]lthough traditionally social contagion is more likely to spread among people who have frequent physical contact with each other, the internet has altered that aspect of the phenomenon" (Clarridge). Because of the internet, the phenomenon spread far beyond physical boundaries and took on a life of its own, but a life with striking similarities to 1981: a digitized form of oral folklore situating phantom clowns as devious, and deviant, folk devils.

Clowns as Folk Devils

Though clowns have been connected with devils through their history, modern folk devils aren't really devils: they are typically a group of people who represent a moral threat because they have been stigmatized or stereotyped as embodying values counter to society. The term folk devil is an interesting one: "'Devil' evokes demonic, almost super-human capacities for evil but these capacities are attributed to particular human individuals or groups. 'Folk' refers to popular perceptions of these beings" (Hindess 50). So what values do clowns represent, as folk devils? One must look to the history and folklore of clowns to understand how they embody disruption and deviancy. In the Americas, for instance, the Hopi's trickster clowns deliberately disrupted serious ceremonies with outlandish behavior (McRobbie). Other Native American tribes also included sacred clowns as traditional figures with a similarly disruptive purpose, notably the Plains tribes' heyoka who were intended to be contrary and unpredictable, speaking or walking backwards, wearing their clothes inside out, crying when they are happy, and being crude or profane during solemn occasions (Mizrach). By behaving in a manner opposite to the norm, they provided a counterforce to order and stability within society. But a clown by any other name is just as strange: the harlequin, for example, is also a clown figure. It appeared as an eleventh-century legend in the story of the Wild Hunt, a European folk myth. In this version, a monk was chased by a group of demons led by a masked giant known as the harlequin, also called the "hellequin" or "host-king" who was an emissary of the devil, roaming the countryside to chase souls into Hell (Radford 6–7). Whether to invoke laughter or spread fear, clowns have long held a place in the folkloric imagination as agents of chaos, disrupting the status quo. As an archetypal figure representing chaos and contrariness, clowns were also capable of inspiring feelings of fear or disquiet. French literary critic Edmond de Goncourt wrote in 1876, "[T]he clown's art is now rather terrifying and full of anxiety and apprehension, their suicidal feats, their monstrous gesticulations and frenzied mimicry reminding one of the courtyard of a lunatic asylum" (Goncourt qtd. in McRobbie). Just as a "lunatic," in Goncourt's words, might inspire fear in the way someone with mental illness might behave unpredictably or out of the socially accepted norm, clowns too make us uneasy because we cannot predict what they will do next. They are anarchists in a society that seeks order.

Yet it is not just this unpredictability that arouses feelings of unease around clowns. By their very nature, they are impenetrable; one can never tell what a clown is thinking or feeling. Not only do clowns have a dualistic nature (i.e. the sad clown vs. the happy clown), but they remain contrary even within this duality. The "happy clown" is only happy because of the smile that has been painted over the lips. For all we know, the person beneath the mask might be very unhappy indeed. This mismatch between inner experience and outer appearance crystallizes a disquiet of the clown, mirroring the fear of a person who is not what they appear to be. Though clowns are human, they maintain an element of the inhuman, as well. This almost-human-but-not-quite nature situates clowns in the uncanny valley, a hypothesis proposed in the 1970s by Japanese roboticist Masahiro Mori. The claim posits that as human likeness of nonhuman entities increases (such as in dolls and robots), it can provoke feelings of repulsion or uneasiness. This may be caused at least in part by perceptual tension between the perceived category membership (i.e. whether the being is human or not) and its deviations from that category. An example given by Roger K. Moore in a study of the psychological phenomena associated with the uncanny valley uses "a humanoid robot" as its basis, which "might appear to be fully human from the cues provided by the overall facial features, but small anomalous movements in the eyes might be sufficient to increase the uncertainty associated with the category membership of that particular cue, thereby giving rise to perceptual tension (and feelings of discomfort) in the viewer" (Moore 2). Much of the creepiness comes from the ambiguity: are they human, or not? Clowns can also create this perceptual tension between their humanlike characteristics and the small anomalies: their corpse-white faces, their fixed red smiles, their bulbous noses. According to psychology professor Frank T. McAndrew, "getting 'creeped out' is a response to the ambiguity of threat and [...] it is only when we are confronted with uncertainty about threat that we get the chills" (McAndrew). Not only do clowns embody ambiguity in their conflicting dual identities of humor and horror, happy and sad, but this ambiguity extends also to their existence in the liminal space between human and monster.

As folkloric symbols, clowns represent disruption of the status quo both through their deviant behavior (i.e. the heyoka's contradictions) and through their deviant nature (i.e. the ambiguity of category membership). They are aberrant from the norm. Such perceived deviancy, whether by clowns or another group, presents a potential threat to society. This is how the perception of folk devils leads to moral panic. Barry Hindess claims that it is the "public debate around 'deviant' behaviour or persons [... that] escalate[s] into panics about perceived threats to social order" (50). How does this escalation occur? Stanley Cohen, in *Folk Devils and Moral Panics*, identifies five steps of moral panic: 1. A group or person is defined as a threat to social norms; 2. The media depicts the threat in the form of a recognizable symbol; 3. The portrayal of this symbol rouses public concern; 4. There is a response from authorities and policy makers; 5. The moral panic results in social changes (Cohen). We can see these steps play out when situating the phantom clowns as folk devils. First, a threat was defined, in this case the danger to children. Then, the media highlighted the clown as symbol of this danger, which sparked public fears over being targeted next. Responses included school closures, laws forbidding clowning, and even some exaggerated reactions such as clown hunting, which sent college students searching for clowns to "hunt." Did the panic result in any social changes? The last step remains uncertain.

Most folk devils are a specific, identifiable group of people which display particular reasons for why society might (rightly or wrongly) view them as deviant, and, thus, a threat. Examples given in Cohen's book include refugees and immigrants, "violent" working class males, pedophiles, single mothers, and welfare frauds. Phantom clowns are a unique sort of folk devil due to their anonymity. They transcend any one particular group by becoming something more than human in their large-scale anonymity. If we were to look at the particular values the clowns represent, however, we might conclude that phantom clowns as folk devils were, at least in 2016, stand-ins for anarchists and school shooters. But unlike single mothers and immigrants, who do not intend to arouse fear by their very existence, the phantom clowns did embody the singular purpose to instill panic, drawing on their power as folkloric figures to play out their threats to society and becoming the boogeymen of the internet age.

The media itself focuses our attention almost exclusively on deviance through news stories of criminals and violence. And indeed, the media play a major role in inciting moral panics. The link between the media and moral panics "is the process of deviation amplification as described by Wilkins. The key variable in this attempt to understand how the society reaction may in fact *increase* rather than decrease or keep in check the amount of deviance, is the nature of the information about deviance. [...] [T]his information characteristically is not received at first hand" (Cohen 11). The nature of the information, in the case of the phantom clowns, never seems to be firsthand; rather, it is transmitted through technology, often mimicking the "friend of a friend" narrative familiar to folklorists and urban legends. The appearance of these clowns is like an urban legend come to life. This manner of recreating legends in the real world is called *ostension* in folkloristics, which involves "retelling legends by acting them out" (Gordon). According to Sarah M. Gordon, Ph.D. in her article "Creepy Clowns Explained, Folklore-Style," the "behavior follows the story, not the other way around. The reason we have people being creepy clowns now is that we already had narratives about creepy clowns. People acting like creepy clowns are, in their own way, retelling a story that existed before them" (Gordon). This mimicry of familiar folktales and legends brings them into the social consciousness through the everyday news cycle, perpetuating the panic and amplifying the fear of clowns. And it can be argued that the spread of the clown phenomenon is wholly media-based; without the internet, the phantom clown phenomenon of 2016 might have fizzled out before it even started, rather than becoming a widespread moral panic with the clown as our new folk devil.

How Clowns Embody a Moral Threat Through Anonymous Reproduction

Thanks to the internet, clowns took over the popular imagination in 2016. No matter where you were, the clowns could find you. The spreading of this panic resulted from the internet's use as a collective space not only to quickly disseminate information, but to interact with and add to that information, creating a new kind of folklore divorced from place and cultural tradition, as described in *Folklore and the Internet: Vernacular Expression in a Digital World*, edited by Trevor J. Blank. In the introduction, Blank claims that folklore has always been a key element of the internet, the purpose of which is simultaneous and instantaneous communication (2). He also suggests that this ability "to quickly disseminate information" makes the internet "an ideal channel for the transmission of folk narratives, due to its anonymity and efficiency" (Blank 9). This anonymity is crucial in the way information is shared, modified, and reproduced on the internet, where "producers" and "consumers" become one in the same "in a single interactive medium as *prosumers*, who can readily create as well as consume the message" (Bronner 24). The action of both consuming and creating the information that is rapidly shared on the internet disregards the role of any original author of the narrative in favor of a collectivist expression of folk information. In doing so, "the Internet putatively liberates artistic communication from materiality" (Bronner 33). The internet inhabits a realm of postmodernity, which, rather than valuing the individual characteristics of an author-creator and physical presence in folk tradition, paradoxically uses distance and anonymity to create a sense of immediacy.

Why even consider how the author-function relates to such a phenomenon? Most folk narratives do not have an individual "author" due to the nature of oral tradition, and the phantom clown narrative follows this tradition even as the oral becomes the textual, as our digital communications on the internet replace the oral sharing of stories. It has no single origin; even Creepypastas, or internet urban legends, have creators, even if those creators are anonymous. Yet the phantom clown story is an internet urban legend that sprang forth from collective anonymity, inviting participants to not only consume but also reproduce, modify, and transmit that story in a way that elevates the story itself above any individual creator. It is also worth noting that this open-source nature of the internet makes it a veritable Wild West of the digital age: lawless, unregulated, and uncensored. And, as young people increasingly engage with the world through the internet, this chaotic realm filled with dubious, vulgar, and pornographic material has become a concern for parents who fear the corruption of their children. But it is a threat far more intangible and elusive than, say, a banned book, thanks to the anonymous nature of the internet.

Due to the digital medium liberated from "materiality," the folklore and artistic expression of the internet is mechanically produced and reproduced ad infinitum. Consider the phantom clown phenomenon: unlike Stephen King's novel *It*, the images and stories of clown sightings had no sole creator or author, no singular point of creation; it was a collective story told, modified, and added to by anyone on the internet capable of tweeting a photo or posting an anecdote. And as the story grew from its assemblage of parts—from snippets of retold encounters—it became more and more real. We might consider, here, the significance of the way stories and art are transmitted in the modern era: through reproduction. Walter Benjamin theorized on the significance of the mechanical reproduction of art and how that affects its authenticity. In particular, he examined film as reproduction and how its creation through an assemblage of fragments produces a sense of realism. According to Benjamin, "the representation of reality by the film is incomparably more significant than that of the painter, since it offers, precisely because of the thoroughgoing permeation of reality with mechanical equipment, an aspect of reality which is free of all equipment" (14). Ironically, the artificial nature of its creation is exactly what removes the sense of artificiality from the work. It is delivered, too, from assembled fragments—just as is the phantom clown phenomenon, which takes the notion one step further even than film (which comes with a screenwriter, director, etc.) into the realm of purely collective grassroots storytelling. And even though it has been, essentially, created hodgepodge within the virtual world of the internet, it penetrates more deeply into our sense of reality.

This can explain why the phantom clown phenomenon created such a panic in a way that stories about creepy clowns told from a clear author-creator do not. Foucault may not have believed that a "transcendental anonymity" is any different than an author, but the difference here is the difference between identifiably made-up clown stories that are less frightening because they are obviously fictional, and the more chilling collective story that frightens through its authenticity and unpredictability. Bruce McClelland points out that when these kinds of stories became reproduced across the internet, "the boundary between the actual and the virtual began to become blurred" (McClelland qtd. in Blank 2). This is partly because the sharing of friend-of-a-friend stories and legends on the internet was just as important (if not *more* important) to the phantom clown phenomenon as the actual experiences of seeing clowns in real life. In this case, "Electronic messages are neither a playscript nor a transcript…. They *are* the event" (Kirshenblatt-Gimblett qtd. in Blank 7). Increasingly, the internet is becoming less a method to transmit information and more another way to live life—in the digital realm. Today's teenagers spend as much time socializing on the internet as they do in "real" life. At that point, which world becomes more real? What they do on the internet becomes part of life. Similarly, the videos and images circulated during the clown panic were not just representations but were *themselves* the phantom clown phenomenon. This closeness to reality makes the phenomenon all the more frightening: if a clown appears in a novel or movie, you are safe, because you are not *in* that novel or movie; but the proliferation of purportedly "real" stories about creepy clowns from various sources on the internet creates a more significant potential threat. It could happen to you.

Save the Children!

Though this potential threat frightened people of all ages during the "clowndemic" of 2016, the greatest threat was aimed at children, as it was in the 1980s. This potential threat—made all the more frightening through its anonymous reproduction on a platform that also represents potential corruption of youth—feeds into our deepest moral fears that our children will be corrupted by deviant forces. Clowns, in both their humorous and creepy incarnations, have long been associated with children. Stephen King's *It*, for instance, gave us Pennywise in 1986, reproduced as Tim Curry in the 1990 TV movie, reproduced again in recent years in *It* (2017) and *It: Chapter Two* (2019). Pennywise is an otherworldly clown who can only be seen by children, on whom it also feeds almost exclusively, returning every twenty-seven years to feed on a new generation of Derry's youth. Curiously, this timeline almost matches up with the thirty-five-year span between the major clown sightings of 1981 and 2016 (interestingly, though, it does line up perfectly with the twenty-seven-year gap between the 1990 mini-series and the 2017 movie). While Pennywise might be the most famous example of the evil clown character, King's creation is by no means the only fictional clown posing a threat to children. Eli Roth's 2014 movie, *Clown*, features an invented folklore around a clown suit (which is actually the skin of a god), that, when donned, transforms the wearer into a creature who must feast on children. In an interview conducted by Clarke Wolfe, Roth discussed the makings of *Clown* and why it was important to stick with the creature's disturbing tastes. He notes both that "[w]e trust our children around clowns" and, regarding the choices in the movie to see the threat realized, "If we're going to stay true to the mythology of fairy tales, then kids are going to get killed." Certainly, much classic folklore involves threats to children—just pick up the Grimm's fairytales to see myriad examples. More recently, in 2018 the SyFy channel's Creepypastas-turned-TV-show *Channel Zero* gave us contortionist clown Pretzel Jack in season 4: *The Dream Door*. Pretzel Jack is presented as the protagonist's childhood "imaginary" friend. The clown is also dangerous, murdering anyone who poses a threat to the protagonist. Curiously, Pretzel Jack begins as a villain character, leaving a swath of destruction behind him, but later in the season becomes something of a hero. This shift is interesting in its moral ambiguity. Is Pretzel Jack a villain or hero? He turns out to be just as unpredictable as the folkloric clown figure, an agent of chaos whose moral compass is dictated by a set of rules that do not coincide with our own.

The changing moral tide of society presents further explanation for this connection between children and phantom clowns. After all, societal changes tend to start with the younger generation. Today's youth, for instance, are more accepting of behaviors and identities previously deemed "deviant," such as homosexuality and transgender identity. Perhaps the older generation fears the younger generation's "loosening" moral values and the ambiguity that can come with these shifts. Folklore, being the stories of the "folk," plays into these changes by reflecting society's major concerns right back at us: "Folklore theory holds that folkloric expression is reflective and serves as a 'mirror' of societal and cultural values" (Blank 4). In this way, the phantom clown, reproduced into the larger collective figure of a folk devil, becomes the uncanny embodiment of our most intrinsic values, and our deepest fears.

Works Cited

Balsamini, Dean, and Melkorka Licea. "Creepy Clown Trend Dates Back to '80s, but This Time It's Different." *New York Post*, October 9, 2016.

Bartholomew, Robert. "Clown Panic!" *Skeptic*, vol. 21, no. 4, 2016, pp. 40–42, 64. ProQuest.

Benjamin, Walter. "The Work of Art in the Age of Mechanical Reproduction." *Illuminations*. Ed. Hannah Arendt. Trans. Harry Zohn. Schocken Books, 1969, pp. 1–26. web.mit.edu.

Biunno, J.B. "Woman Behind 'Flomo Klown' Scare Sentenced to Five Years Probation." *WKRG News 5*, January 19, 2018, wkrg.com.

Blank, Trevor J. "Introduction: Toward a Conceptual Framework for the Study of Folklore and the Internet." *Folklore and the Internet: Vernacular Expression in a Digital World*. Ed. Trevor J. Blank. Utah State University Press, 2009, pp. 1–20. ProQuest Ebook Central.

Bronner, Simon J. "Chapter 1: Digitizing and Virtualizing Folklore." *Folklore and the Internet:*

Vernacular Expression in a Digital World. Ed. Trevor J. Blank. Utah State University Press, 2009, pp. 21–66. ProQuest Ebook Central.
Clarridge, Christine. "Many Factors in U.S. Clown Craze." *Valley News*, October 25, 2016, p. 5. ProQuest.
Cohen, Stanley. *Folk Devils and Moral Panics: The Creation of the Mods and Rockers.* Routledge, 2011.
Coleman, Loren. *Mysterious America.* Paraview Press, 2001.
Dwilson, Stephanie Dube. "Clown Sightings List: Which States Have Reported Threatening Clowns?" *Heavy.com*, December 22, 2016, heavy.com.
Field, Carla. "Clowns in Woods Try to Lure Children with Money, Residents Say." *WYFF*, August 29, 2016.
Foucault, Michel. "What Is an Author?" *Generation Online.* Trans. Josué V. Harari. generation-online.org.
Giaimo, Cara. "In 1981, Clowns Allegedly Appeared Across Boston, Similar to Current Clown Panic." *Atlas Obscura*, September 7, 2016, atlasobscura.com.
Gordon, Sarah M. "Creepy Clowns Explained, Folklore-Style." *Sarah M. Gordon, Ph.D.*, October 5, 2016, sarahmgordon.wordpress.com.
Hindess, Barry. "Folk Devils Rise Again." *Social Alternatives*, vol. 34, no. 4, 2015, pp. 50–56.
McAndrew, Frank T. "The Psychology Behind Why Clowns Creep Us Out." *The Conversation*, September 28, 2016.
McRobbie, Linda Rodriguez. "The History and Psychology of Clowns Being Scary." *Smithsonian.com*, Smithsonian Institution, July 31, 2013.
Mizrach, Steve. "Thunderbird and Trickster." Florida International University, cuyamungue-institute.com.
Moore, Roger K. "A Bayesian explanation of the 'Uncanny Valley' effect and related psychological phenomena." *Nature News*, Nature Publishing Group, November 16, 2012, nature.com.
Radford, Benjamin. *Bad Clowns.* University of New Mexico Press, 2016.
Roffman, Michael. "*Halloween* Turns 35: An Appreciation." *Time*, October 25, 2013, entertainment.time.com.
"10 Years. 180 School Shootings. 356 Victims." *CNN*, cnn.com.
Toledo, Marimar. "Creepy Clown Caught on Video Creeping Around Central Florida." *Orlando Weekly*, September 26, 2016, orlandoweekly.com.
Wolfe, Clarke. "Eli Roth Discusses the 'Clown' Controversy." *Collider*, June 17. 2016, collider.com/eli-roth-clown-interview.
Wright, Bruce. "'Aint Clownin Around' Facebook Hoax? Schools on Alert After Twitter Threat Goes Viral." *International Business Times*, September 30, 2016, ibtimes.com.
Zuppello, Suzanne. "'Killer Clowns': Inside the Terrifying Hoax Sweeping America." *Rolling Stone*, September 29, 2016, rollingstone.com.

From Scream to Screen
"Killer Clown" John Wayne Gacy on Film

BENJAMIN RADFORD

Unlike the Joker or Pennywise, of course, John Wayne Gacy was real. By examining the truths and myths about his role as a clown (as well as how those portrayals are—or aren't—depicted in narrative films about Gacy) we can get a better understanding of the sadistic "Original Killer Clown." Gacy preyed on street hustlers, teenaged laborers, and drug addicts from 1972 to 1978, killing most of them by stabbing and strangulation. As Colin Evans notes in *The Casebook of Forensic Detection,* Gacy had "cruised Chicago's Bughouse Square district, trolling for young males, enticing them into his black Oldsmobile with offers of marijuana. Those who succumbed to his savage sexual demands were released, bleeding and battered; those who didn't were chloroformed into insensibility, raped, and then killed" (Evans 134). Gacy buried 28 victims on his property, most under the crawl-space of his home. The resulting stench from decaying corpses was dismissed as a sewer problem. When he ran out of space under his floor he began dumping his victims in a nearby river. In all, Gacy was accused of killing 33 people, 9 of them never identified. Gacy taunted police even as he was being investigated; according to FBI profiler John Douglas, Gacy "took it as a joke, even inviting two of the detectives to dinner[....] He invited police right into his house, where they smelled rotting flesh" (Douglas and Olshaker 105). That was the final straw, and shortly before Christmas 1978 he was arrested.

Gacy, Pogo, and Patches

As lurid information about Gacy's killing spree made news, one odd and chilling detail emerged: Gacy had been a clown. Police photographs of Gacy's house reveal several paintings and figurines of clowns in his bedroom and recreation room, and neighbors remembered Gacy performing as a clown on occasion.

In interviews Gacy discussed police asking him why he dressed as a clown:

> "I told them because it was fun and was relaxing from my business. Going to the hospitals, visiting kids and old folks, was rewarding as well; and the parades were the most fun, as you could run off into the crowd, kiss the women, squeeze their breasts with husbands and boyfriends watching, and run off with them laughing, thinking it was funny. When you're in make-up clowns can get away with murder and no one gets mad'" (quoted in Barker 93) [see also quoted in Radford 112–113].

Gacy refers to the cultural license afforded clowns, latitude to break the rules of social etiquette for our entertainment.

Gacy's sensational reputation as the "Killer Clown" is only loosely based in fact. Gacy was a building contractor and not a trained or professional clown. Though several seemingly authoritative sources suggest Gacy's clowning was explicitly connected to his killing; a section on Biography.com for example exaggerates both the frequency and circumstances of Gacy's clowning, stating Gacy "frequently performed in clown attire and makeup at children's parties, charity fundraisers and other events[....] When he killed, he sometimes dressed as his alter egos 'Pogo the Clown' or 'Patches the Clown'"; this is false.

But he did volunteer with a local "Jolly Jokers" clown club beginning in 1975, performing now and then as Pogo and Patches at events such as parades and children's parties. Lurid cinema images to the contrary, his occasional clown stints had nothing to do with his grisly trade. He didn't kill anyone while in costume, nor lure children (or anyone else) to him using the clown visage as a ruse. Nor did he use any clown paraphernalia in his attacks. He did, however, use magic and escape artists props (such as handcuffs and ropes) in some of his assaults. Once his victim was incapacitated by alcohol or other drugs, he would "playfully" put handcuffs on him or garrote him with a rope.

Though there's no evidence that Gacy used clowning or a clown costume in any of his murders; a former lawyer who represented Gacy, Sam L. Amirante, in his co-written book *John Wayne Gacy: Defending a Monster*, described the courtroom testimony of one man who Gacy encountered, David Cram. On his birthday in 1976, Cram visited Gacy's house, where the pair drank heavily. Cram testified that, when he entered Gacy's house, Gacy "had a clown suit on. He said that he was preparing for the next day. He had some kind of benefit charity to do with some kids with the clowning, and he thought it would be rather cute if, you know, seeing it was my birthday, that he leave the uniform on, and he was showing me some of his puppets" (Amirante and Broderick 282). Gacy then showed Cram his "handcuff trick," though he did not assault Cram, and the two continued to work together (Amirante and Broderick 282).

Part of the reason Gacy was able to prey on victims for so long was that by outward appearances he was a normal, jovial, and upstanding citizen. The public's perception of mass and serial killers was more akin to deranged, wild-eyed Charles Manson than a stocky family man who organized events and made occasional appearances as a clown. As William Lee of the *Chicago Tribune* noted, Gacy was "described by neighbors and business associates as a pillar of the community: a likable, boastful divorced businessman and Democratic precinct captain who hosted themed neighborhood parties and entertained children as a clown named Pogo. '(The public) would feel much more comfortable if Gacy was this type of creepy, sequestered ghoul that was unkempt and heinous,' [said] Detective Sgt. Jason Moran of the Cook County sheriff's office[....] 'But instead, he dressed as a clown and bounced kids on his knee.'" (Lee 2018). While Gacy's interest in clowns and clowning was sincere—and not, for example, a persona he adopted specifically to avoid suspicion—it certainly helped him get away with murder.

Film posters, books, and magazine articles about Gacy typically exploit the bad clown image to sensational effect. Pop culture has cemented Gacy's gruesome reputation as the killer clown, focusing on an otherwise minor detail in Gacy's life as both dissonant and symbolic.

Gacy himself eagerly cultivated the image. Gacy—having spent over a decade on death row awaiting appeals—became a prolific painter, selling art for profit and notoriety (Garcia-Roberts). Gacy's amateurish art depicts many subjects, from Jesus to landscapes, but he is best known for his dozens of painting of himself as Pogo the Clown. Several of Gacy's best-known clown-related painting are "Hi Ho with Clown," showing himself as Pogo the clown surrounded by the Seven Dwarfs of Snow White fame. "Pogo in the Making" shows himself in three stages of donning his Pogo the Clown costume and makeup, while "Handprint and Clowns" has a life-sized blood-red handprint with two smaller faces—Pogo and a skullfaced clown.

According to Eugene Robinson, editor at large for Ozy.com, he got a "businesslike" letter from the incarcerated Gacy stating "For $300 I will send you a Pogo painting!" Robinson declined but publisher Adam Parfrey became an avid collector of work by Gacy and other serial killers. "'I found Gacy to be quite pleasant,' Parfrey confided by phone. 'The art is not the most sophisticated, but it's great if you like clown art.' And with his eye on dollars, Gacy had price points for any budget and did paint more than clowns. He painted skulls, witch heads, and whatever struck his fancy, usually for a flat fee of $300. With the famous exception of Johnny Depp, who owns a Gacy original and spoke of it quite openly after having bought it, the killer's clientele is mostly anonymous, for obvious reasons" (Robinson).

It wasn't just Gacy's clown paintings that made their way into murderabilia merchandising; his clown costumes did too. Dave Savini, a journalist for CBS 2 discovered that one of Gacy's clown suits—complete with a Cook County police evidence tag still on it to prove provenance—was seen and photographed at a private home in Chicago and later made its way to a museum. Savini notes that "those clown suits became quite valuable. Even though they were collected as evidence and inventoried in his case, Gacy's clown suits […] ended up at the National Crime Museum in Washington D.C." As for how they got there, "In February 1979, Gacy's two hand-made clown suits were taken from his home on Summerdale and locked up in the Cook County Sheriff's evidence room. The Sheriff's Department says they sent the suits to the Cook County State's Attorney's office in November 1979. Then, the trail ends" (Savini). It was allegedly taken from the evidence room after Gacy's trial and sold for $25,000 to a private collector, who later loaned at least one of them to the museum for display.

Gacy's life and clown painting career came to an end by lethal injection May 11, 1994, in Joliet, Illinois. Crowds outside the prison celebrated the night of his execution and the front page of *The* (Ohio) *Chronicle Telegram* the next morning bore the headline "Killer Clown Is Dead: John Wayne Gacy Put to Death," along with a self-portrait of Gacy as a clown and spectators holding a sign reading "No Tears for This Clown." Some of his artwork was burned by those celebrating his execution. Decades after Gacy's death his legacy remains, in both the annals of serial killers and evil clowns.

Gacy Films

There have been about a half-dozen films made about John Wayne Gacy, ranging—as you might expect—from the terrifying to the terrible. The focus here (presented in chronological order) is on features with more than a tangential relationship to Gacy, and in particular those that reference him as a clown. There are a few others. A 2012 film titled *Scary or Die* featured a segment called "Clowned," in which a man is bitten by an evil clown named Fucko (whose facepaint resembles Gacy's Pogo) and slowly becomes a cannibal clown. Michael Emanuel, the director, explained that "a kid who went to my elementary school was John Gacy's first identified victim. Thus the bad clown Fucko is modeled after Gacy's Pogo the Clown. I've always hated clowns but not sure if that hatred came before or after the Gacy incident" (Emanuel). *Bruce and Pepper Wayne Gacy's Home Movies* (1988) is an experimental short (twelve-minute) Canadian film by Bruce LaBruce and Candy Parker, shot on Super 8. It depicts a troubled Gacy household as seen through the lens of a home movie camera held by Bruce and Pepper, Gacy's (fictional) children.

To Catch a Killer (1992)

Two years after *It* terrified television audiences with a two-part miniseries about an evil clown, a fictionalized drama about Gacy titled *To Catch a Killer* was released in 1992. The made-for-television movie stars veteran actor Brian Dennehy as Gacy and focuses less on Gacy's crimes than on police efforts to gather evidence and investigate him. It provides a generally accurate overview of how Gacy became a suspect and was later arrested. It touches on Gacy's reputation as a respectable businessman and pillar of the community who often bragged of his high-level connections.

Gacy is of course the villain; the hero of the story is Lieutenant Joe Kozenczak, who—while battling superiors and wistfully neglecting his family—relentlessly pursues justice for a missing teenager, Gacy's last victim. Because *To Catch a Killer* was broadcast on television for genteel audiences there are no onscreen murders, though several somewhat gratuitous car chases liven up the proceedings.

The killer's turn as a clown is barely mentioned until the final minutes of the first half of the film, with Gacy-as-Pogo performing at a children's hospital when he's confronted by his nemesis, Lt. Kozenczak (upon whose memoirs the script is based). Gacy says "Mr. Policeman, don't you know? A clown can get away with murder," paraphrasing a comment Gacy is said to have made—albeit under different circumstances.

Dennehy stated that Gacy contacted him from prison complaining about how he was portrayed in the film. "Gacy wrote me a letter," Dennehy said in an interview with The Cutting Room Movie Podcast (June 23, 2014), "saying 'You've always been one of my favorite actors, and I'm sorry that you have participated in this fraud' and that he'd been railroaded and so forth … and the greatest line of all, he said, 'Because the fact of the matter is, you know, *lots* of people had access to that crawlspace.'" Dennehy cracked up, seemingly skeptical that Gacy was the victim of unknown nefarious people who buried dozens of bodies under his house without his knowledge.

Gacy (2003)

Gacy (2003), written and directed by Clive Saunders, stars Mark Holton (perhaps best known as Pee Wee Herman's bike-thieving antagonist

Francis Buxton in *Pee Wee's Big Adventure*) as Gacy. The film begins with a title noting that it was "inspired by events from John Wayne Gacy's life."

The film begins in 1953 Wisconsin, where a teenaged Gacy is on a camping trip with his abusive father. The narrative then skips ahead—after another title card informing us that he'd served 18 months for sodomizing a boy—to 1976 Des Plaines, Illinois, where the killer lives with his mother, wife, and twin girls.

He's already begun his killing spree by the time the film begins, as evinced by neighbor complaints about the stench coming from under his home. At one point an eccentric exterminator with a vaguely steampunk backpack makes a valiant attempt to get rid of roaches and worms attracted to the bodies. *Gacy* does its best to mine the clown connection with several gratuitous insert shots of Gacy's living room, which feature numerous clown-themed posters and figurines. About an hour into the film Gacy appears as Pogo the Clown, in a home movie he shows to one of his victims. He later kills one of his victims while in facepaint—not at a party in costume but in his own bathroom, then dragging the body through his home behind his oblivious mother, asleep in their living room in front of a television.

Clunky lip service is paid to a few psychological factors; Gacy hears his father's abusive voice as he kills one victim, for example, and when his wife confronts him with gay porn and handcuffs, he bellows in defiance, "You know how much I hate homos!" But none of them bear much fruit. The last third of the film turns into a police procedural, with the script alternating between depicting Gacy as a clever killer and a sloppy one whose deadbeat ways and carefree attitude seems to invite police involvement. Gacy did indeed decide to kill himself as police closed in on him, as seen in the film, going to various friends and saying his goodbyes.

The film hits on a few mileposts of Gacy's life but fails to build much tension or suspense. Holton brings a strong physicality to the rotund Gacy; we can sense his threatening nature (he also uses it to his advantage, for example feigning a weak heart). The film ends with bodies being excavated by police from under his home's crawlspace, followed by an abrupt final note mentioning his execution and final words: "Kiss my ass." *Gacy* was filmed in Los Angeles and released direct to video.

Dahmer Vs. Gacy (2010)

Dahmer Vs. Gacy, a comedy-horror film written by Andrew J. Rausch, tells the story of a top-secret government laboratory (the project is so secret that the lead scientist has a "Project X-13" logo on the back of his lab coat) hoping to clone infamous serial killers, in hopes of creating a sort of super-soldier. The clones include—as you might expect from the title—Jeffrey Dahmer (played by Ford Austin, who also directed) and John Wayne Gacy (Randal Malone, a part-time actor and bon vivant). This nonsensical plan goes awry when both of them escape, but soon a trailer hick named Ringo (Ford Austin again) is directed by the voice of God coming through his radio to kill both of the killers. Along the way there are occasional fake news interruptions and eventually a troupe of ninjas appear—because, well, why wouldn't they?

Being low-budget camp, it's hard to really pinpoint where *Dahmer Vs. Gacy* would fit in the Gacy film pantheon. By my count Gacy has about ten minutes of screen time and is first seen menacing a Dumpster-diving, rat-gnawing hobo.

The filmmaker has an obvious affinity for dwarves, referencing several including Warwick Davis and Verne Troyer. In fact perhaps the best bit involving Gacy occurs about twenty minutes in, when (in black-and-white, faux vintage footage) a dwarf mime encounters Gacy on a sidewalk. *Dahmer Vs. Gacy* has moments of satire and social commentary, as when three buxom blonde women wearing "I heart serial killers" t-shirts are interviewed on a fake news channel about their serial killer fandom. There's also a Tammy Faye Bakker-inspired televangelist and other badly-dated cultural references.

There are similarities between the two killers portrayed in the film: both were gay, and both preyed on young men, often using drugs to incapacitate their victims. When the pair finally share screen time they bicker like an old married couple, trading inane barbs. The film is also notable for a cameo by Steven Adler of Guns n Roses as a Dahmer victim who gets killed by a power drill to the skull.

8213: Gacy House (2010)

The film *8213: Gacy House*, directed by Anthony Fankhauser, is framed as a pseudodocumentary, ostensibly footage recovered by the Des Plaines police department following the investigation of six murders in a house on a property once owned by Gacy.

Like the Amityville Horror story, the location is said to be haunted—at least in this version of the story. A group of ghost-hunting paranormal investigators for a show called *Ghost Trackers* (imagine, if you can, an even more amateurish *Ghost Hunters*) shows up to investigate.

The group brings along a busty blonde psychic, who says a prayer asking a moon goddess to protect the team—while simultaneously trying to provoke and contact the spirit of Gacy by offering a white t-shirt from her neighbor's teenaged son because "I know you like your boys young." Armed with runes, dowsing rods, and an ample supply of lip gloss, the psychic contacts an evil presence. The team uses typical TV ghost hunting gadgetry such as infrared cameras and EMF detectors, finally getting an EVP (ghost voice) that sounds like "Kiss my ass," which (as the script accurately notes) were allegedly Gacy's last words.

The story is told in a found footage style reminiscent of *The Blair Witch Project* (1999) or *Paranormal Activity* (2007), though the plot owes more to the latter. Much of it is shot with shaky handheld cameras, and is not for those with motion sickness (or, really, any but diehard low-budget horror buffs). Victims are dispatched and lots of people scream hysterically at lights going out or doors closing on their own. It's a kitchen sink approach of haunted house and found-footage clichés, with the only thing really missing being Gacy himself. Despite its title, John Wayne Gacy is wholly absent from the film, and seen only briefly in infrared heat silhouette. It's a generic paranormal team-in-haunted house story, padded out with repeated cuts to different cameras (including, apparently, an exterior walkway that seems to be in daylight for reasons more likely attributable to continuity errors than hidden plot twists; and despite the fact that the entire film takes place over a single night, one of the title cards says "11:54 AM" when it's clearly supposed to be near midnight).

Gacy's real-life home was demolished in 1979, with a new house being built on the property in 1986. It was sold in 2004. In October 2019, a three-bedroom, 2,500-square-foot house (formerly) at 8213 W. Summerdale Ave., went up for sale for $459,000. Like the Amityville home—where real murders took place—the property address was renumbered.

Dear Mr. Gacy (2011)

Along with *To Catch a Killer*, *Dear Mr. Gacy* comes the closest among the films to an accurate depiction of Gacy's life. Unlike the other films, *Dear Mr. Gacy* has little to do with either Gacy's crimes or his capture, but instead focuses on his life in prison.

It is based on the 1999 autobiography of Jason Moss titled *The Last Victim*. In it he recounts being a college student who contacts Gacy—then on death row—for an academic project in criminology. Moss poses as a sexually closeted, sympathetic fan of the killer's and hopes to glean insights into Gacy's mind through correspondence. Moss was deeply interested in famous serial killers, and also corresponded with Richard Ramirez, Charles Manson, Henry Lee Lucas, and Jeffrey Dahmer.

The manipulation goes both ways, however, and *Dear Mr. Gacy* evokes the old platitude, "He who dines with the Devil needs a long spoon." Soon Moss is barraged with collect calls from Gacy, alternately wooing and threatening him. Moss—trying to keep his project secret from his girlfriend and parents—grows paranoid, wondering if Gacy's deadly reach extends beyond his prison walls.

The who's-exploiting-who theme is interesting, and *Dear Mr. Gacy* is clearly the best non-television film production. Gacy's role as a clown is only obliquely referenced a few times, for example in paintings Gacy did of himself as Pogo, one of which he gave to Moss as a gift. Moss later became a lawyer in Las Vegas, Nevada, but struggled with mental illness, eventually killing himself in 2006.

Gacy as Movie Monster

There are of course many films based (however loosely) on real-life serial killers, including *Psycho* (based on Ed Gein), *Henry: Portrait of a Serial Killer* (based on Henry Lee Lucas), *Monster* (based on Aileen Wuornos), *Zodiac*, and many more.

In all these cases, the fictional film versions diverge—often wildly—from the "true story" (Vankin and Whalen xv, 109–113). They are not (and were never claimed to be) the "real story." They are not documentaries but instead scripted fictional narrative films "based on a true story." That is, the film is based on some things that actually happened; that doesn't mean that everything that really happened is in the film, and it doesn't mean that everything in the film really happened. All have scenes, dialogue, and events that never happened, and characters that either never existed or existed but never did some of the specific things they're depicted as having done. Screenwriters must take dramatic license in order to tell an effective story.

Because of this, itemizing which specific aspects of Gacy's actual biography are "accurately" represented in a given film misses the point. The screenwriters are not trying for historical accuracy, so judging the films on that criterion is a fool's errand. Instead a more fruitful approach is to examine how the films drawn upon and reinforce the evil clown mythos as it relates to Gacy.

John Wayne Gacy fits the mold of many masked movie monsters, in particular those starring in popular slasher film franchises such as Michael Myers in *Halloween*, Leatherface in *The Texas Chainsaw Massacre*, and Jason Voorhees in *Friday the Thirteenth*. More recent horror film franchises such as *Happy Death Day, Saw, The Purge, The Strangers*, and *Scream* feature similarly masked killers.

The fact that clowns, like many terrifying cinematic serial killers, are typically masked is important. Early clowns of the *commedia del arte* were masked, including Harlequin and Pulcinella. If a clown's greasepainted smile can vanish with the wipe of a dirty rag, then for all we know the man behind the mask could be very different. They are obviously human (underneath the unnaturally colored skin, wigs, and garish clothes) yet look distinctly inhuman. Clowns are liminal creatures that straddle categories, and thus make us uncomfortable, even if on a subconscious level—the way that any unknown person in disguise who stands near us or interacts with us might. Evil clown films of course make up their own genre, as other essays in this book demonstrate.

Because a grinning, greasepainted Gacy better fits the horror villain stereotype than a sexually sadistic, portly building contractor high on marijuana, it's not surprising that screenwriters depict him that way. An examination of the original official posters and artwork for each film is instructive. Of the five films, three depict Gacy as a clown on the cover art: *Gacy*, *Dahmer Vs. Gacy*, and *8213: Gacy House*; *Dear Mr. Gacy* and *To Catch a Killer* both depict the killer barefaced, though in the latter case later DVD packaging used an image of Brian Dennehy dressed as Pogo.

When Gacy appears specifically as a clown on film, his depiction varies depending on the script's narrative demands. As discussed, in *To Catch a Killer*, for example, Gacy's brief scene explicitly contrasts Pogo's benevolent clowning antics for a hospital room of sick children with the menace that both the audience and the detectives who confront him know he poses; the dual, hidden nature of Gacy's evil identity is revealed. In *Gacy*, the clown costume is essentially irrelevant in his killings; he doesn't use it as a weapon or disguise, as he's in his own house with a victim who knows his identity—though not his motives. In *Dahmer Vs. Gacy* (and to a lesser extent in *8213: Gacy House*), Gacy is basically a bulky masked juggernaut of evil not unlike Jason Voorhees or Michael Myers; as in *Gacy*, the clown costume isn't used to mask his identity or his mission.

Given the public's appetite for horror, to say nothing of the enduring fascination with both serial killers and scary clowns, John Wayne Gacy's posthumous depiction in film will continue. Clowns may be scary to many people, but they are not inherently threatening the way a knife-wielding mugger is. The fear of clowns stems instead from a latent, *potential* harm. We understand that the clown is acting—a fake and fantastical persona adopted for a short time as part of a performance. It can be cute and funny, but we may not want to be around when he decides to stop acting. The fact that many in the community unknowingly worked, drank, and partied with an evil sadist is unnerving enough, but the fact that he did occasional stints as a clown for kids is all the more terrifying.

Though most clowns are funny and silly, it's not difficult to find genuinely (and unintentionally) frightening ones. This is partly because clown features are necessarily exaggerated, sometimes grotesquely so—not out of any malice but practicalities. They often perform in front of crowds who need to see them from a distance. Subtleties work for close-up magic, not clowning. Gacy's amateurish makeup created pointed triangular eyes, something most professional clowns avoid, preferring smoother and less threatening features.

Andrew McConnell Stott, an English professor at the University of Buffalo, attributes much of the fear of scary clowns to the real or imagined contradiction between the clown's public and private personas. No one expects clowns to be manically happy buffoons after their act is over, but to know that one of them killed dozens of innocent people is horrifying. As Stott notes, "For the purposes of sensationalism, at least, killer clowns are an incredibly efficient image. Lurid and overly emphatic though they may be, by placing the pleasures of laughter in close proximity to mortal threat, they embody a particularly tense and volatile contradiction" (Stott 4). For these reasons there's hardly a better—or scarier—embodiment of this contradiction than John Wayne Gacy, the Killer Clown.

Works Cited

Amirante, Judge Sam L., and Danny Broderick. *John Wayne Gacy: Defending a Monster*. Skyhorse Publishing, 2015.
Barker, Clive. *Clive Barker's A-Z of Horror*. Compiled by Stephen Jones. BBC Books, 1997.
Biography.com editors. "John Wayne Gacy Biography." September 9, 2019, biography.com. Accessed December 13, 2019.
Dahmer Vs. Gacy. Dir. Ford Austin. Angry Baby Monkey Pictures, 2010.
Dear Mr. Gacy. Dir. Svetozar Ristovski. Notorious Pictures, 2011.
Douglas, John, and Mark Olshaker. *Journey Into Darkness*. Scribner's, 1997.
8213: Gacy House. Dir. Anthony Fankhauser. The Asylum, 2010.
Emanuel, Michael. Author interview. May 30, 2014.
Evans, Colin. *The Casebook of Forensic Detection: How Science Solved 100 of the World's Most Baffling Crimes*. John Wiley and Sons, 1996.
Gacy. Dir. Clive Saunders. Lionsgate Home Entertainment, 2003.
Garcia-Roberts, Gus. "The Ten Creepiest Paintings by Serial Killer John Wayne Gacy." *Miami New Times*, April 9, 2010, miaminewtimes.com. Accessed December 13, 2019.
Lee, William. "John Wayne Gacy Was Arrested 40 Years Ago in a Killing Spree that Claimed 33 Victims and Shattered the Illusion of the Safe Suburban Community." *The Chicago Tribune*, December 16, 2018, graphics.chicagotribune.com. Accessed December 13, 2019.
Radford, Benjamin. *Bad Clowns*. University of New Mexico Press, 2016.
Robinson, Eugene S. "Grisly John Wayne Gacy, The Painting, Murdering Clown." The Ozy.com, May 6, 2019, ozy.com. Accessed December 13, 2019.
Savini, Dave. "2 Investigators: Were John Wayne Gacy Clown Suits Stolen From Evidence Room?" CBS Local.com, February 10, 2015, chicago.cbslocal.com. Accessed December 13, 2019.
Stott, Andrew McConnell. "Clowns on the Verge of a Nervous Breakdown: Dickens, Coulrophobia, and the *Memoirs of Joseph Grimaldi*." *Journal for Early Modern Cultural Studies* 12, no. 4: 3–25, 2012.
To Catch a Killer. Dir. Eric Till. Creative Entertainment Group, 1992.
Vankin, Jonathan, and John Whalen. *Based on a True Story* But With More Car Chases: Fact and Fantasy in 100 Favorite Movies*. Chicago Review Press, 2005.

Part Three
Interviews and Accounts

Interview with Kevin Kangas (*Fear of Clowns*, 2004)

RON RIEKKI

Why did you get involved with the clown horror genre?

After my first movie *Hunting Humans*, I was looking to do a movie with similarities to one of my favorite horror films, *Halloween*. I knew I needed a big, strong, (mostly) silent killer like Michael Myers. It just so happened that a friend of mine was terrified of clowns, and I'd drawn a couple of pictures of a big clown with an axe to freak her out. As the years went by, I heard of more and more people who had a fear of clowns, and it suddenly clicked that nobody had really done a movie based on that. At the time, there was pretty much only three well-known movies about clowns: *It* (which wasn't *really* a clown), *Killer Klowns from Outer Space* (which was a hybrid horror/comedy) and *Clownhouse* (which was pretty effective for a horror movie, but is now tarnished by the scandal involving the director and one of the child actors). I checked IMDb at the time and there was no *Fear of Clowns*, which I thought was a great title for a movie. I set the story around a woman who has coulrophobia, and it rolled from there. When Lionsgate called me after seeing my trailer, they actually mentioned that they couldn't believe nobody had done a movie with that title yet.

Can you talk a bit more about Lionsgate? How did they find out about the trailer? What did they offer you? Why do you think the trailer was so effective?

I believe they saw it highlighted on the *Fangoria* web site. They offered me a generous advance plus a tiny back-end (which I never saw any money from), plus they offered to double it if I could deliver a sequel within two years. I hadn't planned on doing a sequel at that point, but figured, why not?

As far as the trailer being effective, I think it probably speaks more to how good I am at creating trailers than it does anything else. Before I direct a movie, I always try to see the trailer in my head first. It makes selling your movies much easier. On this trailer—which was actually more of a teaser—it was a simple build-up with a lot of money-shots that hinted at the storyline. But I think a lot of people wanted to see the movie that the teaser promised, so it took off.

What are the top ten clown horror genre films, TV shows, or books? Of those ten, which would you put at number one and why is it the very best of the genre?

Obviously this is my opinion, and everyone's going to have different answers (and I won't include my movies—though I think *Fear of Clowns 2* and *The Midnight Clown* from both *Terrortory* films could compete): *Poltergeist*, *It* (both versions), *Clownhouse*, *Stitches*, *Clown*, *American Horror Story: Freak Show*, *Supernatural* (Episode: "Everybody Loves a Clown"), *Killer Klowns from Outer Space*, *Masters of Horror* (Episode: "We All Scream for Ice Cream"), and *Terrifier*. I didn't love *Terrifier* as far as plot went, but the clown's pretty effective. As far as what's number one, I'd say *Poltergeist* bubbles to the top—even though it's a big stretch to simply call it a "clown horror genre movie"; however, given how many people—when asked what gave them their fear of clowns—respond with that as their answer, I think it deserves the number one slot. If you discount that, then it's the original *It*. Tim Curry's Pennywise is the stuff of nightmares.

For that number one pick, what's the best single scene in the film/show/book and why is that moment so effective?

If it's *Poltergeist*, it's the scene where the clown doll is on the chair when the kid wakes up. He goes back to sleep, or tries to, and then senses something. He sits up and looks, and the clown doll is gone. He checks under the bed—because we all know there's a monster under the bed—but there's nothing there. He sits back up, and it's right there—and tries to strangle him with its long doll arms. If you discount *Poltergeist*, then it's the opening scene of *It* where the clown takes Georgie. The remake version of this might even be better than the original. There's something about that clown peering out of the dark sewer grate that taps into something deep. As a kid we used to play around sewers, and even lose whiffle balls and stuff down the drains, and try to retrieve them, so we're all familiar with them.

How did great, iconic horror movie scenes like that affect your own film directing?

It's mostly subliminal. I started out as purely a writer; I didn't really intend to direct anything. I had immersed myself in so much horror by the time I even thought about directing that the hardest part became not accidentally stealing from them. There's a fine line between homage and theft, and I never intentionally crossed that line. After directing my first film *Hunting Humans*, I took a good look at just why some scenes in my favorite horror flicks were as effective as they are. There isn't any one answer.

In some it's the acting, in some it's the writing, in some it's the editing and direction, and, in most of the greats, it's all of them and more.

What's your favorite line of dialogue from the clown horror genre?
Might sound egotistical, but my favorite line is from the first *Fear of Clowns* movie. When Detective Peters finally captures Shivers the Clown, and the cops are leading him away, Peters says, "That's the biggest fucking clown I've ever seen." Frank Lama, who played Peters, reads it perfectly. He sounds incredulous and disturbed, and it cracks me up every time.

How about a favorite line of dialogue outside of your own films?
Probably "we all float down here" from the original *It*. Or when John Vernon's Officer Mooney says, "Killer clowns … from outer space? Holy shit." It's the dry sarcasm of his reading that makes me laugh every time.

What are your top ten horror films outside of the clown horror genre?
The Thing, Aliens, Halloween, Jaws, The Lost Boys, Tremors, A Nightmare on Elm Street, Fright Night, Night of the Creeps, Predator. The first six are pretty set in stone. The other ones shift in and out depending on the day.

What's your favorite film of all-time outside of the horror genre? And what's your favorite scene from that film? Why do you find it so effective?
This is a nearly impossible question. Can people really answer this? Like, one definitive favorite? If you put a gun to my head, I guess *Jurassic Park* comes to mind very quickly. My favorite scene is the T-Rex attack, which is staged and executed so perfectly that I can still remember the first time I saw it in the theater. Talk about tense. From the moment the ripples appear in the cup of water to the point where Dr. Grant gets Tim out of the tree, it's a rollercoaster. Perfect setup, perfectly written, and perfectly executed. Hell, nobody even noticed for a few years that the geography of the scene doesn't quite work out. The T-Rex seems to come from the direction that later becomes a cliff.

Why are clowns so scary?
We talked about this before we shot, and even feature the question in the making of *Fear of Clowns* (which you can see for free on Amazon Prime). It seems to be because we're afraid of masked people, and what's a clown besides someone wearing a painted-on mask? And even past that, most of them wear deceptive masks—a smile is painted on, even when they're not smiling. I think the bright colors and the paint mask give people "the willies" because something feels very artificial and fake. Your subconscious is raising flags, wondering what this clown's intentions actually are. And we know their intention is probably to kill us, because we know that's what all clowns want to do.

When you say you talked about what makes clowns scary before you shot, is there anything you spoke about along those lines beyond what you mention above? I'm really curious about that, especially in terms of the movie-making, how you really tap into that fear cinematographically/dramatically.

It was more about figuring out why people find them scary. Like, can you just slap clown makeup on a psychopath and he's scary? To an extent, yes. There are countless pictures on Instagram of scary clowns, and, with no context or background, they're legitimately frightening. I didn't have to do too much there other than come up with some cool makeup, which my artist/brother Paul C. [Kangas] came up with, so what I found interesting was the people who are deathly terrified of every clown, even regular, harmless-looking ones. Why are they so scared?

I thought that character trait would be interesting for my protagonist, Lynn. She would have coulrophobia from a childhood run-in with a clown. My early outlines of the script spent more time with the question of whether Shivers was a person or an actual supernatural manifestation from Lynn's paintings. Eventually it morphed into more of a mystery of why this character was painting himself up like the clown in Lynn's paintings and killing people close to her.

Other questions I faced were whether to keep Shivers always in night scenes, as traditionally that's where most of the scares are. I challenged myself to try to make him scary in the day for a couple of big scenes. Whether it worked or not is up to the viewer to decide.

Inevitably I thought it didn't quite work as well as the night scenes, which is why Shivers spends most of *Fear of Clowns 2* attacking at night or in dark places.

What are the clichés to avoid in the clown horror genre?

I don't know if there *are* clichés to the clown horror genre. I think the reason why most of them don't work is that there isn't enough time spent on story or character. A lot of people simply want to put a guy in a clown suit and make him kill a bunch of people. Without a story and a genuine motive other than "he's crazy," it gets old. And the now common thing in horror movies is that the kills are more important than the characters. I've never gotten on board with that. If I don't care about the characters then I may laugh at how cool the kill is, but there will be no impact.

What is the best horror scene you've ever been involved in shooting?

Another one that's hard to nail down. The scene in *Fear of Clowns 2* where we have a fully-naked woman (played by Savannah Costello) get cut in half by Shivers worked out better than I expected. Doug Ulrich, the FX guy, had done a full body cast of our actress, Savannah, but you never quite know how it's going to look on screen, and how well it will work with the shots of the actual person. In this case, it worked great. A lot of scenes in my new film *Terrortory 2* are ones I'm very proud of, especially given its minuscule budget.

What is the best acting performance in the clown horror genre? Why is that actor's performance so effective?

Tim Curry as Pennywise the Clown, hands down. Curry was so good in so many roles, from Pennywise to Wadsworth the butler in *Clue* to Frank-N-Furter in *The Rocky Horror Picture Show* to Darkness in *Legend* … this guy is one of our most criminally underrated actors. And unlike the new Pennywise—which I don't mind—Curry's Pennywise comes off as a friendly clown until he goes evil. It isn't until he morphs and the teeth come out that he becomes *terrifying*. Skarsgård's version of Pennywise seems creepy from his first word, even though he tries for a childlike innocence.

What direction do horror movies need to go in the future? How can the genre be improved?

I think in many cases they're already doing what they need to do: entertain. Tell us good stories with characters we care about. Gore is fine, but it should *always* be in service to the story. Populating your movie with one-dimensional characters that are simply there to be killed is *not* what you want to do. The genre as we know it is really a tale of two camps: Big-budget horror and indie horror. Both camps can be improved by spending more time on the scripts. The big budget horror flicks could be improved if the studios would let the masters—like Guillermo del Toro and James Wan, for instance—do what they want to do. Be there to support them, but don't get in the way. They don't need your input or changes. James Wan's only misstep was *Dead Silence*—a movie that has its share of scares. But he's gone on record as saying there was so much studio interference that he then went on to do *Insidious* for under a million dollars just so he could do whatever he wanted—and he hit that one out of the park. As for the indies, I'd say that they should definitely spend more time on their character development. If we don't give a shit about your characters by page twenty, we're not going to give a shit about them when they're being hunted by your bad guy.

To follow-up on what you just said: It's interesting when I go to horror film festivals and see really badly written horror films in the full-length or short categories, typically done by a director who does everything—writes, directs, edits, everything. And you can tell so little time was put into the writing. And there are all these screenwriters at the same festivals who are there for screenwriting competitions where the festival will get anywhere from two hundred to two thousand scripts and these will be the best of the best and those incredible scripts don't get offers to get shot. All these scripts where the writers have in some cases dedicated their lives to learning the craft, have rewritten till they've got an award-winning script and they don't get made. If I was a horror director, I'd be all over those film festivals, looking to read scripts from those screenwriters. Any thoughts on any of that?

I totally get that, and think you're on to something in many cases. I think there are a lot of fledgling directors who think writing is easy and simple, and in truth it's the hardest part of the filmmaking process. The greatest director in the world can't make a decent movie from a shitty script. Otherwise, Steven Spielberg would have never made a bad movie. These people think they can just shoot anything and use it as a calling card, or perhaps they think their visual style will compensate for an "okay" script. What they should be doing is looking for a script that will complement their directing style and blow people away.

In this day and age of the internet, that's not too hard to find.

On the other hand, when you're working at a micro-budget level there really is no room to take another's work and make it unless it's been very specifically tailored to that budget. Every script I've written has been created with an eye on the locations I know I can get access to, and with stunts and FX I was reasonably sure I could accomplish.

Who is the best horror director in your opinion? What makes them so effective? What's the best cinematographer in the horror genre?

James Wan, if we're talking about current directors. If I knew exactly how he was so good, then I'd just copy him. He knows how to stage very effective scares, and uses very minimal CGI to do it. He also has some great writers with him, like his original partner Leigh Whannell who he's co-written a lot of his hits with (and who's the best writer in horror currently, and an excellent director too—see *Upgrade* if you don't believe me). If we're talking who's the best horror director of all time, I think you'd be hard-pressed to find someone better than John Carpenter.

My favorite cinematographer is Dean Cundey. He's done *Halloween* through *Halloween III*, *The Fog*, *Escape from New York*, *The Thing*, *Psycho II*, *Romancing the Stone*, *Back to the Future* through *Back to the Future Part III*, *Roadhouse*, and more. Nobody beats this guy's filmography, and his movies take me back to my formative days in horror.

What's the most scared you've ever been in your actual life?

I don't tend to have nightmares, and I definitely don't remember them most of the time; however, there was one nightmare I had where I was wandering around lost in a fog. I could sense something was coming toward me that was so terrifying that I could barely breathe. I have never been that scared before or since. It started to emerge from the fog—some sort of thing with an old woman's face but a monster's body. I woke up to the sound of someone whimpering … and I realized it was me. I have never whimpered in my life before or after, but that's how scared I was. I did some research about nightmares later and found out that the "night hag" is a pretty common nightmare. I'm glad I've never had it again.

I hope you shoot *Night Hag as a short someday*…. *One final question that I want to ask, since this last question is being asked a few months after I asked you these questions the first time: what are your top ten horror films outside of the clown horror genre today? (I'm curious to see how your top ten list may have shifted since the last time I asked you.)*

The Thing, Aliens, Halloween, Jaws, The Lost Boys, Tremors, Psycho II, Fright Night, Night of the Comet, and *The Birds*. Like I said, there's always some changing after the first five or six. I love so many horror movies that it's really hard to boil it down to anything under fifty.

Stitches (2012)

Eoghan McQuinn

I came to be involved with the clown horror genre by auditioning for Conor McMahon's 2012 film *Stitches*. I was twenty-one at the time. The film tells the story of party clown hired to perform at a young boy's birthday. He is jeered by the kids at the party and, in trying to sabotage his act, they unwittingly kill him in the process. Several years later he comes back from the dead to exact revenge on the kid and his friends, now teenagers throwing a much rowdier party. The film stars British comedian Ross Noble, but was filmed in Ireland. I had been aware of Conor McMahon since his 2004 feature *Dead Meat*; his enthusiastic approach during the casting process, and indeed in rehearsal and on set, made us all feel comfortable to try things out.

When I read the script I was impressed by the sheer ingenuity of the kills on the page. Whether it involved pulling a rabbit out of someone's throat, using a tin opener to undo their skull and scoop out their brains, stabbing them with an umbrella that sticks through their eye, or making balloon animals out of (my) intestines and jamming a balloon pump into the back of my neck so that my head expands and explodes, Conor was super-excited to bring it all to life on screen. In fact, he told me that mine was his favorite kill, when we were at Bowsie Workshop in the process of creating prosthetics to stand in for my growing head. It was this use of practical effects and excessive blood splatter that gave the film its grungy B-movie quality.

During rehearsals, Shane Murray Corcoran, Tommy Knight, Thommas Kane-Byrne, and myself spent a lot of time together so that our on-screen friendship would feel real. The cast, crew, and extras had fun creating this party atmosphere in the house, complete with our bad dancing and cheesy one-liners ("Vinny, you're about as romantic as a wank in Funderland"). I remember the first day I had dialogue with a group of extras as partygoers at the house, and afterwards at lunch being crowded by a bunch of teenage girls who seemed to hang on my every word. A film school buddy of mine was working as a camera assistant and commented on my newfound "rock star" persona.

I remember the time spent filming my death scene vividly, as a twelve-hour night shoot out in the cold in County Wicklow. Falling onto crash mats, having my mouth refilled with salty fake blood to cough up, screaming my lungs out, and having two different sized heads carefully applied for the finale. I counted myself pretty lucky that I survived so late in the film as my comrades were picked off one by one.

The film premiered at London's Fright Fest 2012. It was fantastic to sit in a large auditorium at the premiere with many of the other actors and the producers, and hundreds of hardcore horror fans. I was so impressed with how Conor, cinematographer Paddy Jordan, and the rest of the crew executed the kill scenes, in particular. Everyone enjoyed Ross Noble's deadpan humor and the fun he had with the role. And my death scene won Best Death of the whole festival! The films later went on general release in the UK and Ireland, with a US release the following year.

It feels pretty cool to be part of that tradition of horror comedy, specific clown horror. It'd be great to see it have a resurgence again with the recent *It* adaptations. Even after several years, I am contacted regularly on social media by young fans asking if I am actually the character "Richie" from *Stitches*, saying how much they love the movie. Horror fans are the most loyal film fans, from what I can tell, the most willing to take chances with an unknown quantity. I see that particularly here in Dublin where we have a five-day Horrorthon every October at the Irish Film Institute. People will literally watch horror movies all day without a break. It doesn't require a huge budget to attract an audience, because it's less about famous faces and more about tapping into that visceral emotion the genre can coax out of the viewer, playing into their most primal fears.

Personally, I like classic psychological horrors the most, like *Rosemary's Baby*, *The Shining*, *Alien*, *Jaws*, *The Others*, *The Village*, *Misery*, and *Carrie*. In terms of slasher fare, *Scream* is always great. More recently off-beat films like *Trick 'r Treat*, *Jennifer's Body*, *Let the Right One In*, and *It Follows* have caught my interest. I've also been very impressed by the films of Robert Eggers and Ari Aster. They are unflinching in their approach, marrying deep psychological unrest with strong plotting and striking imagery. I do enjoy a good popcorn horror from Blumhouse from time to time. I also direct short films myself, so maybe one day when I make a feature I can contribute to the genre from behind the camera.

Interview with Jaysen Buterin (*Kill Giggles*, 2020)

Ron Riekki

Why did you get involved with the clown horror genre?

I chose to get involved with the clown horror genre for one very simple reason: love. Not of clowns, of course, for they are simply foul frightening floppy-footed fiends. No, the love I speak of is actually for my beautiful baby boy, and how I figured it was simply a matter of time before he was invited to a friend's birthday party where the entertainment du jour was "Bubbles the Clown" or some such madness. I figured at that point, I had two options: (1) we come up with a well-rehearsed story about where his Daddy disappeared to, when the truth of the matter is that I was locked in the trunk of my car crying hysterically, or (2) I get over my near crippling case of coulrophobia (the fear/hatred of clowns) by killing them in every way I've ever wanted to … on film. And so, I made *Kill Giggles*, a feature-length film that's also an ill-advised exercise in self-administered cinematic psychotherapy, wherein I was living a dream come true while simultaneously surrounded by my worst nightmare.

What are the top ten clown horror genre films, TV shows, or books? Of those ten, which would you put at number one and why is it the very best of the genre?

Honestly, being a die-hard coulrophobe, there is so much of the clown horror genre out there that I haven't explored, mainly on account of the whole "not wanting to die" thing that comes with looking at, let alone watching, clowns; however, the ones I have been able to bear witness to comprise one hell of a list.

1. Poltergeist
2. Pennywise, from *It*, both film versions and the literary incarnation

3. Vulgar
4. Twisty, from *American Horror Story: Freak Show*
5. *Killer Klowns from Outer Space*

There is one clown horror movie that I know I'm going to have to see and that's Circus of the Dead, simply because I'm such a big fan of Billy Pon and, honestly, how can any filmmaker or film lover *not* be completely in love with Bill Oberst, Jr.? Everything that guy does is just beyond bloody brilliant, so to see these two talents together is something I'm definitely psyching myself up to do. *Clown Fear*, from Avail Entertainment, is another one that's on my list, but it's going to take me a while to gather my courage for that one.

For that number one pick, what's the best single scene in the film/show/book and why is that moment so effective?

I don't know why my number one pick is so terribly and utterly frightening for me, but it's actually just one horrific clown scene from a non-clown horror film. I suppose it's a combination of the cinematography, the score, the actor, the set-up, my young own age at the time that I first watched it, but the clown marionette scene from *Poltergeist* has always been number one with a bullet in my brain as far as what I think of when I think of clown horror.

What's your favorite line of dialogue from the clown horror genre?

Well, I hate to self-promote but I think my favorite at the moment is a two-parter from *Kill Giggles*, from an exchange between Michael Ray Williams and Vernon Wells. Michael: "You know, for a clown named Giggles, you're not very funny." Vernon: "You know, for a monster shaped like a man, you're not very scary." After that, it would most certainly have to be the classic line from Pennywise, "we *all* float down here".... *Still* terrifying to this day!

What are your top ten horror films outside of the clown horror genre?

Oh wow, only ten? Okay, here we go … in no discerning order, it's got to be: *The Exorcist*; *Psycho* (1960); *Halloween* (1978); *A Nightmare on Elm Street* (1984); *Phantasm*; *Bubba Ho-Tep*; *Dawn of the Dead* (1978); *Sleepaway Camp*; *The Exorcist III*; and *Us*.

What's your favorite film of all-time outside of the horror genre? And what's your favorite scene from that film? Why do you find it so effective?

Holy hells, that is a hard question. I think there are at least five fighting in my mind right now for the top spot, so I'll just pick the first one and go with the master of eighties teenage existential levity, John Hughes, and the classic, *The Breakfast Club*! As for my favorite scene, well, I was just thinking about this the other day as I was trying to teach my son how to whistle, because it's definitely the whistling scene in the film, right before they break for lunch. The very first time I saw that scene, I tried whistling along but didn't know quite how to do it yet, so I think all I ended up doing was shooting chewed-up mac and cheese out of my mouth. Well, by the time my tenth or fifteenth viewing of the film had happened, I had completely learned how to whistle, and I owe it all to that scene. To me, even before I truly understood its ramifications and impact, that was always a powerful scene, because it showed that no matter how different or alienated we feel from those around us, there are still the simplest things that can bring us all together, if can we just manage to turn off our brains for a moment. *The Breakfast Club* was a film that always seemed to be on when I needed it to be, and so I would watch it all the time, no matter where it was in the movie. Before I was even old enough to understand everything that was going on, the writing of John Hughes spoke to me on a deeply personal level. With that film, it almost felt like he wrote it just for me; I could see parts of myself in so many of the characters. It was one of the films that made me want to be a writer, and later a filmmaker, long before I ever became aware of it myself.

Why are clowns so scary?

For me, it all comes back to *Poltergeist*; that's really the clown instance that completely unhinged me to the point of some serious coulrophobia. To me, clowns are never funny. They're not cute. They're not whimsical. They're frightening. They're evil. They're a mockery of man at our worst—a man-shaped monster in make-up at best. And isn't that what all the greatest stories throughout history are about, killing monsters?

What are the clichés to avoid in the clown horror genre?

To me, the biggest cliché I wanted to avoid with *Kill Giggles* was the very reason I had for making the film in the first place—everyone has seen the films, heard the stories, of the clowns as the serial killers, the monsters, the murderers. What I wanted to see was a serial killer *of* clowns. So, we decided to take that timeless terror trope of the clown as the killer and turn it on its rainbow wig-covered head by making the clowns the victims instead, and that's just something that hasn't ever been done before.

What is the best horror scene you've ever been involved in shooting?

Hmm, again, not to toot my own clown-killing horn, but my favorite horror scene we've shot so far would be from *Kill Giggles*, where we got to draw and quarter a rodeo clown. It was a scene that myself and cinematographer Jesse Knight plotted and planned for over a year with the FX Director, Joh Harp, and it's one of the signature death scenes in *Kill Giggles*. It was our first time working with live horses, which was just amazingly fun, and it was also a very complex scene to shoot with some intricate prosthetics and FX as well. We had five cameras going at one time as we pulled the limbs from our clown victim, and we thought we would only have one chance at it, so *everyone* on set was sweating bullets by the time I called "*Action!*" We were able to actually get everything back together and shoot another take for safety, but to see that come together in the final edit is just something truly amazing about making movies.

What is the best acting performance in the clown horror genre? Why is that actor's performance so effective?

    I know it might be slightly controversial, but I honestly think that Bill Skarsgård's performance as Pennywise in the new version of *It* was absolutely be*yond* terrifying! Don't get me wrong; there's no topping Tim Curry's incarnation of the foul floppy-footed fiend, but to me his performance was never about horror as much as it was about the excite and delight that goes along with the fright. Also, Tim was Frank-N-Furter, and Frank-N-Furter just isn't scary to me. But what Skarsgård did still haunts me, in terms of sheer terror and performance. When you have an actor who possesses that innate ability to look scary without even trying, by the time you clown them up, it just adds layers of scares. Of course, it might not qualify as the clown horror genre, but I don't think anyone would fault me if I didn't add a memorial homage to Sid Haig's Captain Spaulding either. For something I'm absolutely terrified of, it's a little less scary when I'm laughing too much at lines like "Don't we make you laugh? Ain't we fucking funny?" and "*Tutti fucking fruity!*" There are a lot of clown horror films I haven't seen yet, mostly because of the whole crippling coulrophobia and all, but I'm hoping that *Kill Giggles* provided enough therapy and catharsis that I can start watching some soon.

What direction do horror movies need to go in the future? How can the genre be improved?

    I think I might speak for every indie horror filmmaker ever when I say that I would *love* to see horror movies open up the aperture a bit and focus more on the independent horror film community. Stop the remakes and the reboots and the re-franchising of films and ideas that came out a few years ago. I understand that there's a certain sense of cinematic security with something already familiar but it's time to take a chance on an original and completely unique concept because there are so many absolutely bloody brilliant indie horror films out there that deserve a much broader audience than what they get. I think, I hope, with the massive influx of streaming services and the changing technology available with which to view films, that those viewing options may help shine that light on more filmmakers out there struggling to get their movie magic seen on any screen.

Who is the best horror director in your opinion? What makes them so effective? What's the best cinematographer in the horror genre? The best score?

Oh gods, there are *so* many out there, how can I narrow it down? Alfred Hitchcock (thriller, I know, but still); George A. Romero; Wes Craven; John Carpenter; Mary Harron; Don Coscarelli; Ana Lily Amirpour; Rob Zombie; Sam Raimi; Tobe Hooper; Jordan Peele; Issa Lopez; Mike Flanagan; Karyn Kusama; there's just too many brilliant choices to choose from!

As far as the best cinematographers, I don't know if I'm qualified to make that decision, as I tend to relate it to the top ten that I have, because those films are all-encompassing to me, in terms of what I love about them; however, if I turn the lens towards the independent side of horror filmmaking, holy hells, do I have a list! Jesse H. Knight is absolutely amazing, not only as a cinematographer, but also as a writer/director/producer/brother. The same definitely goes for Justin Reich, Christine Parker, Tommy Faircloth, Brett Mullen—all of whom seem to possess the uncanny ability to be able to pick up a camera and just capture instant magic!

Without a doubt one of the best horror score composers *has* to be John Carpenter. Take the *Halloween* score … something so simple yet so sinister that, as soon as you hear the opening notes of the theme song, you automatically have Michael Myers in your head. Personally, one of my favorite soundtracks of *all* time is the score to *Bubba Ho-Tep* by Brian Tyler! Something about it, maybe the film as a whole, just struck a six-string chord in my soul the first time I saw/heard it. That soundtrack is actually one of five that I always write to as well. And, of course, the great Ron Wasserman, whose score on *Between Hell and a Hard Place* will forever remain one of my most favorites.

What's the most scared you've ever been in your actual life?

Oddly enough, or maybe not so much at all, I think the most I've ever been scared in my life by sheer fear was the very moment my son was born, which was also the happiest I've ever been. But in more of a traditional horror sense, there are several moments throughout my childhood I remember just being utterly unnerved by, but unsure as to how to deal with that. One time, I was left home alone with a stack of horror movies from the local video store, and hearing this cacophonic howling laughter behind me, which was odd, given that I was the only one in the house at the time. Several years later, in a different house, there was an evening where every time I would leave the living room, the lights would switch on and the television would switch off, without fail.

About the Contributors

Dale **Bailey** has a Ph.D. in English from the University of Tennessee at Knoxville, and teaches creative writing and American literature at Lenoir-Rhyne University. He has written eight books, and his fiction has been adapted for Showtime Television, won the Shirley Jackson Award and the International Horror Guild Award, and been a finalist for the World Fantasy, the Nebula, and the Bram Stoker Awards.

Jason V. **Brock** is a writer, editor, filmmaker, composer, scholar, and artist. His fiction and nonfiction have appeared in *Weird Fiction Review* and *Fangoria* and he has also published a monograph, *Disorders of Magniture: A Survey of Dark Fantasy*. He has been nominated twice for the Bram Stoker Award, and his *The AckerMonster Chronicles!* won the Rondo Hatton Classic Horror Award for Best Documentary in 2014.

Jaysen **Buterin** is the creative director for Mad Ones Films. He is the writer/director of the award-winning Tarantino-meets-*The-Twilight-Zone* trilogy *The Gospel According to Booze, Bullets & Hot Pink Jesus*, *Between Hell and a Hard Place*, *Don't Let the Light In*, *The Corner* and *Kill Giggles*.

Jennifer K. **Cox** is completing a Ph.D. from Idaho State University, where she teaches composition, literary theory, and American literature. She has been an editorial assistant for the *Journal of the Fantastic in the Arts*, and her article "From Stage to Page: Adaptation as Survival in Neil Gaiman's *Mr. Punch*" appears in *JFA* 30.2. She researches the carnivalesque in American fantasy and horror.

Kim **Hester Williams** is the coeditor of an award-winning collection of interdisciplinary essays on race and environment, *Racial Ecologies*, published in 2018. She has written a critical review of Jordan Peele's *Us*. Her projects concern Afro-Eco-Poetics and new worldmaking (à la Octavia Butler). Additionally, she writes poetry, which is grounded in the long tradition of African American womanist poetics.

Kevin **Kangas** is a horror writer/director best known for his films *Hunting Humans*, *Fear of Clowns*, and *Fear of Clowns 2*, as well as *Bounty*, *Garden of Hedon*, *Terrortory*, and *Terrortory II*. He has also published a book celebrating Halloween.

Eoghan **McQuinn** is a writer, actor, and filmmaker based in Dublin, Ireland. He is a graduate of IADT National Film School, where he is pursuing an MA in screenwriting. His debut "The Chance of Striking Gold" premiered at the Galway Film Fleadh, while his *Staccato* was selected for the Washington, D.C. Independent Film Festival. He appeared in a supporting role in Conor McMahon's horror feature *Stitches*.

Debaditya **Mukhopadhyay** is an assistant professor of English at Manikchak College. He is completing his doctoral research at Rabindra Bharati University on 20th-century Anglo-American espionage fiction. His work has appeared in *Middle Flight, Muse India, Parenting Through Pop Culture* (2020), *Excavating Indiana Jones* (2020), *Critical Insights* (2020), and *Children and Childhood in the Works of Stephen King* (2020).

Joanna **Parypinski** has a MFA from Chapman University, and teaches English composition and creative writing at Glendale Community College. She has published two horror novels, and her fiction has appeared in *Nightmare Magazine, Black Static, Vastarien, Miscreations,* and other literary magazines and anthologies. Her research interests include the resurgence of folk horror and ecofeminist gothic in response to increasing awareness of climate disaster.

Benjamin **Radford** has a MEd from SUNY—Buffalo. He has written several books on folklore, critical thinking, and Fortean topics including *Bad Clowns* (2016), *Mysterious New Mexico* (2014), *Tracking the Chupacabra* (2011), and *Investigating Ghosts* (2016), winning awards for several of them. He has appeared widely in print, television, podcasts, and film, including the documentary *Wrinkles the Clown* (2019).

Ron **Riekki** is the author of *My Ancestors are Reindeer Herders and I Am Melting in Extinction, Posttraumatic,* and *U.P.* He has edited or coedited *Undocumented, The Many Lives of* The Evil Dead, *The Many Lives of* It, Here, and And Here and Here, Here. He wrote *Thank You for Your Teeth!* (2020 Dracula Film Festival Vladutz Trophy) and *America* (2019 Red Rock Film Festival Audience Award). He was nominated for Best Actor in a Feature Film (*Flesher*) for the 2020 Crimson Screen Horror Film Festival.

Mattius **Rischard** is a Ph.D. candidate, graduate assistant director, and teaching associate at the University of Arizona. He has published several articles, including "*Significación*: A Theory of Political Fashion in Chicano Counter-Culture" in *Transverse* and "The Politics of Regressive Listening" in *The International Journal of Critical Cultural Studies*. His fiction and poetry have been published in *Persona Magazine*.

Kevin J. **Wetmore**, Jr., is a professor of theatre arts at Loyola Marymount University. He has written nine books, including *Back from the Dead: Remakes of the Romero Zombie Films as Markers of Their Times* (2011) and *Post–9/11 Horror in American Cinema* (2012), and edited thirteen, including the Bram Stoker Award–nominated *Uncovering* Stranger Things: *Eighties Nostalgia, Cynicism and Innocence* (2018). He has also written more than 65 book chapters and hundreds of reviews.

Index

Abdul-Jabbar, Kareem 6
Abolitionists 65
abuse 23, 29, 44, 54, 83, 111, 121, 137
Achebe, Chinua 67
acoustics 15
actor 3–7, 19, 28, 30, 43, 50, 52–53, 56, 58–59, 105–107, 109–110, 136, 138, 145, 149, 153, 155, 157, 159–160
Adams, Lulu 4
Adler, Steven 138
adolescent 36, 38, 40–41, 44–47
Africa 67, 84, 86–87, 92, 171
Alabama 122
albino 50, 54
alcohol 2, 24, 38, 133
alien 15, 74–75, 104
Alien 75, 153
alienation 57–58, 64, 69–70, 83, 156
Aliens 147, 151
All Hallows' Eve 57, 67, 69, 71
Allin, GG 53
ambiguity 61–63, 67, 70–71, 101, 103, 119–120, 125, 130
America 9–11, 21, 28, 31, 35–37, 39, 42, 44, 59, 65, 74, 78, 80, 82–87, 89–90, 92, 94, 103, 105, 110–111, 115, 120–121, 124, 159–160
American Horror Story 7, 10, 19, 27–28, 100, 104, 109–110, 146, 155
American Repertory Theatre 4
amoral 57–58, 61, 68–69, 71
Amusement 2008
anarchy 15–16, 18–19, 21, 23, 61, 104, 106–108, 114, 124, 126
Anderson, Harry 19
Anderson, Lew 21
animal 15, 26, 35, 43, 54, 102, 152
Animaniacs 19, 25
anxiety 21, 37, 39, 41, 44, 54, 57, 64, 70, 74, 78–79, 85, 89, 93, 99, 104, 111, 114–116, 123–124
apocalypse 6, 8, 10, 12, 99
Aqua Teen Hunger Force 2

Arabic 64
Arbus, Diane 70
Arctic 42
Are You Afraid of the Dark? 19, 31
Aristophanes 43
Arizona 119, 160
Aryan 59
Asia 63
assault 40, 61, 83, 121, 133–134
Avruch, Frank 21
axe 145
Axegrinder 9

Bach, Steven 59
Bacharach, Burt 37
Back to the Future 150
Back to the Future III 150
Bad Clowns 17, 99, 160
Bailey, Dale 11, 35–48, 159
Bailey, John 115
Bakhtin, Mikhail 16–17, 22–24, 26, 28, 30–33, 43
Bala, Michael 43
Balderson, Steve 6
Barnum, P.T. 115
Barounis, Cynthia 107–108, 111
Barrel, Jean 4
Barthes, Roland 57, 58–62, 66, 68–69
Batman 24, 83, 100, 107–109
Batman 10, 19, 107
Beahm, George 75
beard 1, 6
Beetlejuice 8
Beetlejuice 9
Benjamin, Walter 57, 61, 128
Bentley, Wes 110
Berryman, Michael 4
big top 15, 20, 25, 30, 39, 44, 84
The Birds 151
birthday 5, 23, 133–134, 164, 166
Bitel, Anton 69
Black 3, 23, 25–26, 67, 82–84, 86–87, 89–94, 108, 132, 138, 160

162   Index

blackface 83–84
Blank, Trevor 127, 129–130
The Blob 35–42, 44–47
Blocher, Jay 21
blood 44, 50, 71, 86, 93, 102, 105, 110, 134, 152–153, 155, 157
Blood Dolls 9
Blood Harvest 9, 75
body 4–6, 28–29, 44, 59, 63, 70–71, 78–79, 90, 93, 112, 124–127, 137, 142, 148, 151, 153
The Body Snatchers 104
bogeyman 74–80
Booker, M. Keith 42
borderline 43, 51
Boston 20–21, 120
bourgeois 58, 68–69
boy 20, 26, 28, 45, 50, 70, 83, 113, 121, 137–138, 152, 154
Bozo 15–21, 24, 88, 105
Bradbury, Ray 52
Bradley, Laura 20
Brake, Richard 53
Brandis, Jonathan 19
Brando, Marlon 33, 39, 58
The Breakfast Club 155–156
Brecht 57–58, 68–69
British 65, 109, 152
Brock, Jason 12, 49–55, 159
Brody, Richard 109
Bronett, Sven 4
brother 3, 26–27, 35, 37–38, 40, 44–47, 50–53, 88–89, 112, 148, 158
Browning, Tod 54
Brozo 19, 24
Bubba Ho-Tep 155, 158
Bucknell, Charles 101
Buffy the Vampire Slayer 19, 25–26
Bundy, Ted 50, 105
Bunyan, Paul 86–87
Buterin, Jaysen 12, 154–159
Butler, Octavia 83, 94, 159

The Cabin in the Woods 10, 77
California 7, 88, 99, 119
camera 31, 56, 59, 67, 71, 86, 106, 110, 136, 139, 153, 157–158
camp 31, 107–108, 137–138, 149, 155
Camp Blood 9–10, 77
Camp Blood 2 9
Campbell, Joseph 18
Canio 53, 102
cannibal 44, 69, 121
capitalist 56, 60, 62, 64–65, 70, 103
Capone, Al 107
Captain Kangaroo 21
carnal 45–46
carnie 50, 110
carnival 5, 7, 17, 23, 25–27, 31–33, 46, 50–51, 53–55, 57, 60, 66, 68, 100–101, 104, 110, 115, 159
Carnival of Souls 9, 54
Carnival Row 100
Caroli, Francesco 4
Carpenter, John 53, 121, 150, 158
Carroll, Noël 18–19, 27, 43, 102
castrate 59, 69
Catholic 115
celebrity 43, 51, 71
Central Michigan University 5
Chamberlain, Wilt 6
Channel Zero 130
Chappelle, Dave 3
Charlottesville 94
Chicago 1–2, 4, 121, 134–135
Chicago Tribune 39, 134
child 4, 15–21, 23–24, 26–29, 31, 36–39, 44–47, 50–53, 66, 69, 74–79, 82, 84, 86–88, 90, 100–101, 103–107, 111–112, 114, 116, 119–121, 126, 128–130, 133–134, 136, 141, 145, 148–149, 158, 160
Chiodo brothers 35, 37, 46
Chopper Chicks in Zombietown 35
Christmas 23, 45, 132
church 5, 115
circus 3, 6–10, 15, 25–26, 29–30, 32, 35, 43, 47, 54, 71, 83, 88, 100–101, 111–112, 115–116, 119, 155
Circus of Horrors 8
clairvoyance 85
Clarabell 18–21, 23
Clasen, Mathias 18
Clay, Andrew Dice 3
Clinton 123
Clown, Homey 5, 17, 19, 23
Clown Foottit 4
The Clown Murders 9, 75
Clownhouse 9, 75, 145–146
Clownstrophobia 10
Clöyne 74, 78–80
Coco 31
Cohen, Jeffrey Jerome 43, 45
Cohen, Stanley 121, 125–126
cold 77, 153
Cold War 42
Coleman, Loren 120–121, 123
colonial 86–87, 90, 94
Columbus, Chris 45–46
comedy 1–6, 11, 17, 23, 25, 52, 60, 100–101, 103, 109, 111, 113, 115, 137, 145, 152–153
comic 2–4, 19, 21, 26–27, 37, 46, 101–103, 105, 107, 109, 113–114
communism 42
Connors, Chuck 52
Conroy, Frances 109
conservative 35, 42
Corbet, Brady 67

coroner 71
corpse 4, 49, 61, 71, 87, 92, 125, 132
costume 5, 7, 21, 54, 66, 75, 77, 83, 103, 105–107, 112, 116, 120, 133–135, 137, 141
coulrophobia 26–28, 66, 79–80, 103–104, 114, 145, 148, 154, 156–157
Covey, Edward 91
Cox, Jennifer 12, 99–118, 159
Craven, Wes 45, 51
creep 4, 7, 12, 25, 29, 32, 52, 119, 125–126, 128–129, 134, 149
Creepypasta 127, 130
crime 22–25, 29, 32, 40, 54, 60, 66, 92, 99, 107–110, 112, 121, 126, 135–136, 139, 149
Criminal Minds 6
Crimson Screen Horror Film Festival 6, 160
Cross, David 3
The Crow 9
Crow, Jim 87, 90–91
cruel 54, 56, 58, 60, 68, 71
CSI: Crime Scene Investigation 51
Cummings, Michael David 50
Cummings, Robert Bartleh 49
Curry, Tim 15, 20, 105–106, 129, 146, 149, 157

Dafoe, William 1
Dahmer, Jeffrey 139
Dahmer vs. Gacy 10, 137–138, 141
dance 7, 15, 19, 71, 76, 88, 104, 105, 119, 152
danger 5, 16, 23, 26, 28, 43, 45, 60–61, 65, 74, 78, 80, 92, 113, 121, 126, 130
Danse Macabre 42
dark 4, 7, 28, 42, 46, 59, 86, 105, 109, 111–112, 120, 146, 148
Dark Carnival 9
The Dark Knight 10, 107, 109
Dark of the Moon 4
Darkness 20, 149
David, Mack 37
Davidson, Jon 15
Davis, Janet 43
Davis, Warwick 138
dead 4, 23, 26–27, 42–43, 85–86, 91, 101–102, 109, 135, 137, 140, 152–153, 155
Dead Meat 152
Dead Presidents 9
Dead Silence 149
Dear Mr. Gacy 10, 139–141
death 2, 4, 9, 17, 27–28, 30–31, 33, 42, 46, 51, 53, 61, 69, 75, 84, 86, 88–91, 95, 101, 119, 121, 134–135, 139, 148, 153, 156
defamiliarization 57, 68, 71
de Goncourt, Edmond 124
Deliverance 52
democracy 57, 62, 89–90
Democrat 108, 114, 134

demon 26, 28, 74, 110–112, 124
Demonic Toys 9
De Niro, Robert 109
Derrida 60
Dery, Mark 80
Desfontaines, Henri 8
desire 45, 51, 57, 64, 68, 91, 120
Detroit 9
devil 4, 18, 20, 43, 80, 101, 120–121, 123–127, 130, 139
Devil Girl 9
The Devil's Rejects 9, 52, 54
Diaspora 90
The Dickies 37–38
Diderot 56
diegesis 56–57, 59, 67–71
director 6, 8, 11, 30, 35, 38, 41, 45, 49–50, 52, 58, 69, 101, 106–107, 109, 128, 135–136, 138, 145–147, 149–150, 153, 158–159
Disney, Walt 59, 83, 100
Disneyland 63
disturb 16, 18, 22, 28–29, 43, 50–51, 103, 121, 147
Doherty, Thomas Patrick 36, 44
Douglass, Frederick 91
Driscoll, Catherine 38
Drive Thru 9
Dumbo 100
Dummo 79
Durwin, Joseph 18, 79–80
dwarf 54, 134, 138

Eastwood 54
Egypt 43, 115
8213: Gacy House 10
Eisenhower 35, 42
Eisenstein 57, 68–69
The Elephant Man 54
emergency 41
England 83
Eraserhead 54
Europe 43, 102, 115, 124
evil 3, 16–18, 20, 22, 25, 27–29, 31, 54, 58, 66, 76, 79–80, 88, 94, 101, 105, 112, 120–121, 124, 129, 135–136, 139–141, 149, 156
The Evil Dead 6–7, 160
Evil Dead 2 7
Evil Night 9
exploit 17, 22–24, 28, 37, 52, 54, 58, 68, 76–77, 83, 90, 111, 134, 140
eyes 5, 21, 54, 65, 71, 86, 91–93, 101, 105–106, 109, 125, 134, 142, 150, 152

face 4–8, 18, 26–27, 31, 36, 39, 41, 50, 58, 62–64, 66, 70–71, 74, 78, 88, 93, 101, 105, 107–108, 110, 115–116, 119, 122, 125, 134–135, 137, 141, 151, 153
Falchuk, Brad 114

Index

Fantastic Beasts 100
fantasy 57, 59, 67, 79, 159
fascist 59, 61–62
fear 17–18, 23–27, 33, 40, 44–45, 59, 66, 68, 75, 78–80, 82, 85, 94, 103, 105, 107, 110, 112, 114–116, 120–122, 124–130, 141–142, 145–146, 148, 153–154, 158
Fear of Clowns 9, 77, 145, 147, 159
Fear of Clowns 2 146, 148, 159
Feast of Fools 9
Fellini 54
female 15, 46, 83
fetish 52, 56, 58–60, 68–69
Final Draft 10
Finney, Jack 104
fire 25, 31, 38, 50, 86–88, 91–92, 113–114, 119–120
The First Purge 100
flesh 43, 92, 110, 132
Flesher 6–7, 160
flood 16, 88, 94
Florida 110, 122
folklore 74, 100–101, 119, 123–124, 126–130, 160
fool 23, 40, 60, 104, 111, 140
Fool's Fire 8–9
Foucault, Michel 62–63, 120, 128
Frank-N-Furter 20, 149, 157
Frankenstein 82–83
Fraternity Massacre at Hell Island 10
Frayed 10
freak 4, 6, 27–28, 52, 54, 108, 110–112, 145
Freak Show 10, 27–28, 104, 110, 113, 146, 155
Freaks 8, 66
Freud 64–65, 89, 104
fright 3, 16, 19, 78, 111, 121–122, 128–129, 141, 148, 153–157
Fright Night 147, 151
Fujiwara, Tomomi 63
The Fun Park 10
The Funhouse 9, 52
Funland 9
funny 3, 7, 18, 25–27, 77, 86, 88, 112, 116, 133, 141, 155–157
Funny Games 67
Funny Man 9
future 2, 47, 149, 157
Futurist 61

Gacy 136–137, 141
Gacy, John Wayne 8–9, 11–12, 16, 28, 50, 52, 66, 103, 105, 121, 132–142
The Game 9
gaze 56–57, 61, 67–71
genocide 94
German 22–23, 59, 61
gestalt 53

ghost 1, 10, 25, 28, 32, 85, 92, 95, 104, 111, 138–139, 160
Ghost Hunters 138
Ghost Trackers 138
Ghosthouse 9
Giannelli, Mike 57
giant 21, 29–30, 38, 47, 50, 54, 86, 124
The Giant Gila Monster 36
Gillheeney, Erica Mary 7
girl 21, 23, 28, 30, 39, 45, 86, 94, 110, 113, 137, 140, 153
global 56–57, 60, 62–63, 115
Goehring, Cory 75
Goetz, Bernie 109
Goldberg, Rube 46
Golden Globes 109
Gordon, Sarah 126
gore 20, 149
Gore, Tipper 105
Goth 65, 101, 104, 160
Gotham 107–109
Grand Guignol 103
grave 40, 101
The Greatest Showman 100
Greece 60, 100
green 24
Green, Jonathan 36
Green, Seth 19
The Green Mile 84, 88, 90
Grimaldi, Joseph 4, 43
grin 3–4, 24, 27, 31, 63, 67, 71, 79, 105, 110, 113, 116, 141
grotesque 16–17, 20, 22–24, 26, 28–29, 31–33, 52, 57–58, 105, 107, 114, 141
gun 27, 35, 41, 50, 67, 111, 113, 122, 138, 147

Hack! 10
Hader, Bill 3
Haig, Sid 50, 52–53, 157
hair 21, 24, 29, 88, 102, 105, 110, 114
Halloween 5, 22, 66, 69, 110, 159
Halloween 9, 16, 53, 121, 140, 145, 147, 150–151, 155, 158
Halloween II 53
Halloween III 150
Halttunen, Karen 65
Handelman, Don 43
happy 16, 111–112, 124–125, 142
Happy Death Day 140
Harlequin 124, 140
Harmon, Larry 20
Harris, Jack 35
Harris, Xander 26–27
Harty 4
haunt 5–8, 28, 32, 47, 82, 84–86, 88–89, 93, 95, 104, 112, 115, 138–139, 157
Haunt 10
The Haunting of Hill House 104

Haverhill 50
He Who Gets Slapped 8
heart 5, 15, 20, 22–23, 31, 46, 61
hegemony 58, 61, 83, 88, 90, 92–93, 95
height 6, 64, 101
hell 2, 9, 30, 54, 110, 112, 114, 122, 124, 147, 154–155, 158
Hell and Back 3
Hell Baby 3
Hell Fest 100
Hellbreeder 9, 77
Hellscape 10
Hicks, Bill 3
hillbilly 52
The Hills Have Eyes 49
Hindu 26
hobo 5, 16, 27, 30–31, 87, 138
The Hole 10
Hollywood 3, 6, 36, 59, 69, 102, 110
Holmes, Pete 2
homeless 67, 71, 95
homophobia 93, 114, 137
homosexuality 130
Hooper, Tobe 49, 52, 158
Hop-Frog 8, 52
Hopi 124
horror 3–13, 16–20, 22, 25, 27, 30–31, 35, 37–39, 42–45, 49, 51–52, 54–55, 57–58, 60, 67–71, 75, 77, 79, 84, 86, 88–90, 92–93, 95, 99–107, 112–116, 121, 125, 137–141, 145–160
Hough, Robin 5
house 6–8, 19, 32, 39, 46, 67, 69, 71, 79, 85, 105, 132–133, 136, 138–139, 141, 152, 158
House of Fears 10
House of 1000 Corpses 9, 49, 52, 54
The House on Sorority Row 9
Howdy Doody 19–21, 88
Howl-O-Scream 7
Hughes, John 155–156
humanitarian 57, 65, 68–71
Hume 65
Hutcheson 65
Huxter, Percy 4
hybrid 43, 145

Iceland 78
In Living Color 19, 23
Indian 85
indigenous 85, 87, 101
insane 15, 50–51, 109
Insane Clown Posse 9
internet 51, 119, 121–123, 126–129, 150
interview 12, 21, 24, 50, 52, 58, 63, 106, 130, 133, 136, 138, 143, 145–151, 154–158
irony 24, 35, 52, 105, 107
Islam 64
isolation 58, 60

It Came from Outer Space 35
It: Chapter Two 3, 10, 76, 85–90, 93–94, 105, 129
It! The Terror from Beyond Space 35
Italy 61

jail 29
Jameson, Fredric 64
Japan 10, 44, 63–64, 125
Jaws 147, 151, 153
jester 43, 60, 66, 79, 113
Jesus 95, 134, 159
Jews 59
Jingles the Clown 10, 77
Johnson, John 6
Jojo 38, 44–45, 47
Joker 8, 11, 19, 57–58, 60, 66, 68, 83, 104, 106–110, 116, 132–133
Joker 1, 10, 66, 83, 100, 109–110
The Joker 10
Jones, Jim 114
Juggalo 60, 66
Jung, Paul 4

Kangas, Kevin 12, 145–151, 159
Kansas 9, 27
Keele, Tommy 4
Keeshan, Bob 21
Kelly, Paul 16
Keveney, Bill 66
Key and Peele 3
Kill Giggles 11, 154–157, 159
killer 5–6, 8, 11, 22, 28, 35, 38, 41, 43–47, 51, 58, 63, 66–68, 76–77, 94, 99–100, 102–106, 110–111, 113, 115–116, 121, 132–136, 140–142, 145, 147, 156
Killer Clown 10
Killer Klowns from Kansas on Krack 9
Killer Klowns from Outer Space 7, 9, 11, 35, 37–42, 45–47, 77, 103, 145–146, 155
killing 16, 27–28, 40, 71, 74, 76, 80, 90–91, 94, 103, 108, 132–133, 137, 140–141, 148, 154, 156
The Killing of America 9
Killjoy 57–58, 68, 77, 104
Killjoy 9, 10
Kinane, Kyle 1
King, Stephen 16, 18–20, 42, 66, 74, 80, 82, 84, 88–90, 93, 95, 103, 105, 115, 129, 160
King of Comedy 109
kiss 10, 37, 47, 94, 133, 137, 139
KISS Meets the Phantom of the Park 9
KKK 22, 87
Klovnen 8, 11
Knight, Jesse 156, 158
Knight, Tommy 152
Kohlberger, Glenn 28
Koko 8

166 Index

Korea 63
Krasinski, John 3
Kristeva 58, 63
Krueger, Freddy 47
Krumbholz, Sean 7
Krusty 8–9, 11, 17, 19, 21–22

Lacan 64
Lakoff, George 103
Landis, John 3
Lansdale, Joe 52
The Last House on the Left 51
laugh 2–3, 5, 8, 10, 16–17, 19, 22–23, 26–27, 29–33, 46, 71, 78, 86, 100–102, 109, 111, 115, 124, 133, 142, 147–148, 157–158
Law & Order 51
Leatherface 140
LeBow, Will 4
Ledger, Heath 58, 107–108, 110
legend 10, 20, 78, 102, 104, 110, 113–114, 120, 123–124, 126–127, 129
Legend 20, 149
Leone, Damien 69
Leone, Sergio 54
Lévi-Strauss, Claude 112
Lewis, Gary 22
The Lighthouse 1
liminal 5, 21, 36, 38, 45, 106, 125, 141
Los Angeles 137
Losers' Club 19, 74, 76, 84, 86, 94, 105–106
The Lost Boys 147, 151
Louv, Richard 78
Lynch, David 54
Lynch, John Carroll 27–28, 110
Lynyrd Skynyrd 53

Macbeth 9
magic 5, 27–28, 59, 88, 133, 142, 157–158
Magistrale, Tony 76, 104–105
makeup 4, 6–7, 18–19, 26–27, 29–30, 66, 105, 110, 133–134, 142, 148
male 15, 21, 29, 75, 83–84, 88, 95, 126, 132
The Man Who Laughs 8
El Mañanero 24
Maniacal 9
Manson, Charles 51, 53, 114, 134, 139
Marinetti 61
Martin, Michileen 109
Marx Brothers 51–52
masculinity 69–70, 83–84, 89–90, 93–94
Massachusetts 49, 51, 119
Master of Horror 8
Masters of Horror 10, 146
Masterworks of Terror 8
McCarthy, Joseph 42
McClelland, Bruce 128–129
McDonald, Ronald 88
McGrory, Matthew 50

McManus, Donald 101
McQuinn, Eoghan 12, 152–153, 159
Mears, Derek 3
Mercer, Erin 106
Merchant, Billie 4
The Merchant of Venice 4
metal 2–3
Methodic 10
Methodist 91
Mexico 24, 54, 160
Meyer, Russ 52
Michigan 7
The Middleman 6
militant 61
military 62, 87
Millennium 19, 26
Miller, T.J. 2
minstrel 83–84, 101
Misery 153
Mr. Halloween 10
Mr. Ice Cream Man 9
Mr. Jingles 77
modernity 56–58, 62–67
M.O.N. 9
monster 5, 7, 9, 16, 18–19, 24–26, 28, 32, 35–36, 38, 41–46, 54, 74, 76, 78–79, 87–88, 93, 95, 102, 105–106, 125, 140, 146, 151, 155–156, 159
moon 138
Moore, Roger 125
Mordrake, Edward 28, 110–112
Mori, Masahiro 44
Moseley, Bill 50, 53
Mouse, Mickey 69, 83
mouth 21–22, 24, 27, 29, 42, 88, 93, 101, 105, 111, 113, 153, 156
MTV 47
Mukhopadhyay, Debaditya 12, 74–81, 160
Mulvey, Laura 59
murder 2, 4, 9, 11, 24, 29, 41, 44, 50–52, 63, 66–67, 69, 71, 75, 102–104, 107, 110, 112, 130, 133–136, 138–139, 156
Murphy, Ryan 114
Muschietti, Andy 106
music 22, 36–37, 49–51, 53, 105
mute 21, 29, 50, 101, 112
Myers, Michael 16, 121, 140–141, 145, 158
myth 11, 26, 57–62, 64, 66, 68, 75, 86, 95, 100–102, 113–115, 124, 130, 132, 140

Nanjiani, Kumail 2
narrative 5, 11, 15, 19, 25, 31, 45, 56–61, 67–71, 74, 84, 86, 88, 90–91, 95, 102–104, 106, 120, 126–127, 132, 137, 140–141
nationalist 61, 94
native 80, 85, 115, 124
Natsume, Makoto 63
Nazi 59

Index

netherworld 5
New York 51
The New York Times 39
Newland, John 29
Nicholson, Jack 58, 107
Nicholson, Robert 21
Nietzsche 67
night 1–3, 7, 28, 32, 43, 71, 87, 92–93, 119, 122, 135, 139, 148, 153
Night of the Clown 9
Night of the Comet 151
Night of the Creeps
Night of the Living Dead 51
nightmare 11, 26, 51, 74, 82, 101, 115–116, 146, 150–151, 154
The Nightmare Before Christmas 8–9
A Nightmare on Elm Street 147, 155
Nordic 77–78
nuclear 42, 66, 104

occult 5
October 6, 10, 85, 139, 153
Odd, Dave 2
Olympia 59
100 Tears 9
One Step Beyond 19, 29
oppress 61, 87, 91–92, 95
Oscars 109
Osgerby, Bill 35
Out of the Dark 9
Oxford 64, 69, 103

Pagliacci 9, 25, 53, 102–103
pain 57–58, 60–61, 65, 68, 70, 94, 112
pandemic 79, 115
Parker, Candy 136
Parker, Christine 158
Parks, Craig 123
Parmelee, Caden 122
parody 21–22, 52, 65, 67, 105, 114
Parypinski, Joanna 12, 119–131, 160
Parsons School of Design 51
pastiche 35
patriarchy 41, 52, 59, 93
Paul, Andrew 50
Peacock, Louise 43
Peckinpah, Sam 53
Peele, Jordan 3, 95, 100, 158–159
Pennywise 7–8, 11, 15–20, 27–28, 57, 66, 68, 74–76, 80, 88–89, 91, 93–95, 100, 104–106, 109–110, 129, 132, 146, 149, 154–155, 157
phantom 8–9, 12, 100, 119–123, 126–130
The Phantom of the Big Tent 8
Phillips, Todd 1, 109
phobia 10, 26–28, 66, 79–80, 93, 103–104, 114, 145, 148, 154, 156–157
Phoenix, Joaquin 58, 109

photo 6, 60–62, 64, 70, 121, 128, 132, 135
Pippo 29
Pirandello, Luigi 29
The Pirates of the Caribbean 6
Pitt, Michael 67
plague 80, 85–86, 89
pleasure 38, 45, 47, 51, 57, 59, 69–70, 142
Poe, Edgar Allan 8–9, 52
poetry 58, 61, 159–160
Pogo 11, 16, 52, 66, 121, 132–137, 140–141
police 23, 29, 32, 39–41, 46, 54, 62, 69, 71, 84, 107–108, 116, 119–121, 132–133, 135–138
Poltergeist 9–11, 103, 146, 154–156
porn 52, 56, 65, 67–68, 128, 137
Porter 9
postmodern 66, 127
poverty 5, 111
Powerman 5000 50
Predator 75, 147
presidential 106, 113, 123
Pretzel Jack 15, 130
prison 23–24, 27, 62–63, 84, 112, 135–136, 139–140
privilege 57–58, 61–62, 65, 67–68, 70
producer 35–36, 59–60, 62, 127, 153, 158
profane 69, 124
Prohibition 44, 107
propaganda 62
Proschan, Frank 112
prostitution 21, 54
Psycho 140, 155
Psycho-Circus 9
Psycho II 150–151
psychology 18, 125
psychopath 51, 148
psychosis 83
punk 2–3, 37, 137
puppet 21, 31, 44, 134
Puppet Master vs. Demonic Toys 9
The Purge 140
Pushing Daisies 6–7

A Quiet Place 3

Rabelais 17, 33, 60
race 11, 87, 89–91, 95, 123, 159
racism 84, 86–87, 90–91
Radford, Benjamin 12, 17, 20, 76, 79, 99, 103, 105, 110, 124, 132–142, 160
Rainbow 4
Ralph Breaks the Internet 16
rape 22, 44, 95, 114, 132
Rebel Without a Cause 37
Reid, Terry 53
Reid, Tim 19
religion 5
Republican 109
Riefenstahl, Leni 59, 61

168   Index

Riekki, Ron 1–12, 16, 20, 145–151, 154–158, 160
Ringling 115
Ringmaster 21, 53, 84
riot 50
Rischard, Mattius 11, 56–73, 160
Ritter, John 19
ritual 17, 36, 43, 68–69, 79, 121
rock and roll 10, 36
The Rocky Horror Picture Show 20, 149
Romero, Cesar 19, 107
Romero, George 30, 51, 158, 160
Rose, Jim 3
Roth, Eli 129–130
Roy, John 2

sacred 44, 80, 124
sad 15–16, 60, 65, 105, 109, 124–125
sadist 46, 50, 53, 57–60, 66, 68–69, 132, 141
San Bernardino 88
Sandberg, A.W. 11
Santa Sangre 9
Sartain, Jeff 6
Sartre, Jean Paul 29
satire 23–24, 60, 65, 71, 116, 138
Scahill, Andrew 42
scary 7, 10–12, 16, 18, 21, 25–26, 31, 57, 74–79, 84, 86, 103, 121, 135, 141–142, 147–148, 155–157
Scary Movie 2 9
Schaumburg 1
schizo 58, 64–65
Scooby Doo 10, 19, 25
Scorsese, Martin 53
scream 7, 10, 26, 51, 70, 91–93, 102, 110, 112–113, 132, 139–140, 146, 153
Scream 45
Seasick Steve 1
Second City 4
Secrets of the Clown 10
secular 62
Seinfeld 19, 25–26
Senghor, Leopold 67
serial killer 5–6, 8, 11, 27–28, 50, 52, 66, 76–77, 103, 105, 121, 134–135, 137–141, 156
Serial Killers 9
set design 7
sex 38–39, 44–46, 49, 51–52, 94, 101, 114, 121, 132, 139, 141
shadow 3, 28, 71, 84, 102–103
Shakes the Clown 9
shaman 5, 80
Sharpe, Christina 90
Shelley, Mary 82–83
Shimabukuro, Karra 75
shooting 18, 24, 66, 122–123, 148, 156
Short Straw 6
SICK: Serial Insane Clown Killer 9

Sideshow 9
Sideshow Bob 21
Sigmundsdóttir, Alda 78
silly 16, 25, 141
Silverman, Sarah 3
Simpson, Bart 21
Simpson, Herman 23
Simpson, Homer 22
Simpson, Lisa 22
Simpson, O.J. 51
The Simpsons 9, 11, 19, 21–22
simulacrum 44
sinister 15–20, 22–26, 28–33, 69, 99, 102
sister 16, 32, 121
Skarsgård, Bill 7, 105–106, 149, 157
skin 4, 44, 71, 77, 93, 129, 141
slasher 50, 54, 77, 121, 140, 153
Slashers 9
Slaughter High 9
slave 60, 83, 86, 90–91
smile 10, 15, 27, 63, 65, 68, 70–71, 88, 95, 113, 125, 141, 147
Smith, Adam 65
society 5, 10, 19, 31, 54, 58, 63, 74, 83, 108–109, 114–115, 120, 124–126, 130
Soiree DADA 4
soldier 22, 24, 30, 87, 92, 138
Something Wicked This Way Comes 52
Sontag, Susan 59, 70
South Carolina 119
Spawn 9
spectacle 17, 90, 107, 116
Sssshhh… 9
standup 1, 60
Stanhope, Doug 3
Stanislavski, Konstantin 56
Stitches 10, 12, 146, 152–153, 160
Stokes, Mary Ann 78
story 8, 11, 19, 25, 28, 30, 32, 35, 40, 49, 52–53, 66, 75, 77–78, 83–87, 89, 91–92, 107, 110–111, 113–114, 120–121, 124, 126–128, 136–140, 145–146, 148–149, 152, 154
Stott, Andrew 43, 102–103, 142
stranger 74–75, 78–79, 120–121
Stranger Things 100
stripper 6
struggle 61, 101, 140
suburbia 53, 66, 69, 84
suffer 26, 28, 57, 60, 65, 83, 89
suicide 27–28
Super Badass 9
supernatural 25–26, 74, 77, 148
Supernatural 9, 19, 25–26, 146
supremacist 86, 89, 92–93, 95
Swift, Taylor 47
SyFy 47, 130
symbol 17, 41, 45, 59–61, 83, 88–90, 100–101, 104–105, 108–109, 114, 122, 125–126, 134

taboo 43–45, 56–58, 69
Tales from the Crypt 31
Tales from the Darkside 19, 30
Tales from the Quadead Zone 9
Tarantino, Quentin 52, 159
teen 27, 35–42, 44–47, 86, 105–106, 110, 129, 132, 136–138, 140, 152–153, 155
Teenage Zombies 36
Teenagers from Outer Space 36
teeth 18–19, 27, 29, 44, 60, 71, 89, 95, 149, 160
Terminator 6
Terrifier 10, 69, 71, 146
Terrifier 2 11, 69
terror 17, 22, 27, 29, 32, 66, 79, 82–91, 93, 95, 101, 105, 119, 121, 123, 156–157
Terror on Tour 9
terrorism 79
The Texas Chainsaw Massacre 49, 140
The Texas Chainsaw Massacre Part 2 50
theatre 3–5, 10, 17, 42, 49, 58–59, 66, 68, 83, 100, 106, 147, 160
The Thing 147, 150–151
Thomas, Richard 19
Thornton, David Howard 57
threat 16, 19–20, 24–28, 32–33, 36, 38, 41–43, 45, 89, 92, 94, 102, 104, 110–111, 116, 119–130, 137, 140–142
3 from Hell 53–54
The Three Stooges 44
To Catch a Killer 9, 136, 139, 141
Tolk, Prescott 2
tomb 61
Torment 10
torture 65, 69, 83
Tosh, Daniel 3
Tourist Trap 52
Towlson, Jon 42
Town Without Pity 22
Towsen, John 101, 106, 111, 115
tramp 4–5, 87
trauma 20, 68, 83, 85–86, 89, 93–94, 103, 106
"Treehouse of Horror" 9, 11, 22
Tremors 147, 151
trickster 18, 79–80, 102, 124
Triumph of the Will 59
troll 75, 78, 132
trope 16, 19, 23–24, 28, 31, 49, 57, 83–84, 87–88, 99, 101, 103–104, 111, 156
Troyer, Verne 138
Trujillo, Victor 24
Trump 123
The Turn of the Screw 104
Twilight Syndrome 10
The Twilight Zone 3, 7, 19, 22, 29, 159
Twisty 15, 19, 27–28, 104, 109–114, 116, 155

uncanny 26, 44, 68, 84, 99, 101, 103, 122, 125, 130, 158
undead 32
University of Buffalo 142
University of Houston at Victoria 6
Urban Massacre 9, 20, 62–63, 66, 70, 78, 100–102, 104, 113–114, 120, 123, 126–127

Van Halen 47
Vanity Fair 20
Vatterott, Nick 2
vegetarian 54
victim 16–17, 25, 35, 52, 75, 77, 83–84, 89, 92, 112, 115, 132–139, 141, 156–157
Vietnam 5
vigilante 54, 107–108
villain 58, 66–67, 69, 80, 107, 109, 130, 136
violence 11, 16, 29, 31, 44, 51–54, 56–59, 65, 67, 85, 87, 89, 91, 126
Virginia 94
Voorhees, Jason 3, 140–141
voyeur 51, 57–59, 65, 67–68, 70
Vulgar 9, 24, 128, 155

The Walking Dead 3
war 3, 5, 22, 36, 42, 47, 61–64, 82
Warner, Marina 25, 75, 79
Warner, Wakko 25
water 18, 29, 41, 85, 88, 147
Watts, Jon 12, 74, 77–78, 80
Watts, Naomi 67
Wayans, Damon 23
werewolf 3, 102
Wertham, Fredric 37
West Side Story 37
Wetmore, Kevin 11, 15–34, 160
When Evil Calls 9
white 23, 43–44, 82–88, 92–95, 101–102, 105, 108–109, 119, 125, 134, 138
White, Walter 77–78
White Zombie 49
whiteface 5, 54, 101
The Wild Bunch 53
The Wild One 37, 39
Wiley, Mike 2
Williams, Kim Hester 11, 82–96, 159
Williams, Robert 52
Willy Wonka & the Chocolate Factory 54
Winnicott, Donald 64
witch 78, 80, 134, 139
witchcraft 5
Wolfe, Clarke 130
women 24, 54, 61, 67, 87, 92, 105, 133, 138
Workaholics 2
World War II 36, 64
wrestler 54
Wynter, Sylvia 95

The X-Files 3, 26

Yellow Submarine 9
Yoon-Do-rahm 63
Young, Neil 90
youth 36–37, 39–40, 47, 50–51, 88–89, 121, 129–130
Yucko 17

Zander, Max 23–24
Zedong, Mao 67
Zeebo 32
zombie 12, 43, 77, 115
Zombie, Rob 49–54, 158
Zombie, Sheri Moon 50, 53
Zombieland 10
Zucker, Wolfgang 43